6 00 146535 6

TELEPEN

DATE DU

✔ KU-545-128

Research

FOR RETURN

The Story of Winchester

The Mediæval Towns Series

5s. 6d. each, net

ASSISI. By LINA DUFF GORDON.

AVIGNON. By THOMAS OKEY.

BOLOGNA. By ALETHEA WIEL.

BRUGES. By ERNEST GILLIAT-SMITH.

BRUSSELS. By ERNEST GILLIAT-SMITH.

CAIRO. By STANLEY LANE-POOLE.

CAMBRIDGE. By the Rt. Rev. C. W. STUBBS, D.D., Bishop of Truro.

CANTERBURY. By G. R. STIRLING TAYLOR.

CHARTRES. By CECIL HEADLAM.

CONSTANTINOPLE. By W. H. HUTTON.

COVENTRY. By MARY DORMER HARRIS.

DUBLIN. By D. A. CHART, M.A.

EDINBURGH. By OLIPHANT SMEATON.

FLORENCE. By EDMUND G. GARDNER.

JERUSALEM. By Col. Sir C. M. WATSON, K.C.M.G., C.B.

LONDON. By H. B. WHEATLEY.

LUCCA. By JANET ROSS and NELLY ERICHSEN.

MILAN. By ELLA NOYES.

NAPLES. By CECIL HEADLAM.

NUREMBERG. By CECIL HEADLAM.

OXFORD. By CECIL HEADLAM.

PADUA. By C. FOLIGNO.

PARIS. By THOMAS OKEY.

PERUGIA. By MARGARET SYMONDS and LINA DUFF GORDON.

PISA. By JANET ROSS.

PRAGUE. By Count LÜTZOW.

RAVENNA. By EDWARD HUTTON.

ROME. By NORWOOD YOUNG.

ROUEN. By THEODORE A. COOK.

SEVILLE. By W. M. GALLICHAN.

SIENA. By EDMUND G. GARDNER.

VENICE. By THOMAS OKEY.

VERONA. By ALETHEA WIEL.

WINCHESTER. By W. LLOYD WOODLAND.

KINGS GATE, WINCHESTER, OVER WHICH IS THE
CHURCH OF ST. SWITHUN

The Story of Winchester
by W. Lloyd Woodland
Illustrated by Adrian de Friston

London : J. M. Dent & Sons Ltd.

Aldine House ❧ ❧ Bedford Street

Covent Garden W.C. ❧ ❧ ❧

All rights reserved

FIRST PUBLISHED IN THIS EDITION . 1932

LC32025476

PRINTED IN GREAT BRITAIN

To
D. W. K.

INTRODUCTORY

IF any one man can be said to have laid the foundations of the British Empire that man was Alfred
the Great, King of the West Saxons. If any place
can claim to be the nucleus around which grew up
the British Empire that place is Winchester, capital
of Alfred's kingdom of Wessex.

It was at Winchester that Alfred, scholar, statesman, and lawgiver, as well as king, began the work of
recording Anglo-Saxon history, and those translations
into his native tongue which laid the foundations of
Anglo-Saxon prose. So that Anglo-Saxon-speaking
peoples, whether within the British Empire or
without, may with truth look to Winchester as the
nursery of their language, and the place where the
history of their race began to be set down.

It is a proud claim, but it is well founded. For
centuries Winchester was a royal city indeed. Within
its borders successive Saxon kings delighted to reside,
and in its great church they were given honoured
burial. And there to-day the bones of many of them
still lie, albeit in quaint juxtaposition. Cynegils and
Adulphus, Cenulph and Ecgberht, Emma of the red-
hot ploughshares, wife and mother of four kings, repose
cheek by jowl in ancient chests, their dry yellow
bones but poor reminders of their vigorous fleshly
days. From this strange collection of revered relics
the bones of Alfred are missing; his dust is scattered,
as it were to the four winds, a type of that mighty
spirit which is working yet in lands he never knew.

The history of Winchester in no small degree is the history of England. In the tapestry of Anglo-Saxon story the threads of Winchester are many. It was at Winchester that Ecgberht was crowned king of all England, and it was here that he issued his famous edict abolishing tribal distinctions, and directing that all within the nation should be known by the one name, English. For centuries it was one of the chief centres for minting coinage, and it is recorded that in Athelstan's reign it had no fewer than six mints, when London had but three. Here a standard system of weights and measures was instituted, some of which are in use to-day.

It was in the Anglo-Saxon cathedral at Winchester that Cnut, returning from the seashore after giving his dramatic lesson to his courtiers, hung his crown over the high altar, declaring he would never wear it again.

Here the Conqueror wore his crown every year, equally with London; and here his son Rufus found grudging burial after that tragic hunting expedition in the New Forest in the year 1100. Here successive Plantagenet and Angevin kings gathered their bowmen and men-at-arms when about to embark on their French wars. On the green hill overlooking the city from the east was held each September the great fair of St. Giles, a market for all the merchants of Europe.

To the citizens of Winchester Henry II, in 1184, granted a charter, by which they were privileged and free of all toll in any town and city of the realm. It was the first of its kind. But soon other cities sought charters, with rights "as at Winchester." Henry III, born within the walls of the old city, took its name as his surname. Henry Tudor, seeking to consolidate

x

his position on the throne, brought his queen to Winchester Castle in order that their first child might be born in the ancient capital of the realm; and, in the cathedral, with true medieval pageantry, that child was christened, and named after Arthur, the British king.

Here Henry VIII, using King Arthur's Round Table as his dining board, entertained the Emperor, Charles V, and here Henry's gloomy daughter Mary was married to Philip of Spain. In the Great Hall of Winchester Castle Sir Walter Raleigh confounded his accusers, and in the same place, two generations later, Jeffreys, of sanguinary memory, opened that Assize which forms one of the blackest pages of English history.

On the banks of Winchester's streams fished and ruminated Izaak Walton, and in a chapel in the south transept of the cathedral his remains lie buried. In the grey and green seclusion of the cathedral close gay Charles II dallied with his "Nelly," or some other of that joyous, if scandalous, bevy who accompanied him to Winchester on many a visit. And in still later times John Keats, already stricken by that malady which was hurrying him to an untimely grave, here sought health and inspiration, revelling in Winchester's quaint streets, its quiet walks, and the open downs overlooking the city, where, he solemnly declared, the air was "worth sixpence a pint."

So, incident upon incident, character upon character, crowd into Winchester's story over a space of a thousand years.

And more. For the history of Winchester goes back beyond the Wessex kings, although the records are to be found in other than written page. None can say the date of its founding, although, like Rome, it has a mythical founder, and a legendary date of beginning. For centuries the simple folk of Winchester believed the high-coloured story which was painted on the City Tables, and hung up in the Guild Chamber, setting out that the city was founded by one Ludor Rouse Hudibras, "son of Liel, the son of Brute, the second son of Francke, the great grand-child of the first Brute, 892 years before the birth of Christ, in the age of the world 2295, and 99 years before the first building of Rome."

Such a circumstantial story was no doubt the concoction of some waggish medieval scribe. The bombastic phrasing of the closing lines of these apochryphal tables is of a piece with the beginning. It can be imagined in pompous recitation by the city "bedle" on many a great occasion:

And hath given place of birth, education, marriage, synods, national and provincial, and sepulchres to more kings, queens, princes, dukes, earls, barons, bishops, and mitred prelates, before the year 1239, than all the other cities of England.

CONTENTS

xiii

LIST OF ILLUSTRATIONS

List of Illustrations

List of Illustrations

PART I—THE STORY

CHAPTER I

Winchester in its Beginning

IT is always an interesting speculation, when looking at a town or city for the first time, to determine the reasons for its beginning, and its growing up at just the spot it occupies. Very rarely the site of a town is deliberately chosen. Salisbury is the classic medieval example, and Canberra the very modern one. Generally, however, towns grew up seemingly haphazard. But there is always a reason for the beginning of a settlement at a given place, and, if thought and analysis are brought to bear on the matter, that reason can be discovered.

The reason for the rise of a town on the site where Winchester stands is easy to discover. A brief consideration of the geography of the place will demonstrate that it was certain to be chosen as a site for a settlement. Some towns began to rise at an easy ford; others began at a cross-roads. The site where Winchester began to grow up was at once the meeting-point of several trackways, and a point of easy river crossing. Moreover, it lay in a gap between two vast forest areas, a gap which opened the way from the coast to the heart of the country.

Winchester was certainly a Romano-British town. Was it a British settlement before the Romans came? Or did the Celtic dwellers in the neighbourhood live on the conical hill a mile to the south-east? Hampshire is dotted over with the hill camps of Iron Age and Neolithic peoples, and the museums of the county contain many of their relics, celts, pottery, cinerary urns, and the like. There were Celtic settlements all around Winchester; at Littleton, where there is a

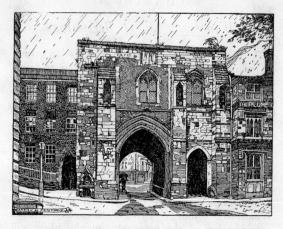

WEST GATE FROM THE HIGH STREET

fine specimen of a disk barrow; at Twyford, where there are evidences of the existence of a miniature Stonehenge; at Worthy Down, where in 1919 an Early Iron Age pit village was laid bare. From Micheldever to Bitterne; from the Great Plain and Quarley Mount to Old Winchester Hill and Butser Hill the early peoples, dwelling sometimes on the hill-tops, and sometimes in water-defended strongholds, moved freely about the country. At the ford at the foot of the chalk spur, now known as St. Giles's Hill, their trackways met. In fact, this spur, pushing

4

out like a huge finger to touch the river in its course north to south, created the ford. It was the only point for some miles north or south where the river spread out on a wide bed of hard chalk and flint to give a crossing scarce ankle deep. What more suitable or more natural place for the uprise of a town? The confluence of many trackways; an ideal ford; a wide green sward sloping gently to the river; steeply rising downs to east and west giving shelter from winter winds; a never-failing water supply; no place more desirable for human habitation was ever found.

But the question has long been debated by archæologists whether the first dwellers lived by the ford, or on the conical hill of St. Catherine's a mile distant. It is of course a commonplace that some of the early tribes feared the low areas, and chose to live on a hill-top, where they were safer from surprise by enemy tribes. But there is ample evidence that there were tribes who did not fear to live in the vales and by the rivers. The many finds of the remains of Neolithic men at several points in the Itchen valley, e.g. at Bishopstoke, Compton, Bitterne, prove that not all the early dwellers in the county were hill-top men.

It seems very probable that the successive waves of Celts—Goidels, Brythons, and Belgæ—invading the county from the continent, and establishing themselves by force of arms, needed to live in strong fortifications. They would fear reprisals by the tribes they dispossessed. St. Catherine's Hill has been proved to be, not a Roman camp, as used to be popularly supposed, but a Celtic stronghold, probably Brythonic.

Some careful excavations, carried out on the hill

5

from the year 1925 onwards, by several zealous Wykehamists, have demonstrated that it was used as a dwelling-place for some centuries. Sections were cut through the earthen ramparts, and a number of dwelling-pits were excavated within the enclosure. Many relics have been found, the earliest being placed by archæologists in the period 700–500 B.C., but most belong to the period termed La Tene I, about 500–300 B.C.

The excavations appear to show that the first dwellers on the hill lived there without fortifications. The deep fosse, a hundred feet across from lip to lip in places, which girdles the hill like a crown, though pygmy in size when compared with the mighty earthworks at Maidun Castle in Dorset, is nevertheless impressive at close quarters. The recent excavations would seem to point to its having been constructed about 400 B.C. If this conjecture be correct the likelihood is that the men who made it belonged to the Brythonic race, iron users who had displaced Bronze Age men. They used iron not only for weapons, but also for money, in the form of flat bars not unlike a long sword in the rough. Specimens of these currency bars, as they are called, were found in Winchester in the middle of the last century, and in 1919 a hoard of thirteen was found at Worthy Down when excavations were being made by the Royal Air Force to enlarge one of their hangars at that aerodrome. The hangar proved to be almost in the middle of an Early Iron Age pit village. The bars were found about a couple of feet below the modern ground level.

The earthworks thrown up on St. Catherine's Hill by these Iron Age people made the camp one of some strength. There was an entrance gate on the north-east side which had, in its latest period at least, a timber guard-house on either hand. The excavations made in 1927 showed clearly that the camp had been taken by storm, and the guard-houses destroyed by fire. Correlative evidence would seem to show that this capture and destruction took place about 250–200 B.C. The traces of any subsequent occupation of the hill are extremely few. The assumption which may be drawn from these discoveries is that the Belgæ, a warlike tribe of Teutonic origin, who invaded the country about 200 B.C., were the conquerors of the Brythons, who lived on the hill, and that they themselves, scorning to live in a hill stronghold, founded a settlement at the ford.

The earliest name of Winchester, Caer Gwent, is Celtic, and is said to mean the White City. Possibly this was from the chalk hills and downs around. But some philologists have identified the name with a Celtic word which means selling, hence Caer Gwent would mean the Market Town. Either interpretation would have fitted Winchester in its early days, for the white chalk is everywhere, and the settlement at the ford would undoubtedly have been a place of general trade. The first syllable in the modern name, Win, is no doubt cognate with the Celtic word, Gwent.

It may thus be taken as highly probable that the Celtic Belgæ were the first founders of Winchester on its present site, and that they were the people living there when the Romans invaded the island in A.D. 43.

The Belgæ, so far from being the rude, ignorant savages suggested by Roman writers, were people of considerable culture. They were skilled artificers in the metals, and they had an art of designing in

7

enamel which was approved even by their conquerors. By the date of the Roman occupation they had become very numerous south of the Thames, and there is a tradition that Gwent was their metropolis. It is recorded by Milner and other historians that the task of subduing them was entrusted to Vespasian, then a rising officer in the Roman army, and that he had to fight thirty battles and capture twenty towns before his task was completed; but the story rests on unsatisfactory evidence.

The strategic importance of Winchester in the business of subduing the island, and establishing the *Pax Romana* within its borders, must have been seen at once by the conquerors, and they seem to have established a military station here very early in their occupation. It was ideal for their requirements. It was a comfortable day's march from their landing-place at Clausentum, modern Bitterne, and there was the advantage of the river Itchen as a means of conveyance for heavy goods and munitions. Moreover, it lay right in the gap between the great forests and on the road to the heart of the country to be subdued and controlled.

Whatever kind of a town the Romans found here they certainly, on coming into possession, planned the place according to their usual formula, with two main streets crossing at right angles in the centre. The present High Street unquestionably follows the exact line of the Roman street running from west to east, but as it strikes straight at the ford it may well have been also the main street of the Belgic town.

The Romans built a strong wall around the city, with four gates opening on to the principal roads at the four points of the compass. It is uncertain

8

THE CATHEDRAL FROM THE NORTH-WEST; EARLY MORNING

whether the city wall built in medieval times followed
the line of the Roman wall, but the probabilities are
that it did, at any rate, for a considerable part of its
length. The Roman town was probably smaller
than the medieval city, and lay slightly higher up the
slope from the river. The line of the Roman street
running north and south is uncertain. It may have
been a little to the west of the present London-
Southampton road.

Very early in the occupation Winchester, or
Venta Belgarum, as the Romans called it—"Belgarum" being necessary to distinguish it from the
two other Ventas in the island, one in Norfolk and
the other in Monmouthshire—became a station of
importance. This is evident from the number of
Roman roads running from it. There were five.
From the east port, across the ford, went the road
over the downs to Portus Magnus, now Portchester,
with a divergence to Chichester possibly. From the
south port went the road to Clausentum, or Bitterne,
keeping close to the Itchen most of the way. Out of
the west port, up the steep downs in the rear of the
city, and no doubt traversing a British trackway,
went the road to Old Sarum, and to the lead mines in
Mendip. From the north port went two ways, one
north-westwards to Cirencester, and the other north-
eastwards to Calleva Atrebatum, now Silchester.
This last was also the road to Londinium.

Dean Kitchen, an esteemed historian of Winchester, reckoned a sixth Roman road to emerge from
the East Gate, and strike north-eastwards towards
London or Dover, on the line of the modern road to
London, over Magdalen Hill. The straightness of
this modern road for about four miles at first sight
suggests a Roman road. The learned Dean supposed

10

that the Romans began to make a road toward Dover, but desisted on finding the difficulty of penetrating the dense forest of the Andredesweald. The idea is a mistaken one. The straightness of the road has been satisfactorily established as due to the Turnpike Commission which was operating in the middle of the eighteenth century.

The disposition of the buildings in Roman Winchester is surmised to have been that usual in Roman towns, e.g. the public buildings in the south-west, and the religious buildings in the south-east. It is even conjectured that a Roman temple stood upon the site of the present cathedral, and that, in turn, upon the site of a Druid circle. In each case it is sheer supposition. The idea rests solely upon the vaguest tradition. Moreover, the fifteenth-century story, told by the monk Rudborne, that here was the first Christian church in the island, founded by a supposed King Lucius, is a priestly concoction, as also is the story from the same source that the Emperor Constantine founded at Winchester a Christian college.

The nature of the site on which the present cathedral stands, as disclosed by the preservation works which were carried on during the years 1905–12, would appear to show that the site in Roman times was too swampy, certainly at the east end, to have allowed of the erection of any substantial building. It is not an unreasonable assumption that at the beginning of the Christian era the river Itchen was fuller in body, and the fringing marsh much wider, than would be the case to-day were the site still wild. More than half the present cathedral was built upon a wedge of peat twenty-four feet thick at the east end, and thinning down to nothing when nearing the west end. The Normans built upon a raft of beech logs placed on the peat. That the Romans built a temple in such a morass calls for some credence, especially when it is obvious that there was solid ground farther up the slope to the west. The fact that the Anglo-Saxons built a cathedral there five hundred years later proves nothing concerning a Roman temple. The Anglo-Saxons, coming from the flats of north Europe, would have been quite at home in such marshy ground. The only scraps of evidence which may in any way be held to support the idea of a Roman temple being erected on the site of the present cathedral are: (1) the existence of two very ancient wells in the crypt directly under the tower; and (2) the discovery, during the works 1905–12, near the south-east corner of the nave, of old foundations, faintly suggesting an apse, and a fragment of tessellated pavement. Each of these bits of evidence may just as reasonably point to the existence of any building other than a Roman temple; and even the scrap of tessellated pavement may have belonged to a Roman villa.

Many Roman remains have been dug up in and near the present city; indeed, they continue to come to light with every extensive excavation which is made. Remains of eight or nine buildings have been found within the ambit of the medieval walls, and three just outside. Roman cinerary urns and other evidences of human burial by Romans have been found on three sides of Winchester, in each case close to the highway emerging from the city port; while one has been found just inside the medieval boundary. It is right to note, however, that this last is considered by many authorities to be doubtful as a Roman burial. It was discovered in 1838, five feet below the surface, on sloping ground just behind the present Corn Exchange, and very close to the modern highway known as Staple Gardens.

While allowing that the evidence indicating this interment as Roman is slight, e.g. some Roman coins found near it, it may be urged that here, possibly, is some proof that the north wall of the Roman city

ANCIENT BRIDGE AT HYDE ABBEY, WINCHESTER

stood a little to the south of the medieval wall, and nearer to the Via Principalis, or High Street. The site of this burial was one hundred and twenty yards inside the medieval north gate. The Romans made their burials outside their cities, and by the sides of their highways. There is some ground for supposing that the Roman road crossing the Via Principalis took the line now followed by Staple Gardens. This burial, if indeed a Roman one, may have been made just outside the north port of the Roman wall. The fact that very few Roman relics of any kind have

13

been found north of the High Street, and not a single vestige of a Roman building, helps the argument that the Roman wall probably took a line farther to the south than the medieval wall. All definite traces that have been found of Roman buildings have been on or to the south of the High Street.

Portions of foundations of Roman buildings have been found in or close to the High Street at the following points: Hammond Passage, the south end of Upper Brook Street, and, as lately as 1928, Colebrook Street. These remains in each case included fragments of tessellated pavement, that found in 1928 being of plain red tile, coarse in size, and possibly belonging to some outbuilding or walk.

During some excavations in Minster Street and Symonds Street in 1878 a large piece of tessellated pavement of geometrical pattern, ornamented with dolphins, was found at a depth of 11 ft. 8 in. This may have belonged to a villa extending somewhat to the south for, two years later, another fragment of pavement was found in a garden on the other side of the Close wall not many yards away. The piece of pavement found in Minster Street was taken up with care, and may now be seen in the city museum.

Some fragments of pavement which were found, along with evidences of the foundations of a building, during the erection of supporting buttresses on the south side of the cathedral nave in 1910, were judged to be Roman. The tesseræ were taken up, and laid, in the order as found, in the porch of the deanery where they may be seen by the curious.

In the early part of the nineteenth century a large piece of tessellated pavement of a coarse pattern was found a little to the north-east of Wolvesey ruins, as well as a couple of fragments of Samian ware.

14

Winchester in its Beginning

Sir Christopher Wren found a tessellated pavement somewhere in the precincts of Winchester Castle when he was preparing to build a new palace for Charles II on the site now occupied by the barracks. A century and a half later, when the London-Southampton railway line was being cut, further discoveries of a Roman building or villa were made slightly to the west. It is thought that Wren's discovery, and the remains laid bare by the railway cutting, were all part of the same villa, which would certainly have been outside the circuit of the Roman walls.

On the east of the city remains have been found of two villas, both outside the walls. The one on the eastern side included a tessellated pavement, the other, roof tiles and foundations. Two further finds are doubtful as to date, one on the south, and the other on the north.

Chief among the smaller relics of Roman occupation found in Winchester is a small altar, now in the British Museum. It was discovered in Jewry Street in 1854, is of blue sandstone, and measures 19 in. by 8 in. When discovered it was imbedded in the foundations of the street boundary wall of the old gaol, which was then being demolished. Obviously it must have been picked up elsewhere and built into the foundations by workmen who were quite ignorant of its real character. It is even possible that it had served as a piece of building stone for one or other of the religious edifices of the city which were destroyed at the Reformation, and were subsequently treated as quarries by the builders of the neighbourhood.

This altar is the only fragment bearing a Roman inscription which has been found in the city. Although a few letters are missing, it can be satisfactorily deciphered. The letters remaining are in this order:

MATRIB

ITAL S GER

MANIS

GAL · BRIT

· NTONIVS

· CRETIANVS

· F · COS · REST ·

The agreed reading is:

Matrib(us) Ital(i)s Germanis Gal(lis) Brit(annis) (A)ntonius (Lu)cretianus (bene)f(iciarius) co(n)s(ularis) rest(ituit).

To the Italian, German, Gallic, and British Mothers, restored by Antonius Lucretianus, beneficiary of the governor [of the province].

It is suggested by Professor Haverfield in the *Victoria County History* that this relic may very likely date from the latter part of the first century, because of its reference to the mothers of four countries, that being a period when a legion recruited from all those countries was likely to have been quartered in or near Winchester. A beneficiarius was a soldier promoted to some special service, but exactly what kind of service is not known.

Other Roman relics found in Winchester include pottery of New Forest make, Samian and other pottery, ampullæ, cinerary urns, a bronze tap, and earthenware lamps. One of the last named, found near Orams Arbour, is exquisite in design, and is imprinted with the potter's mark, a naked foot.

Coins of many dates have been found in several parts of the city, and scarcely a year passes without

16

one or more being added to the store. There is, however, a preponderance of the coins of the usurpers Carausius and Allectus. One of the latter was found as lately as 1929 during excavations on the north side of High Street.

One reference has already been made to a supposed Roman burial. Others, more definitely Roman, have been found in Hyde Street. When digging out a cellar near the corner of Hyde Close a row of urns was found in 1780; and in the nineteenth century, when building a brewery about thirty yards to the south, more urns were discovered. This was probably the site of a fairly extensive Roman cemetery. Other relics of burials, with Roman coins accompanying them, were laid bare in 1842 about a furlong to the west. Roman cinerary urns have also been found in St. James's Lane, on the south-west of the city; also on the slopes of St. Giles's Hill, where, in 1878, two lead coffins were found 4 ft. below the surface. One contained the skeleton of a woman, and the other of a man. The latter had a coin of Constantine at the head.

With few exceptions all the Roman relics and pave-ments have been reached at a depth of 10 ft. to 12 ft. below the present ground level. This accords, roughly, with the depths at which Roman remains have been found in other towns similar to Winchester in Roman occupation.

CHAPTER II

Winchester before Senlac

WINCHESTER must have remained continuously under Roman rule for three hundred and sixty-five years. One of the earliest towns to be swept into the Roman scheme of government, it must have been among the very last to be abandoned when the Romanized population was left to its own devices after the withdrawal of the last legion in the early years of the fifth century. It was too near the "Saxon Shore" and too much under the menace of the pirates from the continental seaboard to be given up until the last moment. Its position on the main line of the middle route to the continent, through Clausentum and the Gallic peninsula where now stands Cherbourg, would make it a point of importance to the very end of the period of Roman dominance, as well as during the long struggle between the Romano-British inhabitants and the Teutonic invaders.

The Roman period is a long one; few people realize how long. It is more than twice as long as that of the British rule in India to date. It is as though the Claudian invasion took place in the year Shakespeare was born, and the legions were only now on the point of departure. It was a period in which the whole population of Winchester, and the area around, must have become thoroughly Latinized; as Roman as the Romans in speech and social habit.

18

Hampshire in those three and a half centuries became a very fertile country, certainly in its arable areas. It must have been covered with the villas of affluent Roman or Romano-British landowners. The sites of over fifty of these villa farmsteads have been discovered in the county. In many cases complete foundations have been laid bare, proving buildings of considerable size to have been reared upon them. And it may reasonably be assumed that many more such sites still lie hidden beneath the soil of centuries. Winchester, then as now, was the centre of the agricultural activities of the district.

There is evidence that Winchester was not only concerned with cereals, being in the middle of a corn-growing district, but it was also a place where there was an imperial factory for the weaving of wool. In a list of Roman officials, made probably in the fourth century, there is a reference to a director, or manager, "of the imperial weaving works at Venta in Britain." (Procurator gynaecii in Britannis Ventensis.) The country around the Norfolk Venta was, and is, unsuited to sheep farming and the raising of wool, and the area of the Monmouthshire Venta is equally inappropriate for the purpose. Winchester, on the other hand, is now, and has been for many centuries, an ideal district for sheep raising, hence it may reasonably be assumed that the Venta referred to in this early record is Venta Belgarum, or Winchester.

At that time Winchester was a peaceful, residential town, and probably had been such for some three centuries. It was far removed from the scene of the Pictish border troubles, and from the British forays along the Welsh marches. An analogy may be drawn between the Winchester of those days and a jute-weaving town of Bengal to-day in contrast with the North-West Frontier of India. No doubt a great proportion of the corn grown in the country around, as well as much of the woollen cloth woven in Winchester, passed to Rome via Clausentum (Bitterne) and the Cherbourg peninsula, just as did much of the pig lead from the Mendip mines.

But the legions departed, and with them went the alien defence which had for so long held off the Saxon marauders who swarmed in the narrow seas. Whether the Roman or Romano-British owners of the many villa homesteads in the county and the Isle of Wight departed at the same time there is no evidence to show. Even at Silchester, most complete and extensive of all the Roman remains in Hampshire, there is no evidence to support the tradition of a storming invasion, and such destruction as would be expected if the Saxon invaders dispossessed the Romano-British occupiers with fire and sword. The actual evidence is all the other way. Silchester appears to have been vacated and allowed to fall into natural decay. What happened at Winchester no one knows. The earliest Saxon records are too mythical, and were written down too long after the supposed events to have any real value as history.

It is interesting, however, to note what these early stories say. Cerdic and Cynric, Saxon chiefs, are said to have landed at the head of Southampton Water early in the sixth century, and driving the Britons northwards, they broke the native resistance at Charford, near Salisbury. The story goes on that the victorious Saxons turned and stormed Winchester, and, subduing all the area which is now Hampshire, they laid the foundation of the Wessex kingdom. The first part of this story is now believed to be substantially true,

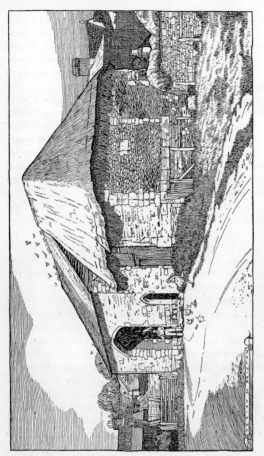

GATEWAY AT HYDE ABBEY

mainly because of the prevalence of undoubted Saxon characteristics in the native population of the Avon basin, the route of the first Saxon advance in this part of the island. But, whether that part of the story which deals with Winchester is true or myth it is very difficult to say.

The evidence of Silchester rather suggests that Winchester also was vacated by the Romano-British without a fight, and that the place was left as a dead city to decay as it would. It may have been many years, perhaps generations, before the Saxon immigrants decided to use the site for one of their tribal "tuns," and built their city of Wintonceaster upon the Roman ruins.

The reason for thinking that there was a long interregnum before the Saxons settled at Winchester rests upon more than the fact that the earliest date that the place is mentioned in the *Anglo-Saxon Chronicle* is A.D. 643. There is the curious and significant dislike of the high road displayed by the Saxon everywhere in the county. There are scores of villages of Saxon foundation, bearing even now in their names the evidence of their Saxon origin, all of which are off the great trunk roads of the Romans. It is plain from the fact that scarcely a single genuinely Saxon village can be found upon any one of the Roman highways, that the Saxons had a racial dislike of broad highways, and preferred to have their little "hams" or "leys" in clearings hidden away in the forest approached only by narrow winding ways. Assuming, then, that the area which is now Hampshire was occupied by these reticent Saxons, who preferred seclusion to the publicity of the high road, the cross-roads and the ford, it is reasonable to suppose that it was quite a long while before they overcame their racial dislike of such a place, and elected to build a Saxon "tun" at Winchester.

The Jutes, or "Meonwara," smallest of the three north European tribes to strive for a footing in Britain, were probably the first to arrive in Hampshire. They settled in the Isle of Wight, and on either side of Southampton Water, particularly in the Meon Valley, to which they gave their name. But there is no evidence whatever that they got as far as Winchester. The high downs between their settlements and Winchester, as well as the old British defences at St. Catherine's Hill and Old Winchester Hill, may have been quite sufficient to deter them from adventuring thus far. Their settlements probably began immediately the well-organized Roman opposition to such immigration was removed, and no doubt went on throughout the middle years of the fifth century.

The tradition that King Arthur rallied the British forces at Winchester, and that Winchester was Camelot, is utterly wrong. Camelot can much more justifiably be fixed in Somerset.

The eclipse of Winchester in Anglo-Saxon story during the fifth and sixth centuries and the greater part of the seventh is conclusively proved by the fact that Southampton, a Saxon port of importance, and not Winchester, gave its name to the shire. Not Wintonscire, but Hamtunscire, was the name given to the area, and to this day the official name of the shire is the County of Southampton, though popularly Hampshire.

Some authorities, arguing from the scanty records in the *Anglo-Saxon Chronicle*, consider that the occupation of Hampshire by the Saxons was much later than A.D. 508, that it was an occupation effected

with very little fighting, and that it was an invasion
by way of the Thames valley, and southwards through
Reading, probably in the last two decades of the
sixth century. This theory of the Saxon settlement
in Hampshire seems to be borne out by the fact that
the centre of the West-Saxon kingdom in the early
part of the seventh century was somewhere in the
Thames valley; and when the Christian missionary
Birinus converted the West-Saxon king Cynegils to
Christianity in A.D. 634, it was at Dorchester, Oxford-
shire (Durocina of the Romans), on one of the tribu-
taries of the Thames, that the West-Saxon bishop's
see was fixed.

Not for forty years was Winchester to be the seat
of the bishopric, although the first move towards the
old Celtic and Roman centre was made in 643, when
Cenwalch, son of Cynegils, in obedience to his father's
orders, began to build the first great Saxon church
or minster within the ambit of the ruined Roman
walls, approximately on the site where stands the
present cathedral. But it is extremely probable
that Hampshire had been "shorn" off from the rest
of the Saxon kingdom (the word "shire" meaning
an area shorn off from another area) some years
before, probably as early as the beginning of the
seventh century. The shire was defined roughly on
the same boundaries as now, but it must have been
half a century or more before Winchester began to
see the renaissance of civic life within its walls. The
building of a great Saxon church there was probably
part of a larger plan in the minds of Cynegils and his
Witan, namely, the deliberate choice of Winchester
as the centre of civil government, as well as ecclesiastical rule, and as the centre, ultimately, not only
of the shire of which it was as near as possible the

geographical centre, but also of the whole kingdom of the Gewissas, or West Saxons.

However that may be, it is undisputed that Cenwalch (or Kenwal) began to build the first Saxon minster in A.D. 643, or soon after. The *Anglo-Saxon Chronicle* (Ingram's translation) says: "This year Kenwal succeeded to the kingdom of the West-Saxons, and held it one and thirty winters. This Cenwalch ordered the old church at Winchester to be built in the name of St. Peter. He was the son of Cynegils."

In A.D. 676, by which time it may be assumed that the Saxon minster at Winchester was completed, the see of the bishop of the area was transferred from Dorchester to Winchester. Hedda, or Haeddi, was the bishop who carried out the transfer. Nor was the see alone transferred; the treasured relics, including the bones of the sainted Birinus, missionary, and first bishop of the West Saxons, who had been buried in the cathedral church at Dorchester, were also taken to the new church at Winchester.

Another story tells how Cynegils himself began the building of the minster at Winchester, and endowed it with the land for seven miles around Winchester, but, dying before the completion of the church, he laid it upon his son to finish it, which he did. Although there is so much that is mythical, or of a deliberately fictitious character concocted during the Middle Ages concerning Winchester Cathedral and its origin, it nevertheless seems safe to accept the middle of the seventh century as approximately the date for the founding of a Christian church or cathedral on or close to the present site.

With the founding of the cathedral, and the consequent shifting of the centre of the ecclesiastical rule to Hampshire, Winchester became the capital of the West-Saxon kingdom. It was from Winchester that King Ine, or Ina, one of the greatest of the Saxon kings, issued a famous code of laws for his people. He is said to have initiated the tax known as "Peter's Pence," levied on every family in the kingdom for centuries, and cordially hated by the people. Originally an impost to pay for the upkeep of an English college at Rome, it was later taken by the Popes as an ecclesiastical tax. It was abolished at the Reformation.

During the next century Winchester no doubt recovered all its lost importance as one of the chief cities of the south. A monastery on the Benedictine plan and rule was founded by the side of the minster church, encouraged and helped, doubtless, by the pious Ine. A royal palace was built near by, at Wolvesey, a water-defended stronghold lying between the monastery and the fast flowing river Itchen.

But notwithstanding its restored importance as the principal town of Wessex, Winchester in the eighth century showed no sign in itself, or in its rulers, of its future importance as the nucleus of the British Empire. Quarrelling, and even assassination, mark the reigns of several Wessex kings. Cenulph, after a long period of rule, was unlucky enough to be surprised at the home of his mistress not far from Winchester, and was killed before her eyes by Cunehard, brother of the deposed Sigberht, whom Cenulph had succeeded. Cenulph was buried in the minster at Winchester, and, according to the inscription thereon, his bones still repose in one of the mortuary chests in the present cathedral.

But, at the court of Brethric, Cenulph's son and successor, was his cousin Ecgberht, a handsome young

prince of the Saxon line, who was destined to become
the supreme ruler of all England, and the ancestor
of all future English sovereigns save four, i.e. Cnut,
the two Harolds, and William the Conqueror.
Brethric was jealous of Ecgberht, and his harshness
drove Ecgberht away from Winchester to France,
where for a while he found honourable sanctuary at
the court of the mighty Charlemagne. Then Brethric
died suddenly, poisoned, it is said, by his queen, and
Ecgberht was recalled to Winchester, where he was
crowned King of the West Saxons in 802.

The seventh century saw the supremacy of the
Kingdom of Northumbria under Eadwine. The
eighth century saw the overlordship of England pass
to Mercia under such great kings as Æthelred,
Æthelbald, and Offa, the last named being the
greatest king that England had yet seen. With
different succession, or with better fortune, the
British Empire might have been founded at York, or,
under Offa's successors, at Northampton or Bedford.

But the destiny of Empire was otherwise. Offa
died, and under his successor Beornwulf, Mercia's
overlordship was challenged by the young Wessex
king, Ecgberht. After successful campaigns in
Kent and Sussex, and then in Cornwall, Ecgberht
attacked his overlords the Mercians. A great battle
was fought at Ellandun in Wiltshire, Beornwulf was
killed, and Mercia came under Ecgberht's rule. He
then made preparations to attack the Northumbrians,
but, tired of civil war, and also perceiving a bigger
danger threatening from without, they sent to
Ecgberht acknowledging him as overlord. Ecgberht
was soon after crowned King of the English at
Winchester (A.D. 826). It was the moment of the
beginning of the British Empire; for, although

27

England was afterwards split by the Danish invasions, from Ecgberht sprang the ruling house, and in Wessex was nurtured, through all the dissensions of the ninth and tenth centuries, all that was finest

MORTUARY CHEST IN CATHEDRAL, CONTAINING BONES OF KINGS CANUTE AND RUFUS, QUEEN EMMA, AND ST. ALWYN

and best of Anglo-Saxon spirit and tradition. Moreover, for over two hundred years Winchester flourished, not only as the capital of Wessex, but also as the political hub of the whole realm.

One of the factors which helped to bring about the union of the English kingdoms under the strong rule of Ecgberht, was the growing menace of the Danish invasions. These began with a swooping raid on Wareham in Dorset in the year 787. Nothing more was heard of the raiders for six years, and then, in 793, came a very destructive foray at Lindisfarne. The Danish attacks became more and more frequent after this, no part of the seaboard being safe from their daring onslaughts.

Ecgberht dealt with the Danes with a strong hand whenever they essayed to strike inland. But his lack of sea power prevented him from coping with them on the coast, and consequently the coastal townships suffered severely. In his lifetime he kept the Danes out of inland Wessex, but the midlands and the northern shires were frequently penetrated by their marauding bands before Ecgberht could organize an effective resistance. The other parts of the country seemed to look to Wessex to lead the attack against the foreign foe. Hence it came about that when the Danes became settlers instead of mere raiders, it was in the East Midlands and the northern shires that they secured their best footing.

Things became worse after the death of Ecgberht. His son, Æthelwulf, besides being far less of a soldier than his father, had to meet a fiercer and a more widespread invasion. The destruction wrought by the invaders was appalling. Many large towns had been burnt; monasteries and churches had been destroyed and their occupants slain, while their priceless treasures of jewelled vessels and illuminated manuscripts were carried away. It seemed as though the supreme lust for destruction was vented primarily upon everything Christian. As a result most of the scholarship and literature, which had made the English Church noteworthy among western nations, disappeared at this time.

29

Wessex, relatively safe during Ecgberht's reign, at last began to suffer the common fate of the rest of the realm. By the time that the grandsons of Ecgberht came to reign, three of them successively in the short space of fourteen years, the Danish raids on Wessex were frequent. In 860 a big Danish fleet sailed up Southampton Water; the raiders disembarked, and pushing swiftly up the Itchen valley, "destrued Winchester al out."

This was the most daring raid the Danes had yet made, for it was a stroke at the very heart of England. Their success was due, doubtless, to the swiftness of their onslaught, and the consequent difficulty of spreading the warning along the countryside so that the native defences could be roused and mustered. But the temerity of the invaders was met by a successful, if tardy ripost.

The ealdormen of Hampshire, Osric and Æthelwulf, unable with their small forces to stem the rush of the invaders, were obliged to leave the city to its fate. But they hastened to beat up the "fyrds" of Hampshire and Berkshire. A large native force assembled near Romsey, possibly at Toot Hill, and, led by Osric and Æthelwulf, they fell upon the raiders as they were straggling back, laden with booty, to their ships at Southampton. The Danes had to leave their spoil and fight for their lives. Many were killed in this historic fight, and it was a very depleted fleet which eventually succeeded in escaping.

This disastrous raid must have meant the complete destruction of Winchester as a city, for most of the houses were built of wood, or wattle and daub, and all with roofs of thatch, or wood shingles. The scene after the raid must have been ghastly, the once fair city nothing but a smoking pyre, and hacked

30

corpses lying in dreadful nakedness where, but a short while before, had been bustling life and activity.

But the great monastery, then, as now, chief of the buildings of Winchester, went unscathed. This was because Swithun, appointed prior a few years before, had built a great wall of flint rubble around the monastery buildings, a sufficient obstacle to the Danish raiders. The lesson of the raid of 860, and the immunity of the monastery because of the foresight of Swithun, was not lost upon the people of Winchester who had survived the raid by timely flight. The old Roman walls were probably entirely destroyed, or at best in ruins. Speedily the site of the city was encircled with a wall, like the monastery wall, of flint; and the houses were rebuilt within the defensive ambit. When, a few years later, another marauding band swept eastwards from Southampton, penetrating even as far as Alton, which they destroyed as they had done Winchester in 860, Winchester now escaped, the raiders having to be content with deriding the townsfolk, who watched them from the wall as they passed on their way back to their ships.

The ninth century saw three great men arise in Wessex and Winchester: Ecgberht, Swithun, and Alfred, grandson of Ecgberht. It is possible that much of Alfred's greatness was inherited from his grandfather. It is certain that the foundation of his learning was laid by Swithun, who was his sagacious tutor.

Swithun was the greatest as well as the humblest man of the age. In his younger days tutor to the royal princes, he later became prior of the great monastery, and at length bishop of the diocese. The records declare that he it was who caused the first stone bridge to be thrown across the Itchen at the great ford, and that, while the bridge was a-building, he used to sit near by, speeding the builders and admonishing those who were of a mind to idle. When he died his innate humility was shown by his directions for his interment. His wish was that he might lie, not in any place of honour in the great cathedral church, but out in the open where men might walk over his head, and where the rains of heaven would fall.

He was buried as he requested, just outside the old minster, but with the passing of the years a tradition of sainthood grew up around his name. Hence, when the greed of monastic establishments for the possession of the relics or bones of saints grew beyond the bounds of reason, they dug his body up, and encased it in a magnificent shrine which they housed in the cathedral for pilgrims to adore.

No wonder that there arose another tradition, that rain upon the day of his canonization, the 15th of July, will mean rain for forty days thereafter. Men said that the very heavens wept on the day of his sacrilegious translation from the grave of his choice to the pompous shrine within the cathedral, and they would continue to weep for the mystic period of forty days as a sign of the saint's displeasure at their impious disregard of his dying wish.

Alfred, apt pupil of the pious and scholarly Swithun, was the youngest of the four sons of Æthelwulf. His chance of kingship must have seemed slight indeed when his father died in 857, leaving the crown to his sons in order of age. Yet Æthelbald, Æthelbert, and Æthelred in turn ruled, the last being killed in a battle with the Danes in 871, their combined reigns totalling fourteen years. Alfred, who had lived in comparative obscurity, was crowned at Winchester, succeeding to a kingdom which was overrun by enemies, and menaced by alien fleets in all the seas.

He was but twenty-two years of age when the burden of monarchy fell upon him. He had already proved his valour as a soldier in hand-to-hand fighting. He was now to prove himself statesman and scholar as great as any the realm has known before or since.

The story of how he at length broke the Danish menace belongs to the greater canvas of English history. It must be passed over here, for the fighting went on for the most part at a distance from Winchester. Only one isolated raid, which took place after the Danish treaties had been made, appears to be connected with Winchester. A body of Northumbrian Danes broke the treaty by coming into Hampshire on a marauding excursion. They were dispersed, and some of their number captured. Alfred had those who were captured brought to Winchester, where they were executed, their bodies being hung out over the walls of Wolvesey palace, facing the river, a grim warning to others of their race to abide by the treaty.

There is still at Warsash, in Hamble creek, off Southampton Water, the wreck of an ancient galley which is visible at low tide. It is an oaken craft with triple planks, clinker-built, fastened with iron bolts, and its length is about one hundred and thirty feet. Tradition says this is one of the Danish ships which Alfred sank in a sea battle with his enemies. A small portion of this vessel has been detached, and now hangs in the Winchester Westgate Museum. It is a reminder of the fact that Alfred, perceiving that the best defence of England must be a force upon the sea, built a number of ships larger and faster

D

than those of the enemy, and thus he was enabled to defeat them on their own element. He may, therefore, justly be regarded as the founder of the British Navy.

Another very important part of his scheme of defence, and one which exhibited his comprehensive grasp of the essentials of generalship, was the organization of a chain of beacons throughout the country, with wardens at each beacon always in readiness to light the pile of wood, the flame or smoke of which would give swift warning to the whole countryside of the approach of the enemy.

After his triumph over the Danes Alfred spent most of his life at Winchester. His palace at Wolvesey, surrounded by water and marsh, could not have been a healthy spot. Possibly the periodic illness which harassed him for so many years, and shortened his life, was malaria.

Although often prostrated by disease, Alfred's industry was prodigious. For a healthy man his achievements would have been remarkable; for him, with his heavy handicap of ill-health, they were stupendous. He codified the laws of the country, making them plain and intelligible to his people, so that long after his death they were known as the "Laws of Alfred."

This "Codex Wintoniensis," or code of the Laws of the Saxons, was kept at Winchester, in the Old Minster. It was also known as the "Domboc," or Doom Book, i.e. the book recording the "doom" to be pronounced for this or that offence or trespass. But the word "Domboc" has led historians astray, and caused the incorrect statement to be set down that Alfred caused a "Domesday Survey" to be made of all his realm, and the results recorded in a book called *Liber de Winton*. This is entirely wrong. There was no "Domesday Survey" made by Alfred, and the statement that there was a *Liber de Winton* rests upon no more than the misapprehension concerning the real meaning of "Domboc," and the famous forgery of Ingulph.

Alfred's work in the revival of learning was perhaps the greatest of all his astonishing achievements. The Danish wars during two generations had left the churches in ruins, and the monasteries deserted, their former inhabitants either slaughtered by the marauding Danes, or fled to the Continent. Sadly surveying the pitiful situation of his realm from his royal palace at Winchester, Alfred wrote: "There is not one priest south of the Thames who can properly understand the Latin of his own church books, and very few in the whole of England." He set about getting scholars from the Continent to come to London, Winchester, and Oxford to found schools where Englishmen could be instructed. It is even claimed that Alfred's action at this time was the beginning of the University of Oxford.

He himself spent much of his time at Winchester in literary work, in the translation of Latin works into the English tongue. He gathered a band of scholars around him, and directed the translation of a number of works into English. In the Bodleian Library at Oxford is a translation of Pope Gregory's *Pastoral Care*, which Alfred had made at Winchester, the preface to which is thought by some to be in his own handwriting. This particular copy was sent to Worcester, and there are two other similar copies in existence. But perhaps his greatest literary monument is to be found in the *Anglo-Saxon Chronicle*, which he began at Winchester, and which was continued after his death for nearly three hundred years.

Alfred raised England from the lowly position it occupied when he ascended the throne to a leading place among the nations of Western Europe, not only as a nation of naval and military strength, but a nation of increasing scholarship and of enlightened social order. Ever devoutly religious, he caused to be built anew the churches of the land, and for his own royal city of Winchester he had a fond dream of two new monastic foundations to be built within its walls, one for men and another for women. But, like David of old, he died ere his dream could be realized. Worn out by disease, and no doubt by the rigours of his early days, he died in 901 at the comparatively early age of fifty-three.

He was buried in the Old Minster or cathedral church, which had been built by Cynegils and Cenwalch, but it was intended that when the New Minster of which he had dreamed, and which by his will he directed his son to build, was completed, his body should be removed there. New Minster was accordingly built by his son, Edward the Elder, to the north of the Old Minster, between it and the High Street of the city. It is said that the monks of the Old Minster, as soon as the New Minster was completed, could hear o' nights the ghost of the great king wandering about in their church, and they begged that his remains might be speedily removed, in order that his ghost might be at rest. So his remains were translated to the New Minster, the church of his dreams, in the heart of the city where he had lived and worked so long. And near by, a few score yards to the east, the other part of his dream was fulfilled by the erection and establishment of the Nuns'

Minster, known for centuries as Nunnaminster. This was destroyed at the Reformation, but the site is now covered by delightfully kept public gardens, and the memory of Nunnaminster is preserved in Abbey Gardens, Abbey Mill, Abbey Passage. Abbey House, which stands in Abbey Gardens, is the official residence of the Mayor of Winchester for the time being.

But Alfred's bones were not destined to remain in the church raised by his son. Less than two hundred years afterwards the monks of New Minster built a new and larger church and monastery at Hyde, a couple of furlongs outside the north wall of Winchester; and when they moved from the New Minster to Hyde Abbey in 1110 they took with them not only the relics of their imported saint, St. Judocus, popularly St. Josse, but also the bones of Alfred and his son. Tradition says they were buried reverently and with utmost honour before the high altar of the new church at Hyde. But even there they were not to rest undisturbed for ever. The Abbey of Hyde was destroyed at the Reformation, and the tombs of Alfred and his son were defaced and ruined. The leaden caskets containing their bones lay hidden for two centuries more, and then, grubbed up by workmen who were employed by the County of Hampshire to clear the site for a bridewell about the year 1780, the leaden coffins were sold for the sum, it is said, of two guineas, and the money spent on beer, and the once honoured dust of England's greatest king, and of his able son, was scattered no man knows whither. One relic of this wicked despoliation alone remains, but it is not in Winchester. It is at Corby Castle, in Cumberland, whither it was taken by an officer who happened to be serving in Winchester when the bridewell was built. This relic was almost certainly

37

the inscription stone which lay on the great king's tomb, for it is inscribed:

ÆLFRED

REX

DCCCLXXXI

The importance of Winchester was greatly enhanced by Alfred's work. It had been a royal city, as well as the seat of the bishop, for two hundred years before his time, but he raised it to a supreme position in the government of the realm, and by his literary work and ecclesiastical organization made it renowned throughout the Western Church. Even after his death its importance grew. Within its walls were three great monastic establishments. Its bishop ranked next to the archbishop in dignity. At the great Benedictine monastery there grew up the most renowned school of illuminated script in the West, a school where the finest British art vied with the best the Continent could produce, and created works which were unsurpassed in Europe.

Two great figures help in the steady rise of Winchester in ecclesiastical importance, St. Dunstan and St. Æthelwold. Dunstan, a man of outstanding mental ability, and resolute will, had one ambition to which he devoted his life. That was to bring the English Church into line with the papal demands by the extension of the monkish system, and by the enforcement of celibacy among the priestly orders. It was an ambition antagonistic to English sentiment in each feature. The common people had a decided preference for a secular priesthood, native born, and they saw nothing improper in their priests being married men with families; they resented too much interference from Rome, and they looked with disfavour upon the foreign monks who, all too often, helped to make up the strength of the monastic establishments. It was in keeping with English tradition and sentiment that the priests holding office at the Old Minster at Winchester were secular canons, and not regulars. But all over Europe the

THE CITY BRIDGE AND MILL

regular monkish orders, backed by the papal see, were gaining ground, and Dunstan, a monkish zealot to his finger tips, helped on the movement in England.

As a young man he had lived for some time at the Benedictine monastery at Winchester. Later he became Abbot of Glastonbury, then Bishop of Worcester, and at length Archbishop of Canterbury. Swift to perceive the help he could be to the papal schemes, the Pope made Dunstan his legate in England, with the widest powers.

Dunstan soon made his intentions known. He

39

had already marked down for drastic purging the old monastery at Winchester, which had harboured and instructed him as a young man. At this distance of time it is impossible to say whether the charges of corruptness, neglect of spiritual duty, levity, and even immorality, brought against the canons by those who hankered after the monkish regime, were true or false. No doubt plenty of evidence was speedily available to support any charge, however baseless in fact. And the monkish chroniclers who came afterwards saw to it that the case of Dunstan and Rome was presented to posterity in unassailable fashion.

To carry out his purposes at Winchester, Dunstan chose one whom he had known at Winchester and Glastonbury, a man after his own heart. This was Æthelwold, a son of an affluent Winchester citizen. Æthelwold had no doubt received his early education at the school of the Old Minster. He seems early in life to have decided upon the career of a secular priest, but, preferring the severer order of a regular monk, he left Winchester and entered Glastonbury Abbey as a regular. His scholarship, zeal, and pious asceticism marked him for certain preferment. He was made abbot of the thriving abbey of Abingdon-on-Thames, and he soon transformed it into a model of monkish regime. Having accomplished this work Æthelwold was called by Dunstan to the bishopric of Winchester, with the expressed instruction to purge the church in that diocese. It was a fateful moment in the history of the Church in England. It was the beginning of the triumph of the regulars over the seculars. Æthelwold was welcomed by one of his own monks as

A prelate whom the Lord hath caused to be head of the church of Winchester, truly understanding how to preserve the fleecy lambs of Christ from the malignant arts of Satan.

It was, of course, one of the "fleecy lambs" who set down this unctuous tribute.

Æthelwold's method of purging the Old Minster was, to say the least, dramatic. Having secured the support and presence of the king on the first Saturday in Lent, 964, he entered the church of the Old Minster accompanied by a monk who carried on his arm a number of Benedictine cowls. Waiting outside the church were a number of Benedictine monks from the abbey at Abingdon. After a severe homily to the assembled canons on the subject of the necessity for holiness in life, Æthelwold called upon them each to don a cowl, abjure their secular condition, and their wives and families, and conform to the stern rules of St. Benedict, or relinquish their canonries. Only three accepted the conditions. The remainder left their stalls, and the Abingdon monks, waiting outside, were summoned to take their places. It is said that the supplanted canons were pensioned out of the revenues of the monastery.

The displaced canons appealed to the king, who ordered a council to be held at Winchester. But the scales were weighted against the disgruntled clerics, for Archbishop Dunstan himself came from Canterbury to preside over the deliberations, which were held in the refectory of the monastery. The evidence of neglect of duty was overwhelming, and, as though this were not enough, a fortuitous miracle happened, as though Heaven itself approved the change. The great figure of the Christ, looking down from the wall of the refectory, sometimes upon convivial scenes, but now upon bitter quarrel, suddenly spoke with human voice in favour of the newcomers. The controversy ended incontinently and the great monastery entered upon a regime of rigid order.

The scholarship which Alfred had made famous was pursued with even greater diligence; but in nothing did Winchester craftsmen excel more than in illuminated script, which at this time reached its high-water mark. The Benedictional of St. Æthelwold is one of the masterpieces of the time. Scattered, with other priceless books and documents, at the Reformation, and in the Puritan upheaval in the seventeenth century, it passed into private hands, and is now in the possession of the Duke of Devonshire. Although the owner has in recent years presented a copy of the work to Winchester Cathedral, that is but poor solatium for the loss of the priceless original.

Æthelwold must have been a man of unusual energy, far-seeing, and eminently practical. In days when civic hygiene was unknown, and water companies a millennium away, he inaugurated an efficient water supply, not only for the three minsters, and Wolvesey, but also for the city itself. Tapping the Itchen above the city, he led the water by a number of streams through the main streets. Those streams are running yet in the same channels, although some are now culverted. The principal water-course which he constructed still flows through the abbey grounds, past Wolvesey and Winchester College. It is known to Wykehamists as "Logie."

Æthelwold undertook a much greater work, nothing less than the rebuilding of the old minster of Cynegils. For those days it was a mighty undertaking. It was magnificently carried out, if the testimony of contemporary and medieval church historians is to be believed. Built of stone, on a far larger scale than the old minster of Cynegils, which had stood for over three hundred years, this new church of Æthelwold's was so full of chapels, winding passages, towering pillars, that none save the regular habitués could venture in for fear of being lost! In order that the pilgrims, who came from all parts of the realm to see this new wonder of Saxon architecture, might venture through its vast area, special guides were appointed. Truly the vergers and lay clerks of to-day have a long ancestry.

Nor were the services "plain." In common with the other arts music had made great strides at Winchester, and many books of tunes had been written. The craft of organ building, too, had advanced, and it was ordered that a great organ should be built for this magnificent church. One of the books of music written for it is now to be seen in the Bodleian Library at Oxford. It was, there seems little doubt, the most magnificent instrument to be found in Europe.

Two skilled musicians were needed to play this organ, for there were two keyboards, a marvellous thing indeed for those times. Each player had "his own alphabet," for each key was marked with the letter of the note, yet the musicians played "in unity of spirit," sending forth jubilant notes as they thumped the keys with their fists. Organ playing in those days was indeed manual labour. The blowers of this mighty organ had even a heavier task. No fewer than seventy were needed to supply the wind chest, stamping to and fro on many bellows, and all the while shouting and cheering each other on to greater exertion. The organ had a scope of no fewer than four hundred pipes, and, according to a

43

contemporary poet who sang its praises, "the ear cannot abide the brazen bellowing as you draw near. All through the city its music can be heard."

But Æthelwold's church and organ are both gone. After the Conquest the Norman Walkelyn, despising Anglo-Saxon architecture, and no doubt finding Æthelwold's church in bad repair, built a Norman cathedral close by, and then had the old church destroyed. What happened to the organ no one knows.

But, although the Church was gaining in power and increasing in usefulness by the development and perfection of the arts, the state, after a century of beneficent rule by the house of Alfred, fell under the calamitous dominion of Æthelred the Redeless, so named because of his unwillingness to accept advice from his counsellors. Profiting by the weakness of this king the Danes returned to their old practices, harrying the land in many parts. Æthelred's chief defence was to buy the raiders off. For this purpose he imposed a new and hateful tax upon every hide of land, a tax known for centuries afterwards as Danegelt. It was a futile plan, for no sooner had the Danes received the first payment than they returned for more. Then began periods of alternating truce and warfare. During one of the periods of truce Æthelred committed the maddest act of his foolish reign. From his palace at Winchester he issued secret orders that every Dane in the kingdom should be assassinated.

It was a moment when there were many Danes in the country carrying on peaceful trading, but the king's orders were obeyed without question The killing began at Winchester on St. Brice's Day, 1002, and among the slain were the sister of King Swegen (or Sweyn), the Dane, and her children.

WINCHESTER CASTLE HALL, SHOWING ARTHUR'S ROUND TABLE

Swegen exacted a terrible vengeance. For four years, using Hampshire and the Isle of Wight as his base, he burnt, slaughtered, and plundered all over the south of England. Æthelred fled to France to the court of the Duke of Normandy, whose daughter he had married. Seeing no other way to end the terrible warfare the English Witan, gathered at Winchester, solemnly chose Swegen to be King of England. But Swegen's death followed soon after, and he was never crowned. Æthelred was recalled, but he died very soon after his return. The Witan met again at Winchester and chose Cnut, son of Swegen, as king, for the Danes were still in possession of the whole of Wessex and the midland shires. The Londoners refused to accept the vote of the Winchester Witan. They elected Edmund Ironside, son of Æthelred, as king. Seven months of fighting between Cnut and Edmund followed, and then, each respecting the other's prowess, they agreed to share the realm. But Edmund died shortly afterwards, and Cnut became the undisputed ruler of England.

In the nineteen years that he ruled England Cnut proved himself a great king. He strove to understand his English subjects, and succeeded so well that he became almost more English than the English. He spent much of his time at Winchester, and used Southampton as his port for contact with his native country. It was at Southampton that he gave his immortal lesson to his courtiers, although Bosham in Sussex also claims that honour.

Cnut was a generous donor to the monasteries of Winchester. To Alfred's New Minster he gave a massive cross of gold and silver for the high altar. To the Old Minster he gave a more permanent offering, nothing less than "three hides of land

46

called Hille." This is none other than St. Catherine's Hill, which, with the land around, has been held by Winchester Cathedral for nearly nine hundred years continuously. In 1930 the hill was purchased by Old Wykehamists, and presented to Winchester College.

Dying in 1035 Cnut was buried in the Old Minster. Centuries later his bones, in danger of being scattered, were gathered up, together with those of his wife Ælgyfa (or Emma), and bestowed in a chest of wood. And there they are to this day, on one of the screens of Bishop Fox. In the same chest are said to be the bones of a couple of bishops!

Winchester became of less importance in the reign of Edward the Confessor, for that king preferred Westminster to the older capital. But he was crowned at Winchester and, every year, he "wore his crown" there, as well as at Westminster and Gloucester. This "wearing the crown" was something like an annual coronation, followed by a gorgeous procession through the streets of the city. And Winchester was still too important a place not to be visited by the king frequently for the purposes of government and the administration of justice, most of which took place in the king's presence, if it was not actually dealt with by himself. It was two centuries later that the administration of justice began to be deputed to itinerant justices.

Winchester during the Confessor's reign was the centre of the English, or anti-Norman party, the head of which was Earl Godwine, and the Dowager Queen Emma. The Confessor banished his mother to Nunnaminster, and there she lived out her last days, triumphantly surviving the calumnies which were brought against her by the Norman interlopers

47

who thronged her son's court. The story of the ordeal of the red-hot ploughshares in Winchester Cathedral is, however, spurious, and probably a monkish invention of two or three centuries later.

Among the property which Emma (or Ælgyfa, to use the Anglo-Saxon form of her name) held in Winchester was the manor of God Begot, on the north side of the High Street. Æthelred the Redeless, her first husband, and father of Edward the Confessor, gave her this manor in 1012. On her death in 1052 she bequeathed it to the Old Minster, in which possession it remained until the Reformation. Its interesting story will be dealt with more fully in a later chapter. Emma lived many years in Winchester, being known as "The Old Lady."

It was during one of the Confessor's visits to Winchester that tragedy overtook his enemy, Earl Godwine. On Easter Monday 1053 Godwine was dining with the king in his palace at Winchester, when, heated with wine, the Confessor revived the old accusation that Godwine had had a hand in the murder of his brother Alfred. Twice before had the Confessor made the charge, but each time, by oaths and gifts, Godwine had denied it, and he doubtless thought the matter was finished with. The renewal of the accusation threw him into a fury. "May this crust of bread that I am eating choke me," he shouted passionately, "if I had any hand in his death." As he spoke his countenance became turgid, he fell on the floor, in a fit, dying four days later. The incident may have been adorned by medieval historians, but it is unquestionably true that Earl Godwine died tragically after a banquet at Winchester, collapsing in the king's presence. Having regard to the fact of the king's brooding

48

suspicion, and his hatred of Godwine because of his power as leader of the English party in the realm, such a singular tragedy suggests that the Confessor may have resorted to poison to rid himself at once of his most powerful enemy, and the man whom he believed to be his brother's murderer.

Godwine's son Harold succeeded him as Earl of Wessex, and, on the death of the Confessor, the Witan elected him as king. But a few short months later he fell at Senlac, with many another from Wessex, including the valiant abbot of the New Minster at Winchester, and a number of his monks whose dead bodies were found on the field near by the body of Harold. The flower of the thegnhood of southern England perished in that momentous conflict, and the alien Norman entered into possession.

There is a legend, spurious beyond doubt, but interesting because of its likeness to other tales of dead heroes (Frederick Barbarossa, Prester John, and others), namely, that Harold did not perish on the hill of Senlac, but that he was found next morning wounded, but alive. The story goes on that two thegns brought him secretly to Winchester, where he was nursed for two whole years by a Saracen woman skilled in leechcraft; that, after many adventures in fruitless attempts to gain help to recover his throne, he became a recluse at Chester, dying at a great age. The story cannot be accepted. Harold never lived to see Winchester again. His body, buried first near where it fell, was later translated to Waltham Abbey, where his tomb was an object of veneration until the Reformation.

E

CHAPTER III

Norman Winchester

THE appalling news of the disaster to the English arms without doubt reached Winchester within a few days after the event by survivors of the Hampshire fyrd returning to their homes stunned by the magnitude of the blow which had slain their king, and wellnigh every thane in the shire, as well as the aged abbot of New Minster, and his twelve monks. How many citizens of Winchester also fell at Senlac there is no means of reckoning, but it may be taken as certain that there would have been some Winchester men among Harold's house carles who died to a man around their king.

The disaster was complete, and the burghmote of Winchester doubtless realized that further resistance would be useless. They had heard of Duke William before. In the weeks following the great battle the citizens waited with trepidation for William's next move. Sooner or later he would certainly descend on Winchester, and possibly wreak vengeance for the opposition offered to his claim to the throne. The one hope for the city was that it was the dwelling-place of Queen Eadgyth, the Norman bride of Edward the Confessor.

William made himself master of London, and then turned westward with the intention of subduing Wessex. Of necessity he had to keep his army on

50

the move in order that it might live upon the country. A day or two was as long as it could stay in any one place, for supplies were speedily exhausted. Domesday Book affords evidence of the course which the army took by the severe reduction in value which certain manors showed in the year they were handed to new owners. In many cases three values are given, i.e. in the time of Edward, in the time when given to the new owner, and at the time of the Survey. Many Surrey manors show these three values in a ratio of 10–6–10, the inference being that there was severe spoliation about 1066–7.

Calculating partly from this evidence, and partly from the military exigencies, and the routes which would be possible to an army in the middle of winter, it may be taken as fairly certain that William moved along the old Stane Street, past Ashtead, Burford Bridge, and Dorking, then turning along the old track past Guildford and Compton to Farnham. From Farnham the army followed the old Harrow Way, probably the most ancient trackway in the country, passing south of Crondall, then to Nately and Basing, afterwards striking through Ellisfield and Dummer to the then valuable manor of Micheldever.

It has been plausibly argued that it was somewhere at this point that William sent to Winchester demanding its submission. He received it promptly. A contemporary poem appears to suggest that it was from Canterbury that William sent to Winchester, but it seems far more reasonable that he would have waited until he was within striking distance of the city before sending his demand for surrender. Besides, it would have been at about this point in the army's progress that news came of the approach of reinforcements from the south, thereby strengthening

William's position in the sheer number of his troops, and also further overawing the citizens of Winchester by the knowledge that the invaders were moving upon the city from the south as well as the west.

Soon after the success at Senlac William had sent over to Normandy for reinforcements, and directed his ships to move them to Chichester, a reasonable military procedure, having regard to the importance of Winchester in the ultimate subjugation of the country. Taking note of reduced values of Hampshire manors, as recorded in Domesday, the path of the reinforcements would seem to have been through Fareham, Wickham, Bishop's Waltham, Droxford, Exton, Warnford, the two Meons, Easton, and Alresford. Having regard to the contour of the country it is likely that the two forces linked up near Easton, about four miles from Winchester.

Contemporary stories state that William left Winchester on one side, after its formal surrender, as an act of courtesy to Emma. "In courtesy William does not move to seize her city, he requires only tribute and fealty." But, in fact, William had something more pressing on hand, the subjugation of the shires. Winchester's prompt surrender set him free to push on with his task. The city might have chosen to fight, as did Exeter, when its turn came, and Chester, York, and Durham, but the result in the end would without doubt have been defeat, as those other cities found to their bitter cost. Winchester, by her prompt submission, not only saved herself much misery and material loss, but also ingratiated herself with the new king. A royal city from early times, she meant to keep her royal status if swift change of fealty could serve her. Therefore, King Harold being dead, long live King William.

52

So, leaving Winchester untouched, William's army moved in two columns north-westward, one striking through Micheldever, Sutton Scotney, Highclere, up into Berkshire, while the other took a more westerly route through Crawley, Clatford, and Tidworth, into Wiltshire, then swinging into Berkshire, to keep touch with the easterly column. No real resistance was met anywhere, which is not surprising seeing that almost all the Saxon thanes who could have organized resistance had been slain on the fatal 15th of October.

Crowned King of England at Westminster on Christmas Day, 1066, it was not until Whit Sunday, 1068, that William was crowned, with his wife Matilda, in the Old Minster at Winchester. But it is certain that he must have spent much time in the city before that, getting the reins of administration into his hands. By all accounts the Winchester ceremony was far more elaborate than the hasty coronation in London. During the great banquet which followed, a mailed champion rode into the hall, amid a great blast of trumpets, and, throwing down a gauntlet, challenged any one to deny that William was truly King of England. This custom of challenging any one to assail the right of the newly crowned sovereign was kept up until the nineteenth century. The last time a royal challenger appeared at a coronation banquet was when George IV became king.

Although William appreciated the growing importance of London, he nevertheless regarded Winchester as the real capital of England. Ever after his great victory he was more at home in Winchester than anywhere else. Although at Whitsuntide he "wore his crown" at Westminster, and in midwinter at Gloucester, it was at Winchester that he wore it at

Easter, chief feast of the year. Thus he followed Saxon custom.

Notwithstanding the fact that Winchester had been the chief home of Harold, and the Earls of Wessex, the submission of the city was so whole-hearted that William had no need to build a mighty fortress there, as on the banks of the Thames, and at many another place. The dwelling he built at Winchester, as soon as he was able to settle down, was a palace, a kingly residence, and not a defensive castle, with huge forbidding keep. For one thing, at Winchester he was very near his native Normandy, by way of Southampton, or Chichester, and Cherbourg, or Havre. For another thing, and that, to William, a very important one, Winchester was a very suitable centre for his hunting expeditions in the Forest of Bere, and later in that New Forest of his, the making of which chroniclers in his own and later ages considered one of his worst sins. How completely Winchester accepted William, and how thoroughly his Norman following took hold of the reins of government in Winchester and Wessex, is proved by the fact that the Domesday Survey was organized from Winchester, and there all the findings were sent, and it is proved also by the significant omission of the city itself from that momentous record.

William was not content with a crowning once and for all. He had need to impress his kingship upon his subjects, therefore there should be an annual crowning, "wearing his crown," as it was said. The third time he was crowned at Winchester was perhaps the most impressive of all, for it was performed by no fewer than three papal legates who had been sent by Rome to bless this son of hers who was going to give his help to the papal see in a campaign which was then on foot for the complete submission of the English Church and people to the successor of St. Peter.

Many of William's judicial acts were ordered at

EARLY NORMAN FONT IN CATHEDRAL; NORTH AND WEST SIDES

Winchester. It was at Winchester that he imprisoned Stigand, the arch-pluralist, who held both the archbishopric of Canterbury and the bishopric of Winchester. It was said that William held Stigand in prison awaiting the time of his death when he might lay hands upon the reputed enormous wealth which the miserly prelate had amassed. Old chroniclers say that at Stigand's death a key was found hanging from a cord around his neck, a key

55

which unlocked a casket containing parchments telling of the whereabouts of this treasure, some of it in the beds of flowing streams! Whether this story is true or false, it is certain William gathered Stigand's hidden treasure to himself.

The new king built his palace in the very centre of the city, taking for its site land adjoining the New Minster, some say actually overrunning the New Minster precincts. Rudborne, a fifteenth-century monk of Winchester, repeated, if he did not invent, a story that William confiscated the land, along with much more belonging to New Minster, because the old Abbot Ælfwig and his twelve monks fought against him at Senlac, William's grim judgment being, "The abbot is worth a barony, and every monk a manor," his total confiscations running to twenty thousand acres.

But the Domesday Survey seems to mark this story as fiction. It may be that in the heat of the moment William, who was notoriously hasty of temper, finding the dead bodies of the Winchester clerics among his slain enemies, made some dramatic estimation of the material worth of these supporters of Harold; but Domesday records prove that, whatever he may have done immediately after his victory, in later years he favoured New Minster exceedingly, even to the extent of giving ample land elsewhere in exchange for that upon which he built his palace. And the verdict of the Winchester assessors was that he had given far more land than the site of the palace was worth.

Not only did he build a palace here, but he set up also his mint and his treasury, his storehouses, and even his stables. The stone pillar still to be seen on the west side of the passage-way by the Butter

Cross is undoubtedly Norman in construction and ornamentation, and is thought to be a relic of the Conqueror's stables. The rest of the palace has disappeared, unless some very old work in cellars of shops close by the Butter Cross can be identified as part of it.

It was at Winchester that William consummated the supreme blunder of his reign, the execution of the English earl, Waltheof. Arraigned before William and the Great Council, at the Midwinter Gemot at Westminster in December 1075, for treason, no decision was come to, and the earl was transferred to Winchester for safe keeping, until William should have made up his mind what to do with him. It is unquestionable that there had been a conspiracy against William, but it is doubtful if Waltheof had ever been more than an unwilling listener at the councils of the conspirators. At any rate, as soon as he was able, and before the conspiracy could make headway, Waltheof had gone to William and made full confession of what he had heard.

Waltheof lay in confinement at Winchester until May. It is said that William was disposed to pardon him, but that his purpose was turned towards execution by the vehement accusations of Waltheof's wife, Judith, William's own niece. Possibly, hating her English husband, she saw here an opportunity of ridding herself of him for ever. Although it was his boast that he had never shed blood, save in the exigencies of actual warfare, William listened to the angry woman, and departed from the rule of his life. The case was again brought up for trial, and this time Waltheof was condemned to death. It would seem that the cause was argued in the absence of the prisoner, for the sentence was pronounced at the

57

Pentecostal Gemot at Westminster. The order was sent to Winchester, and on the 31st of May, very early in the morning, Waltheof was ordered to prepare himself for execution.

The early hour was deliberately chosen. The earl was highly regarded by the English. They looked upon him as their last champion. So the execution was hurried forward in order that the king's sentence might be carried out before the city was astir. And that there might be less chance of a public disturbance, the earl was taken outside the walls through the east gate, up the steep hill of St. Giles. Here, looking out over the fair valley of the Itchen, Waltheof, clad in his earl's robes and insignia, went to his death.

But, early as the hour was, a few had got wind of what was astir, and had followed the hasty procession. A few clerks, who had perchance heard whispers overnight of what was toward, and some labouring men who rose with the light, were all, save the officials, who were present to witness one of the most momentous acts in all William's reign. Waltheof spent some time in prayer, too long indeed for the headsman, and for the minions of William who were fearful lest the people of Winchester might hear what was doing, and attempt a rescue. When admonished to cut his devotions short, Waltheof pleaded that he might say the Lord's Prayer for himself and for those around him. He began the petition, but the impatience of the headsman was too much for him; with the last phrase of the prayer still unsaid the sword fell, and the last English earl was no more. But men said that as the severed head fell on the grass the lips concluded the prayer, "Libera nos a malo."

58

The dead clay was hurriedly buried beneath the grass where the earl had fallen. But at the earnest petition of the monks of the Abbey of Crowland, founded by Waltheof, William consented to the removal of the body to Crowland, as, after Senlac, he had allowed the removal of the body of Harold to Waltham. The petition of the Crowland monks was, strangely enough, backed by Judith, either from remorse, or, as was more likely, from a desire to look well in the eyes of men.

The execution of Waltheof proved to be the turning point in William's life. Hitherto he had been fortunate beyond most men, even seeming untoward accidents being turned to his advantage. But, thereafter, his good fortune deserted him, and ill hap followed him even to the day of his ghastly burial.

Perhaps the greatest event of the Conqueror's reign, as far as Winchester was concerned, was the building of a Norman cathedral to replace the Old Minster of St. Æthelwold, possibly then in indifferent repair. In Domesday the Old Minster is referred to as St. Peter of the Bishop, while the New Minster next door, the foundation of Alfred, and his son, Edward the Elder, is styled St. Peter of Winchester. Each held much land in the county and elsewhere.

The work of substituting a Norman for a Saxon cathedral was undertaken by Bishop Walkelyn, who had been appointed to the see after the deprivation of Stigand. It is said that Walkelyn was a cousin of the king, but the evidence of the relationship is slender. The work of building the new cathedral upon the scale contemplated by Walkelyn was a stupendous one, and called for the utmost resources of the see. Æthelwold's cathedral had been considered by its builders to be the wonder of the age,

59

but it was certainly despised by the Norman church-men. While the military followers of William were busily engaged in building defensive castles, Walkelyn was aiming at the creation of the most massive edifice in Wessex, if not in England, and he spared none in the pursuit of that aim. Even King William himself was made to suffer for the sake of the new cathedral. The story of the levelling of Hempage, or Hampinges, Wood has often been told. It was a wood, full of magnificent timber, near the road running between Winchester and Alton. The crafty prelate begged some of these timbers for the roof of his new cathedral, and the king, not realizing the resource of Walkelyn, agreed to give him as much timber as he could cut and carry away in three days. Walkelyn gathered an army of woodmen, and swept the wood clear in the allotted time. Many of the roof beams so obtained may be seen yet, above the stone groining put in by Wykeham. William was furious when he realized how he had been tricked, but, his anger cooling, he forgave Walkelyn, saying he had been too generous a giver, and Walkelyn too grasping a taker.

Walkelyn made others to suffer as well as the king. He raised the "ferms" of all the lands of his bishopric, and bitter was the complaint of those who had to pay the increased demand. Meon was raised from £30 to £40, and the comment at the time is, "but it cannot bear it long." His Fareham lands were raised from £16 to £20, and his Isle of Wight manors from £16 to £40. And it may be imagined that the army of masons, carpenters, and labourers swinked and sweated under the zeal of the bishop. From the quarries in the Isle of Wight, in flat-bottomed boats, and in rude carts, a stream of stone flowed to Winchester to further the great ideal.

The work was begun in 1079, and finished sufficiently for occupation in 1093. It was consecrated on St. Swithun's Day, nearly all the bishops and abbots of England being present. At its core the present cathedral is that of Walkelyn, although it has been so altered and amended, curtailed and added to in later years. But the north and south transepts, save for a few minor alterations, remain as Walkelyn built them, and, from them, the general appearance of the Norman nave can be imagined.

Winchester saw the beginning of the papal campaign for the complete subjugation of the English Church to Rome, with the full assent and support of the new king. It was his side of his bargain with the Pope. The first part of the scheme was soon plain to everybody. It was nothing less than the substitution of Continental prelates and abbots for the Englishmen now holding bishoprics and abbacies. Walkelyn's appointment was only one of many.

Another great aim of the papacy at this time was the subjugation of the civil to the ecclesiastical power, and, as a means to that end, strict celibacy of the clergy was to be insisted upon wherever the Pope's word was law. On 1 April, 1076, a great synod was held at Winchester, from which the order went forth throughout England that those within the Church's orders, even the seculars, must be celibate. No canon was to have a wife, and no marrying would be allowed in future by any in priest's orders.

Strangely enough, Walkelyn appears to have been one who favoured a more easy system among the occupants of the great monastery over which he now ruled. He wished to reverse the rule of Æthelwold, and substitute canons for the monks. He even went

the length of having forty canons ready to take the
places of the monks when they should have been
ejected, thus exactly reversing what had been done
by Æthelwold a century and a half before. But
the Pope and Archbishop Lanfranc would have none

CHURCH OF ST. PETER, CHESIL

of it, and so the monks remained, and in fact continued in possession for four and a half centuries
longer.

One important edict of William's, issued from
Winchester, was the order of curfew. In those days
of wooden dwellings and frequent fires it was a
salutary order. Curfew is, of course, *couvre-feu*

62

Englished. The order was that on the ringing of a bell at eight o'clock at night all fires and lights should be extinguished. The curfew has been rung at Winchester for nine centuries, and each evening it still rings from the tower of the Old Guildhall, over the clock in the High Street. It did not, however, prevent some serious outbreaks of fire from time to time. In 1161 a disastrous fire wellnigh destroyed the city, and again, in 1180, another outbreak, beginning at the Mint, destroyed more than half the houses.

At this time, as well as in earlier reigns, Winchester was the place of the dower house of the dowager, or widow queen. Here Cnut's widow had lived out her widowhood, dying just before the victory of William; and here Eadgyth, widow of Edward the Confessor, came likewise to end her days. Although Eadgyth was the sister of Harold, and of the House of Godwine, she was nevertheless held in the highest honour in William's court at Winchester. The dower house was situated on the north side of the High Street, just below the West Gate, at that time, no doubt, one of the choicest positions for a residence in the whole area within the walls.

Although William built his palace in the very centre of Winchester, cheek-by-jowl with the two minsters, at some time in the twenty years of his reign he built, or began the building of a stone castle on the high ground to the west, and overlooking the city. There was no imperative military need for such a castle, but the Norman love for a massive defensive structure, built upon high ground either natural or artificial, may well have induced William to build, in so suitable a spot, a castle worthy alike of his kingship and of the ancient capital of the realm. That castle at once surpassed Wolvesey in importance, and for several centuries ranked with Windsor as the royal residence.

Two other great events of William's reign were the making of the New Forest and the ordering of the Domesday Survey. The first was, perhaps, little more than the declaring of a large part of West Hampshire, much of it naturally infertile land, a new royal forest. There were natural forests still existing in plenty in the south of England. Most of the vast forest of Anderida in Sussex then remained. To the west and south of Winchester stood the Forest of Bere, already royal by William's edict. But these were not enough to satisfy the hunting zeal of William, or, more likely, he preferred the west Hampshire country, with its varying character—coppice and woodland, and wide spaces of heather-covered clearings.

Tradition tells of a vast and ruthless depopulation of a rich countryside in order to satisfy the selfish desires of the alien king. How far this tradition is based on fact it is difficult at this distance of time to say. It is certain that the stories of wholesale destruction of villages are exaggerations. The general nature of much of the land in the New Forest is such that it could never have carried a large population. It is too infertile. There may have been some depopulation of the countryside, as in the case of the Scottish crofters in modern times, but it is unlikely that there could have been such a wholesale destruction of village community life as the monkish stories suggest. Some villages certainly were left, and new ones were formed, no doubt by verderers, and other forest officials, for, in several places in the Forest, there are evidences of the erection of Norman churches.

64

The severity of the forest laws, however, made men hate the whole system, and nothing was too bad to be believed about the king's doings concerning this new forest of his. Men were swift to see a Divine vengeance in the fact that two of William's sons, as well as a grandson, died violent deaths while hunting in this New Forest. Richard, his son, was killed there in William's own lifetime, and Richard, natural son of Robert, was killed there scarcely three months before Rufus met his death in identical fashion in the glades of Malwood.

The Domesday Survey of 1085 must have made the Winchester clerks exceedingly busy. For months the returns poured in, to be collated at Winchester into the great record which was considered at the time to be comparable only to the very *Book of Doom*. It is now valued by the nation as one of its most priceless literary possessions. It was a census of land, of men, of beasts, and even of field utensils. It was the first time such a complete record had been made in any country in Europe since the fall of the Roman Empire. With good reason men regarded it with hatred, and with apprehension of exactions and oppressions to come.

Domesday is of profound interest to-day for its picture of Hampshire in 1085. Something like two-fifths of the land of the county was held by the Church. For his own purposes the Bishop of Winchester held over a score of manors, and, for the support of the Old Minster, of which he was ex-officio abbot, he held about thirty more. The monks of New Minster held over a dozen of the richest manors in the county, notably Alton, Micheldever, North Stoneham. Nunnaminster (St. Mary's Nunnery) held five. Moreover, several Hampshire manors

F

were in the possession of monasteries in William's Norman dominion.

The king was, of course, the biggest landowner in the county; and when he made demands upon his subjects by way of extra taxation they grumbled that he did not "live on his own," i.e. make his manorial dues suffice. The remaining manors, almost without exception, were held by the alien followers of William. Scarcely any Saxon earls or thanes were in possession of their paternal holdings. They had either fallen at Senlac, or had since been dispossessed. One Norman baron, Hugh de Port, held nearly sixty Hampshire manors direct from the king, and he held others as underlord, doing knight service for the Bishop of Winchester.

While the people in other parts of the country hated William, and detested his usurpation of the English throne, it is more than likely that the citizens of Winchester on the whole approved the change. With the preference of Edward the Confessor for Westminster the importance and prosperity of Winchester had been dwindling. The advent of William, and his decided recognition of the old capital as the centre of government, arrested the commercial decadence which had been going on since the beginning of the Confessor's reign. William's love for the New Forest, and his general use of the "Hampshire Gate" to the Continent, each helped to enhance Winchester's prosperity. There is evidence that the population of the city increased materially during the rule of William and his two sons.

From the first it had been William's aim to make as little change in the government of the country as possible, consistent with his determination to have things ordered as he wished. It was his pleasant fiction that he had come over, not as a conqueror, but as the rightful heir to Edward the Confessor. Hence he thought it politic to preserve, in outward form at least, the old Saxon customs of government. As Winchester had been the old capital for so long, what more natural than to keep Winchester as the hub of his English dominion?

So Winchester flourished exceedingly under the smile of the alien king. Hordes of alien officials thronged her streets, and inhabited the many new houses which had been erected in the green gardens within her high walls. Here was the increasingly important office of the scaccarum, or exchequer, with its many officials. The zeal of these officials brought home to all in the kingdom what the change of king really meant. The eyes of all men turned towards Winchester as the place into which flowed more and yet more taxes for the support of the king and his wars. Here, too, was carried out a large part of the work of making the king's currency, thus following the Anglo-Saxon tradition, for, in the previous century it was recorded that Winchester had six mints, while London had but three. A mint at this time probably meant no more than a small workshop carried on by an individual "moneyer," who made each coin by hand, hammering it out on an anvil die.

Not a little of Winchester's new prosperity was most likely due to the great increase in the military establishment, not only of the rank and file, but also of the Norman nobles, a number of whom had houses built in or just outside the city. The arrogance of these strangers was no doubt exceedingly galling to the old inhabitants of Winchester, but the wealth they brought to the city was a welcome solatium.

67

Moreover, the citizens were no doubt greatly pleased at having recovered their old supremacy over London, and they may be imagined as being kept in a continual round of excitement with the comings and goings of the king and his court.

After the ghastly end of William the Conqueror at Rouen, his son, William Rufus, or The Red, continued the Norman association with Winchester. To the rest of the country Winchester now became a place of execration. It was the lair of an infamous king and his sardonic minion Ranulf, or Randolf, Flambard. William I had been hot tempered and overbearing, but, according to his lights and subject to his desires, he was, in a rough sort of way, just. But his son, William Rufus, had scarcely a redeeming feature. He had all the vices of his father in an exaggerated degree, and he had others of his own. He soon gained for himself a reputation for wickedness unequalled even in that age of wickedness. While allowing for probable exaggeration by monkish writers, who regarded with horror his blasphemous attitude towards the Church, it appears fairly certain that he was a man who not merely preferred evil for its own sake, but was ferociously antagonistic to everything good. Such a fiendish spirit of mockery of everything which had to do with religion and goodness had never been known before, and men feared the vengeance of God, not only upon the wicked king himself, but also upon the very places and people where and with whom he lived.

In Flambard William Rufus found a minister and a companion after his own heart. Flambard was as diplomatic as a Machiavelli, and as avaricious and unscrupulous as a Borgia. He set out to advance himself by serving the king in any way required.

He built himself a sumptuous residence just outside the North Gate at Winchester and, with true Norman arrogance, blocked up the road by building his house directly across the thoroughfare, for no other reason, apparently, than that it pleased him so to build it. "From his lair at Winchester," say contemporary chroniclers, Flambard devised new and drastic methods of squeezing vast sums from the English people for the benefit of his profligate master.

One of the ways by which money flowed into the coffers of the king, and one which aroused the universal execration of the Church, was by the refusal of the king to allow fat ecclesiastical offices, bishoprics, and the like to be filled, he himself appropriating the incomes meanwhile. It was probably a device of the wily Flambard. The protests of the angry clerics were of no avail. The saintly Anselm, who had been made Archbishop of Canterbury upon the nomination of Rufus himself, came down to Winchester to remonstrate with the king. The audience is said to have taken place in the great hall of the new castle which had been built on the rising ground to the west of the city. The remonstration ended in an open quarrel between king and archbishop, and Anselm left the realm in despair of persuading William to give up his evil courses.

Then came a mysterious illness, and Rufus tasted the fear of death. It was indeed a case of the devil, being sick, a saint would be. He called to his bedside the holy men he had formerly mocked and scorned, and "for the good of his soul," but perhaps more truly for the health of his body, he made eager grants to the Church. To the Bishop of Winchester he made the historic grant of a three-days' fair, to be held in August on the hill of St. Giles, overlooking the city;

and with the grant was given the right to suspend for the duration of the fair all other trade within a radius of seven leagues of Winchester. It was a most valuable grant and, added to by successive kings until the three days had been drawn out to sixteen, the bishop's fair at Winchester became one of the greatest in Europe, known from the Mediterranean to the Baltic, and from Russia to Spain.

It may have been at this time, and not immediately after his succession, that Rufus carried out the last behests of his father, although the *Anglo-Saxon Chronicle* gives him credit for it in 1087.

William the Second went to Winchester and inspected the Treasury and the riches which his father had before gathered. It was not to be estimated by any man how much was there gathered in gold, and in silver, and in vessels, and in gems, and in many other precious things which are difficult to recount. The King then did as his father had commanded him before he died: he distributed the treasures for his father's soul to every monastery that was in England; to some he gave 10 marks of gold, and to others 6.

It is supposed that the two archbishoprics got ten marks each, and each of the bishoprics and abbeys six marks. The mark, either of silver or of gold, was only a denomination for so many silver pennies, the only coin then existing in the realm.

In 1098, not long after the illness which so frightened him, Rufus wanted his money back. He sent to the aged Walkelyn demanding the return of a large sum "without a moment's delay."

But Walkelyn, well knowing that he could not do that at the moment without plundering the poor or rifling the treasury of the church, was rendered weary of life by this and other things of the like sort, and, having offered up a prayer, begged that he might be delivered from his unhappy existence.

And, says the *Chronicle*, Walkelyn actually did die ten days later. The king did not get his money, but as a large sum in treasure had disappeared from the Church's coffers at Winchester, it was thought that William had carried it off. The six gold marks which Rufus had given to the Church at Winchester had gone. It was a very large sum to disappear, being between eight and nine thousand silver pennies. Where had the money gone?

This problem was not solved until a Sunday afternoon in June 1833. On that day four little boys were playing in a field at Beauworth, about seven miles from Winchester, when they unearthed a leaden box containing a very large number of silver pennies of the last issue of William the Conqueror. There was a scramble by the villagers for these coins, and many disappeared, but an official of the British Museum examined six thousand five hundred of the coins, and estimated that the leaden box had originally contained between eight thousand and nine thousand laid in rolls.

Now this field in which the leaden box was found was originally attached to the Manor of Beauworth, and the manor itself belonged to the bishops of Winchester. The strong inference is that Walkelyn, perceiving that Rufus would despoil the Church of the money, resolved to hide it where the king could not get at it, but where the Church could recover it when the menace of so wicked and rapacious a king had safely passed. As the sum in the box corresponds almost exactly to the value of six gold marks, and as all the coins when found were new and fresh as if they had just come from the moneyer's die, it seems fairly certain that it was the money which Rufus had first given to the Church, and then wanted to have back again. The reason why it was lost to the medieval Church was because Walkelyn died suddenly, or almost so. There is evidence that he had something on his mind when he died, and was not able to unburden himself. Can one doubt he was striving to disclose the hiding-place of this treasure of the Church, a hiding-place which was to be inviolate for seven hundred and thirty-five years? The remains of the leaden box, and several of the "Pax" pennies that were found in it, are to be seen in the museum at Winchester to-day.

Rufus, as has been said, was free with his gifts to the Church while sickness held him in its grip, but, with the passing of his illness and the return of his normal health, came a return also of Rufus's old spirit of godless wickedness. The saint was a devil once more. But the privileges he had given, and the grants he had made, he left undisturbed. The old profligate habits were resumed, and the revelry at the new castle, whenever Rufus was in Winchester, was once again a byword among the citizens. There was, however, less open antagonism to the Church. Flambard, possibly taking his cue from his master, became a notable church builder. He began a pretentious Norman church at Christchurch-Twynham, at the confluence of the rivers Avon and Stour, where had already grown up a flourishing offshoot of the Benedictine foundation at Winchester. A great deal of Flambard's work may yet be seen at this church at Christchurch.

Perhaps for his zeal as a church builder, possibly for his assiduity as a tax-gatherer, but certainly not for his piety, Flambard was made Bishop of Durham on the nomination of his master. At Durham he began the building of a cathedral which was to out-

72

WEST GATE FROM WITHOUT

rival the one which had just been completed at Winchester by Bishop Walkelyn. One may imagine that Rufus looked upon the church-building zeal of his minion with amused toleration, thinking it a kind of insurance against the ills of the flesh.

Then came that fateful Lammastide in the year 1100, when Rufus set out from Winchester roisterously, as he had done so many times before, with a crowd of boon companions, to hunt in the New Forest, but to return stark and lifeless, ingloriously borne on the rudest of vehicles. The story has been told many times, yet to this day it remains a mystery whether the Red King met his death by fortuitous circumstance, or whether he was deliberately murdered. The commonly accepted story, told by William of Malmesbury, and repeated in similar form by many following writers, is that as Rufus and one of his companions were following a stag, they became separated from the rest of the hunt; the king shot at the stag, missed his aim, then called upon his companion to shoot "in the devil's name," which the companion proceeded to do; and his shaft, likewise ill directed, struck a tree, was deflected, and found its billet in the king's side, so that he fell dying from his horse, while the unlucky bowman, fearing for his life, fled to the coast, and got a ship for France.

The appearance of this story in so many histories does not make it true. The habit of historians of past days to copy from earlier histories without question is sufficient to account for the persistence of the story. In some accounts the king's companion in those last fatal moments is definitely named as Sir Walter Tyrrell, and his Christian name is tacked on to the king's command to shoot at the stag which he himself had missed. What may be significant is

74

that there is, near Ringwood, a ford over the River Avon still called "Tyrrell's Ford," and it is indicated by the rustics as the point at which Tyrrell crossed the Avon in his haste to get to Christchurch, or Twynham, then one of several flourishing south-coast harbours.

But Tyrrell later solemnly swore that he was not near the king on the fatal day. This oath of non-complicity may be set alongside the fact that other records of the time strongly suggest that the current belief was that the king had been murdered deliber-ately, and that the murder had been carefully planned before he left Winchester. Few wanted to discuss the subject afterwards. The rest of the hunt would seem to have dispersed swiftly as soon as the fatal shaft was loosed, and possibly some even returned to Winchester without making any search for the body of their king. In fact, it was not until the next day that the corpse was found by a charcoal burner, lying where it fell at Malwood, not far from Lyndhurst. No mention is made in any of the chronicles of the king's riderless horse, which would almost certainly have galloped back to the rest of the hunt, thus giving warning of the tragedy. If, in actual fact, the death of the king was the result of pure accident, it is inconceivable that his companions would not have sought for his body, and themselves brought it to Winchester. The circumstantial evi-dence points to murder, to which probably many of the hunt were privy or consenting.

The tragedy seems to have made a very deep mark upon local tradition. Many other sovereigns have lived in Winchester and Hampshire, but none other has left place-name or tradition. It is as though wickedness is more enduring in men's memories than goodness. The narrow way from Malwood, via Romsey and Hursley, along which the murdered king's body was brought home to Winchester, has for eight centuries been known as the King's Way, or King's Lane, and, although some of it is little better than a bridle path, it can still be traversed from Rufus's Stone to Winchester. And, moreover, there are in the district many who boast their descent from Purkess the charcoal burner who, in his rough cart, brought the king's stiffened body to Winchester.

Picture the entry into Winchester of that humble wain. Already whispers of tragedy must have been abroad, and the conspirators must have been agog to know what was happening to the body of their victim. Even the heads of the Church could not have been unaware that something momentous was afoot. Ever since the last "wearing of the crown" at Pentecost there had been omens of evil threatening the king.

Then comes galloping from the west road one who declares, with frantic voice, that the body is on its way to the city, is even now at the great South Gate. There is a rush to the gate, and the awed populace see the pallid corpse of their king borne in on the rudest of biers, the rigid body jerking to and fro as the solid wheels, groaning on a crude axle, drop in and out of the ruts in the highway.

Few, if any, there were to mourn that home-coming; many to rejoice. Surely no other king could be so bad, or so oppressive, as he who now lay lifeless. Only remained his obsequies, and they were brief. Not for three generations had an English king been brought to Winchester for burial. The Old Minster, sepulchre of successive Wessex kings, had been replaced by the new cathedral which had never yet seen the burial of a king. Although the wickedest of men, Rufus had been King of England. It was unthinkable that the body of one who had been a king should be buried anywhere but in a sacred fane. Rufus must be buried in the cathedral church of his capital city. And had not his brother Richard, killed like himself while hunting in the New Forest, been buried in the minster while it was yet a-building? The relics of the Wessex kings, queens, and bishops had been gathered up, and had been sepultured in Walkelyn's great cathedral, while the body of Walkelyn himself had been buried at the foot of the great dais in the nave. Rufus, who had much greater need of salvation, should be remembered for his grant of the Fair of St. Giles, and should be buried in the very heart of the sacred building in the centre of the choir beneath the four-square tower. So, not stopping to unclothe or shroud him, nor even to withdraw the bloody shaft from the wound, possibly lest men should know from whose bow it had sped, the priests thrust him into a massive sarcophagus, and so buried him.

Controversy still rages around the tomb which is even yet pointed out as that of Rufus. The tomb was opened in 1868, when the almost perfect skeleton of a man was found within. Measurements of the bones by surgeons seemed to indicate that the individual must have been about 5 ft. 8 in. or even 9 in. in height during life. This, and other evidence, inclines some people to deny that the skeleton could be that of Rufus, who was reputed to be stocky. On the other hand, there is the common people's saying, when the cathedral tower fell down a few years later, that the fall was caused by the fact that the wicked king had been buried immediately beneath.

England was not left long without a ruler. The

Conqueror's eldest son, Robert, probably thought his way to the throne was now open. If so, he reckoned without his youngest brother, Henry, who had not only inherited all the brains of the family, but had been educated to make the best use of them. There is reason to believe he received his education in a Grammar School at Winchester. Henry was in England at the time of his brother's death, and he saw his opportunity to seize the throne. He realized, moreover, that the key of the position was the national treasury. Within a few hours of his brother's sepulture he reached Winchester, and, as the Conqueror's son, took possession of the royal treasury and its revenues. From that moment there was never any doubt about Henry's position. Robert made an effort to establish his right to the throne, as the eldest son of the Conqueror, but the wily Henry bought him off, and then settled down to rule England with an iron hand.

It was during the reign of Henry I that the Winton Domesday was made, probably about the year 1115. It was made under the direction of Bishop Giffard, and, like the greater Domesday Survey, it was made to ascertain the amount of the king's dues, his "gafol," or "landgable," a fee-farm rent receivable from tenants or burgages in the king's dominions. This "gafol" was not a rent; indeed, it was generally far less than the actual rent. For instance, one house with a rental value of twenty shillings, a very high rent for those days, paid only sixpence "gafol" to the king. In another survey, made in 1148 by Bishop Henry de Blois, many houses are shown as paying sixpence a year to the king. At a later date still other curious payments to the king are recorded; for instance, "tangable" at the rate of one penny is paid to the king by a tanner for the right to have a board, i.e. a counter, in the High Street; butter sellers pay one penny similarly for what is called "smear-gable"; shoemakers pay similarly for "shoegable," or "scogable." There is also an enigmatical "brueg," which may possibly be "brewgable."

A remarkably fine copy of the Winton Domesday is in the possession of the Society of Antiquaries. The survey was made by the Bishop of Winchester and other commissioners, and all the principal burgesses appear to have assisted in the work. It was a very thorough business. They began at the bottom of the High Street, by the East Gate, and having worked up the High Street on the north side to the West Gate, they came down on the south side, leaving no tenement or messuage unmentioned. They then surveyed all the houses of the barons and important people. The survey shows that in the time of Edward the Confessor—referred to in this, and in the Domesday Survey, as "T.R.E."—sixty-three burgesses in the High Street were paying dues to the king. When the middle of the south side of the High Street was cleared to make room for the Conqueror's palace, which it will be remembered also encroached upon the grounds of New Minster, twelve burgesses were evicted. Of the remaining fifty-one burgesses the survey revealed that only eighteen were paying dues to the king. It may be assumed that this serious leakage of royal income was promptly stopped.

The survey also shows that even at this time there was an extensive suburb immediately outside the West Gate, a fact significant of the peace and sense of security which had grown up under the strong Norman rule. But it is certain that most of the working-class people of Winchester still lived within the security of the city walls. Their dwellings were also surveyed in the streets running off the High Street. The names of these streets sound strange to-day. There were three on the south side, Gere, or Gar Stret, now Trafalgar Street; Gold Stret, now Southgate Street; and Calpe Stret, now St. Thomas Street. The last name is rather puzzling to new-comers to Winchester because St. Thomas's Church now stands in Southgate Street. But this is a modern edifice; the original St. Thomas's Church actually stood in St. Thomas Street, and was pulled down in 1848, the site being still left open. The dedication is to St. Thomas of Canterbury, the original church having been built shortly after the murder of Becket.

The streets running from the north side of the High Street, reckoning from the West Gate, were first, Snithelinga (or Sniderling) Stret, i.e. Tailors' Street, but now Tower Street. This took its later name from a hermit's tower, or grotto, which is said to have stood in medieval times on the high ground at the north-west corner of the city. The other streets successively were named Bredene, Scowertene, Alwarene, Fleshmangere, Wenegerene (or Wongar), Tanneres, and Bucchestre. Only the last persists in its modern form, Busket Lane. All the others have completely changed their names, and one, Alwarene, has ceased to exist. Its site lies along the gardens of Jewry Street and St. Peter Street.

The dwellings in these streets at this time must have been constructed of wood, wattle, and daub, roofed with thatch and very vulnerable to fire. The edict of curfew had good reason behind it. Although Winchester was doubtless as civilized as any city

WINCHESTER'S EARLIEST CHARTER IN THE POSSESSION OF THE
CORPORATION OF WINCHESTER

(*Photo by F. A. Grant, Winchester*)

in the realm, compared with modern standards it must have been very insanitary, and devoid of almost every convenience which to-day is a commonplace. Chimneys had not yet been invented; chairs, tables, bedsteads, and the like, were only for the well-to-do; the domestic water supply of rich and poor alike was the open stream, into which inevitably trickled the seepage from the domestic midden piled up close to each house; windows were as yet mere openings, covered possibly in the worst weather by wood louvres, or parchment; for glass, if in use at all, was only for the very wealthy. The thoroughfares of the city in bad weather must have been very unpleasant to traverse, although, as a set-off, there was, of course, very little heavy-wheeled traffic to cut up the surface.

The local government of the city in the twelfth century was still carried on in the traditional way through the burgh-mote, or town-meeting, which every citizen of standing must attend. But the business of collecting the king's revenues, market tolls, etc., was in the hands of the sheriff of the county nominally. The sheriff appears to have appointed a provost, or reeve, to carry out the work of collection in the city. Although Winchester was not a royal manor in the strict sense, the king was lord of the city, and he was reckoned to own all the open land within its borders. Hence, no market-stall could be set up without paying toll for it to the king. The imposition of an outsider to collect dues within the city was a source of great bitterness to the citizens. The first step on the road to municipal freedom is taken when, at the urgent petition of the citizens of Winchester, they are allowed to collect the dues themselves, and render a fixed sum per annum to the king's treasury. This was first permitted, so far as the existing records show, by King John in 1208, and the sum agreed upon between the city and the king was £142 12s. 4d., a large sum for those days. The only domestic tax paid by the citizens severally was the "murage," for the upkeep of the city walls.

Winchester claims to be the premier mayoralty in the kingdom; to have been the first chartered city; to have been a pioneer in a new form of municipal right, copied by many another city thereafter. According to tradition Winchester was the first to get its municipal freedom, and the right to elect from its own body, as head of the town government, a mayor (instead of, as heretofore, the king's provost or reeve, who had been the dominant figure in the burgh-mote), and this is said to have been granted in the year 1184. London got the same privilege in 1188, and by definite charter. Winchester, alas, can show no charter so early as 1184. Its claim to be the pioneer mayoralty is based upon tradition, strengthened, it may be, by the record of a fierce disputation which took place between the representatives of the city of London and of the city of Winchester for precedence at the crowning of Richard I. It may be assumed that at the time of this dispute the actual date of the beginning of the new order in Winchester was thoroughly well known, even though no royal document existed to prove it.

The mayor, as chief magistrate, was an official entirely new in English town government. He stood, not only as the town's representative to any outside authority, but also as the living symbol of the newly-won freedom of the municipality. In the last quarter of the twelfth century and the first quarter of the thirteenth century the idea was eagerly taken up by many English towns, and in a number of instances the king was asked for rights, "as at Winchester." Gloucester, for example, got a duplicate of Winchester's rights. Indeed, all over Europe, cities were

NORMAN NORTH TRANSEPT, WINCHESTER CATHEDRAL

seeking to establish their freedom, and to entrench themselves against unfair treatment by king or baron. It is the time which saw the rise of that very remarkable confederation of cities in North Europe, termed the Hansa League, a kind of medieval League of Nations. To the citizens of Winchester the change

from provost to mayor must have been as the change
from darkness to light. The provost was the king's
man, imposed from without by the chief county
official, signifying that Winchester was merely a part
of the county; whereas the mayor was the city's own
man, elected from within, signifying that the city
had now an entity separate from, and every whit as
important as, the county.

Later charters confirm this, and accompanying
trading rights which may have grown gradually by
prescription or by charter. Sometime before the
traditional date for the beginning of the mayoralty
Winchester had obtained a valuable trading charter
from Henry II. This was between 1155–8, and one
of the witnesses is none other than Thomas Becket,
later styled martyr of Canterbury. This first charter,
now in the city archives, is a grant to the trading guild
of Winchester. Another charter of about the same
date gives rights to the citizens as a body. Later
charters deal with a very jealously guarded right,
namely, that no gentlemen shall be compelled to
plead anywhere outside Winchester; they have the
right to be tried in Winchester only.

Returning to the period of the survey of Winchester it should be noted that the record shows that
there were many clerks (i.e. churchmen) living in the
city or its suburbs. Then, as now, the atmosphere
of ecclesiasticism must have hung strongly about
the place. It was a city of many churches, infinitely
more, it would seem, than could possibly have been
needed for the spiritual wants of the inhabitants.
It has been estimated, although possibly upon somewhat thin evidence, that the population at the end
of the twelfth century was about twenty thousand,
that is, not much below the present figure. It is

difficult to believe that it can have been so large, even though Winchester was one of the two largest cities in the realm. To-day, with a population of twenty-three thousand in round figures, about thirty-five churches, chapels, and meeting-houses cater for the spiritual and ethical needs of the population, yet it has been reckoned that at the end of the twelfth century there were upwards of seventy churches, all of course under the one great Church of Rome, about sixty being parish churches. But in those days everybody was a church-goer. Traces of some of these churches come to light from time to time in the course of building operations in the city. In 1924 a very fine brick-groined crypt had to be destroyed in the process of preparing for the erection of a shop for Messrs. W. H. Smith and Son at the corner of High Street and Parchment Street. The crypt undoubtedly belonged to one of these early churches. Remains of others now exist in walls of other buildings, as, for instance, St. Peter Macellis in the walls of Messrs. Kingdon's workshops in St. George's Street, which stand on the site of the old church.

The twelfth century was a momentous one to the city in another and a far more terrible direction. The peace which had endured in and around the city during the reigns of the Conqueror, and his two sons, William Rufus and Henry Beauclerc, came to an end when Henry died in 1135. Henry had wedded an Anglo-Saxon princess named Edith, who had sought shelter at Romsey Abbey from the boisterous attentions of William Rufus. Henry took her from the abbey after he had seized the crown, and by marrying her he consolidated his own position on the throne of England. Two children were born of the marriage, a boy and a girl. The former, when a young man, was drowned in the disaster of the *White Ship*, thus blasting his father's fondest hopes. The girl grew up to marry Geoffrey of Anjou, and to become her father's nominated successor to the throne of England. It was a disastrous nomination for the people of Winchester, for they soon found themselves, and their city, the very centre of the bitterest faction, bloodshed, and destruction.

Henry de Blois, nephew of Henry, was made Bishop of Winchester about six years before Henry's death. He was not only the astutest prelate of his age, but he was probably also the most ambitious. Whatever his saintliness may have been he was certainly a very great statesman, and a militarist of considerable ability. When King Henry died, Henry the Bishop saw a chance of advancing his brother Stephen to the throne, and thereby strengthening his own position as a prince-bishop, at the same time, perchance, helping him in his own ambitious schemes, one of which was to make the bishopric of Winchester into an archbishopric, equal with Canterbury and York. It was true that King Henry had nominated his daughter Matilda, or Maud (according as the English or the Norman form of the name is used), as his successor, but the idea of a woman as ruler was repugnant to many; while on the other hand, the prospect of having an easy-going man as king was very attractive to many of the barons. The weak, lackadaisical character of Stephen was well known to the barons, and, when his name was put forward at a great assembly in London as King Henry's successor, he was elected.

Stephen at once repaired to Winchester, where he was welcomed as king by Henry the Bishop, and by the chief citizens. Henry the Bishop had tried, but unsuccessfully, to get hold of the royal treasury at Winchester when King Henry died, just as, thirty-five years before, Henry himself had done when his brother William was killed in the New Forest. Then, as now, the possession of money meant power. On

ANCIENT GRILL-WORK IN PILGRIM GATES, WINCHESTER
CATHEDRAL, CIRCA A.D. 1093

the arrival of Stephen as king, the keeper of the royal treasury had nothing to do but to hand over the keys of his charge. The two brothers, Stephen the King and Henry the Bishop, got their fingers on the vast wealth which had been accumulated by King Henry. Stephen used his share as bribes among the barons, to win them the more securely to his cause. Henry used his in preparation for the warfare which he saw was inevitable. He began to build a vast stronghold at Wolvesey, on the most up-to-date Norman pattern.

And not only at Wolvesey, but also at Merdon by Hursley, at Waltham, and at Farnham; indeed, Matthew Paris tells that in the year 1138 Henry the Bishop was busy with the building of no fewer than six castles.

Following the lead of their bishop it may be assumed that the citizens of Winchester sided at first with Stephen and the barons who supported him, especially as at first there must have been much money flowing from that direction; but later on they went over to the side of Matilda. Between the two factions Winchester soon began to suffer exceedingly. Fire and bloodshed raged in the city, aye, and even to the suburbs as far as Hyde Abbey, some of the buildings of which shared in the destruction. The inflammable character of most of the dwellings, and of the roofs of such buildings as were constructed of stone, would have made the city an easy prey to deliberate incendiarism, as well as to the fire-balls hurled by the combatants on either side.

The period of anarchy which began with the election of Stephen to the throne lasted nearly twenty years. Henry the Bishop was first on one side and then on the other, and in between times he made honest endeavours to patch up a peace between his brother and Matilda. At first a strong supporter of his brother, Henry went over to the other side because Stephen attacked two bishops for the offence of building castles without permission. To Henry the Church and its leaders were inviolate, and not even his brother could be permitted to arraign or seek to punish a bishop. Zealous for the honour of his Church, Henry summoned his brother to appear before an ecclesiastical council at Wolvesey Castle. Such was the fear which even kings had of the

Church in those days that Stephen appeared at the council, and was severely censured by Henry.

In the next year Henry openly supported the cause of Matilda, who came with a great army from Sussex, and halted on the downs to the east of the city. Here Henry went out to meet her with pomp befitting so great a prelate. Matilda made him many promises, among them that he should be her chancellor when she should rule as queen. Prelate and lady journeyed down into the city together, both attending service in the cathedral, but there was no ceremony of coronation there. Matilda had a reputation for a haughty and overbearing manner beyond most, and it was not long before she began to show her real nature to Henry. It was a grave tactical error, for no prelate of those days, much less Henry de Blois, would suffer haughtiness from any other, even a woman; and so it was that Henry once more changed sides. Matilda got possession of the Norman castle on the west of the city, and set about the task of subduing the wily bishop. Henry, meanwhile, had fortified himself to withstand a siege at Wolvesey, and, when summoned by Matilda to meet her, he enigmatically replied that he would "prepare himself."

It was at this period that Winchester suffered most, being, as it were, between the upper and nether millstones. Very many of the buildings in the city were destroyed, including many churches; while the Conqueror's palace in the centre of the city, which had been considerably damaged by a fire early in the reign of Henry I, was completely destroyed. In between the hostilities Henry the Bishop removed the stone of the palace to Wolvesey, and used it in hasty building of further defences there. Evidence of this rapid building can still be discerned in the ruins at Wolvesey to-day, in the uneven courses, and the inferior workmanship in the upper parts of the keep.

It is said that the garrison at Wolvesey was under William of Ypres, and was composed mainly of Flemish mercenaries, skilled in the art of medieval warfare. It was their fire-balls, thrown by catapults erected on platforms high up in the keep, which destroyed much of the town occupied by the troops of Matilda. The chief of Matilda's forces was her half-brother, Robert, Earl of Gloucester. Very soon assistance arrived for the support of the bishop in the person of Stephen's queen (Stephen himself was a prisoner at Bristol, having been captured at Lincoln), and a large number of barons who were supporting Stephen's cause. It is said that Winchester was the prey of faction for nearly two months at this time. The skilled Flemish engineers at Wolvesey had some of the finest artillery of the time, and were frequently hurling their flaming missiles out over the city. There seems little doubt that the almost complete destruction of the city was due to their zeal, and, considering that they probably had little interest in anything but the success of their engines, this is not to be wondered at. Every building to be fired was one more proof of the excellence of their artillery and the accuracy of their aim. There is no official record of the opinions and feelings of the worthies of Winchester at this time, but it may easily be surmised that they were all in black misery at the destruction which had fallen upon their beloved and beautiful city. It was probably a worse disaster even than when the Danes sacked the city centuries earlier.

In the end Stephen's party triumphed, because, it is said, of shortage of water in the castle on the west. That must always have been its vulnerable feature in any dry summer. Matilda was forced to fly the city, and a circumstantial story is told by the historian Knighton that a false report of her death was spread abroad, and that during a truce she was carried out in a coffin, so escaping to Oxford. Her half-brother and chief commander was captured, and was later exchanged for Stephen himself. The strife dragged on until Robert of Gloucester died, and Henry, the young son of Matilda, grew old enough to dispute with Stephen his right to the throne. It ended in a compromise, Stephen being left in the position of king for his life, with the proviso that his successor should be Matilda's son Henry.

It was high time some strong ruler came to rescue not only Winchester, but all England, from the terrible grip of faction. Following the pernicious example of Henry of Blois, the barons had been building castles everywhere, and filling the land with anarchy and oppression. The security which had characterized the reigns of the Conqueror and his two sons was gone.

The destruction which fell upon Winchester during Stephen's reign helped to bring the city down from its proud position of capital of the realm, though the economic and geographical factors were more potent in raising London to take her place. Some of her citizens had perished in the war, but others had departed to find a place in the now greater town, so that the population of Winchester, after the long conflict, was sadly diminished; some of her public buildings were in ruins; and even the strongholds of Wolvesey, and the king's castle on the west, bore many signs of destruction wrought by the bitter conflict. It must have been a dismal prospect for the proud citizens. They might, it was true, build their city anew, but what of that if they were to lose their cherished pre-eminence among the cities of England? There were promises of renaissance in the reigns of Henry III and Charles II, but these promises failed to materialize. The Thames, not Southampton Water, becomes more and more the waterway of the kingdom's commerce with the continent of Europe, and, while London goes on from strength as the centre of the trade of the nation, Winchester recedes into the background.

Nevertheless, it was not an immediate and complete decadence. The citizens laboured and strove with all their power to regain their former position. They were aided by one important factor: her population might dwindle, and kings might come less and less often within her walls, yet Winchester continued to maintain her high ecclesiastical position until the time when Henry VIII broke with the Pope. The Bishops of Winchester were scarcely less powerful in the realm than the Archbishops of Canterbury; indeed, often they were more powerful; and some of their reflected glory fell upon the name-city of the see. And generally the see of Winchester was a more coveted prize in the medieval church than either of the archbishoprics. There was solid financial reason for the saying attributed to one Bishop of Winchester, when he was refusing a translation from Winchester to Canterbury, "Canterbury may be the higher rank, but Winchester is the deeper manger."

Two other things helped to retard Winchester's decline. One was the great Fair of St. Giles, which brought commerce from all parts of Europe in

August of each year. The other was the uprise of the custom of the Great Pilgrimage from Winchester to Canterbury, which began after the murder of Thomas Becket. A well-defined route, known as the Pilgrims' Way, led from the shrine of St. Swithun at Winchester to the shrine of the newly canonized Saint Thomas of Canterbury.

It was a royal pilgrimage, for it was unwittingly initiated by Henry II himself. Landing at Southampton, after the murder of Becket (for which he was held morally responsible by the Church), he hastened to Winchester, visited the shrine of St. Swithun, and, by confession to the monks there, began his penance. He then journeyed, *sans* regal pomp, along the old way to Farnham and Canterbury, not omitting to pay his devotions at every shrine and church on the way. And countless thousands of pilgrims after him did likewise, through wellnigh four centuries.

Throughout the Middle Ages there were, at distances of about a mile from the city, places of devotion on every road leading out of Winchester. On the Pilgrims' Way there was the little Saxon tower, with its rood clumsily cut on its wall, at Headbourne Worthy. On the Southampton road there was the newly established Hospital of St. Cross. On the north-west road was the little Church of St. Matthew at Weeke. On the road to Portchester, or near to it, was the little Church of St. Catherine, crowning the hill to the south; and a little later arose another hospital for sick people, or lepers, the Hospital of St. Mary Magdalene, on the road running over the eastern downs.

CHAPTER IV

Medieval Winchester

THE momentous agreement between the warring factions of Stephen and Matilda, that Stephen should hold the crown of England during his life, and that Matilda's son, Henry, should be his heir, was ratified at a great council of the barons held at Winchester Castle in November 1153. Homage was paid to both king and his heir by all present. It was a welcome settlement to the long-drawn-out struggle, and, as events turned out, a beneficent one to the realm. Stephen did not keep young Henry long waiting for the supreme honour; he died within a year of the settlement.

The accession of Henry II ushered in a new period for Winchester, and the citizens regained much of their former prosperity. The Treasury and the Mint were again established in their midst, so that they may have imagined their former glory of pre-eminence would return. But Henry had too large an empire to control, and many of its elements were too turbulent, for him to spend much time in England. So that Winchester did not see much of him. In thirty-four years he paid a score of visits to the city, and every one would seem to have been relatively brief, mostly only a day or two, when passing to and from Portsmouth or Southampton.

But Henry was generous to Winchester. To clothe his troops for a war in Ireland he placed an order with the Winchester weavers, probably through their guild, for two thousand ells of their famous woollen cloth, termed "burel." In 1184 he granted them their first charter, or so tradition says, for documentary evidence is lacking; but they paid substantially for the grant.

In August 1172 Winchester Cathedral was the scene of the crowning of young Henry, the king's son, with his wife Margaret of France, as it had been of Henry himself when he came to the throne. Young Henry had been declared the heir, and, according to continental custom, he had been crowned at Westminster. But Margaret, his wife, was not with him at the ceremony, whereat her father, the King of France, became furious at the supposed insult. The double crowning at Winchester Cathedral served to placate the angry Louis.

It was now as though there were two kings of England. Young Henry's ambition, stirred no doubt by his crafty mother, Eleanor of Aquitaine, began an insurrection against his father, and his younger brother Richard embarked on a similar enterprise in other parts of the vast territories nominally held by Henry. But the father was more than a match for his turbulent sons. He made defensive preparations in many places. Among the castles which were strengthened at this time was that at Winchester. The bishop's castles at Wolvesey, Merdon, Bishop's Waltham, and elsewhere, had been reduced years before.

Winchester Castle must have been at that time a place of great strength. Its outer works covered an area of some eight acres; the walls were of unusual massiveness, as befitted a royal stronghold, and around them ran a deep moat. Although dry in

Tudor times this moat was undoubtedly filled with water in the days of the Plantagenets. It has frequently puzzled people in modern days to divine how the moat was filled with water seeing that its lowest level was far above the level of the Itchen and its divergent streams. The solution of the problem would appear to be that the moat having been well puddled with clay throughout its whole length, until it became watertight, springs then flowing freely on the slopes above were fed into it. Some of these springs existed until well on into the nineteenth century, but since the establishment of waterworks on the hill they have disappeared.

Henry de Blois, the great Bishop of Winchester, who had had so much to do with the inception of the war between Stephen, his brother, and Matilda, lived on for nearly twenty years after the famous settlement. His earlier life was marked by disappointments. His advocacy of his brother's claim to the English throne had plunged the realm into a long and dreadful spell of bloodshed and horror. Nor was his great ecclesiastical ambition any more successful, namely, that dream of making Winchester the centre of a new archbishopric, composed of the seven south-western dioceses, with, of course, himself as the new archbishop. It was an idea which came very near to fulfilment. Not being fully cognizant of the views of the leaders of the English Church, the Pope at first gave his assent to de Blois's proposal, and actually sent him a pallium. But a swift outburst of English ecclesiastical feeling caused the Pope to withdraw his approval; Henry realized that the opposition was too strong, and reluctantly he had to relinquish his cherished dream.

But in the later years of his life Henry of Blois

CATHEDRAL FROM DEANERY KITCHEN-GARDEN

H

devoted himself to his diocese, his cathedral, and the city in which it stood. He it was who procured for the cathedral the curious font of black Tournai marble, which stands on the north side of the nave. In it was christened Henry III, and also Arthur, first child of Henry Tudor. The ruins of the great castle which de Blois built are still to be seen at Wolvesey, a grim reminder of that terrible time of civil war; but his greatest and most enduring memorial is the Hospital of St. Cross, which for nearly eight hundred years has dispensed charity in medieval fashion to black-gowned brothers who daily remember the name of their great founder. He failed in his effort to make Winchester an archbishopric, but, in his splendid foundation of St. Cross he built for himself a more enduring and more worthy monument. He held the bishopric of Winchester for more than forty years. There were few of his successors in that great office down to the Reformation but were closely associated with the government of the realm, and, in one way or another, left their mark upon the life of the nation. Among them were De Lucy, Edyngton, Wykeham, Beaufort, Waynflete, Fox, Gardiner, and Wolsey.

Although Winchester had lost to London its premier place in the government of the country, nevertheless she saw not a little of royalty as the years went on. Richard I, in one of his brief visits to England, the one in fact after his release from captivity, came to Winchester in order that he might be crowned a second time, and, as it were, purified and re-consecrated in his kingly office after the degradation of foreign imprisonment. Seated upon a great throne in the nave of the cathedral he heard mass, and, although not re-crowned, was blessed by the Archbishop of

Canterbury. After the service he dined with the monks of St. Swithun in their refectory. But his stay in Winchester was short. Soon he was off again to the Continent, whence he never returned.

The Bishop of Winchester at this time was Godfrey de Lucy, one who left his mark, not only upon the cathedral, where he introduced a new and beautiful style of architecture at the east end, but also in Hampshire, for he developed the waterway of the Itchen, making it navigable for the small vessels of the period as far as Alresford, where he had a palace.

Winchester saw a great deal of John. It was at Winchester that his queen gave birth to the prince who became Henry III, and was named Henry of Winchester. It was during John's evil reign that Winchester and the country round suffered the supreme indignity of a foreign invasion. Some of the English barons, furious with John for his ill-government of the kingdom, declared him deposed, and invited Louis, the prince-royal of France, to become King of England. Louis came over to England with an army of Frenchmen. But he soon found there was more opposition than welcome awaiting him. The realm was divided, and civil war began. The defence of Winchester was entrusted to Savaric de Mauleon, who proved himself a traitor, no doubt being secretly favourable to the invader. When Prince Louis approached Winchester with his army de Mauleon slipped away, leaving the city open for Louis to enter without difficulty.

So it was that, for a while, Winchester was invested with French mercenaries, and Hampshire, and a considerable area of the south of England, became a province of France, a most hateful happening in the eyes of the patriotic Englishmen who remembered the time when their king, Henry II, ruled from Northumberland to the Pyrenees. Winchester was the invader's base. But with the death of John in the midst of the turmoil came the promise of better things. The barons agreed to recognize the nine-year-old prince, Henry of Winchester, as king. A peace was patched up with Prince Louis, who withdrew to France, speeded upon his way by a present of ten thousand marks.

Henry III, born in one of the rooms of Winchester Castle, throughout his life cherished a kindly feeling for the city of his birth. He frequently came to the city, and he made an especial point of keeping Christmas there, banqueting sometimes in his own castle, but sometimes at Wolvesey, at the expense of the bishop. As the bishop in the early years of his reign was the rapacious Peter des Roches, a man after Henry's own heart, it may be imagined that the feasting at Wolvesey was more roisterous than befitted the residence of a bishop. Peter was Henry's evil genius for several years. Under the wicked tutelage of this foreign priest Henry set at naught many English laws and customs, so that at length the Great Council of England, led by the Archbishop of Canterbury, called for Peter's dismissal from the office of bishop and from the realm. Frightened by the storm which he had raised, Henry bowed to the will of the Council, and des Roches was banished.

Meanwhile Winchester flourished again under the sun of royal favour. The clergy and the barons might suffer as the result of the counsels of Peter and Henry, but the citizens, safe under the protection of their charter, found trade improving, while the common folk benefited by the frequent presence of the king and court.

At length, however, Henry's autocratic misrule brought on civil war. Simon de Montfort, a former royal favourite turned enemy, and a foreigner "more English than the English," led a faction against the king. Now it was that the peaceful traders of Winchester began to see that there were dangers in royal favour; for the very fact that Henry spent so much time in the castle of his birth, brought the civil war to their very doors. The citizens took one side in the faction, and the monks the other. Open warfare occurred in the streets. The citizens attacked the monastery of St. Swithun, swarming down the narrow street leading to the Close Gate. They stormed the gate, burning it and the buildings adjacent. The flames spread to King's Gate near by, destroying it and the guard house. It was when King's Gate was rebuilt, towards the end of the thirteenth century, that the little Church of St. Swithun was set upon it, to be a place of worship for the lay servants of the monastery who lived without the Close Gate, and to be at the same time one of the very few churches in the country to be built over a thoroughfare. There had been a church for the lay attendants before this time, but whether or not it had been built upon the gate which was burnt in the de Montfort fighting is uncertain.

But the genius of Henry's son Edward ultimately overcame the de Montfort faction, and the closing years of Henry were peaceful, and his rule more beneficent, a foreshadowing of the great reign of Edward I. Men saw, in this change for the better, the hand of the young prince. When but a youth at Winchester Castle Prince Edward had distinguished himself by sallying out as far as Alton where he challenged to single combat a lordling bandit who had

UNIVERSITY
COLLEGE
LIBRARY
NOTTINGHAM

been persistently taking toll from travellers going from London to Winchester. This adventurer, Adam de Gurdon, or Gordon, was overcome by young Edward, who, however, gave him his life, thereby making him a staunch and lifelong supporter.

De Gurdon was not the only highwayman of the day. The lonely tree-lined roads of Hampshire were notoriously dangerous for travellers in the thirteenth century. No longer could men boast, as they were wont to do in the Conqueror's day, that a man might travel from end to end of the kingdom with a bosomful of gold and none molest him.

During his period of residence in Winchester Henry III was made furiously angry by one of these roadside thefts. Some Brabant merchants were robbed as they were coming to Winchester. Unlike other sufferers, they took their grievance to the king himself, and called upon him to give them justice. They were aided in their suit by the foolishness of the robbers, who had about the same time robbed a convoy of wine destined for Winchester Castle.

Henry was ever a man who loved a foreigner, even before his own subjects. He was also a man who wished to do everything himself. To discover these robbers who had plundered honoured foreign merchants was a task after his own heart. The theft of his own wine made him rampant with fury. With unusual zeal he summoned a jury of men of Winchester and the district and, putting them upon their oaths, bade them declare the culprits. Here, it may be noted, is an instance showing the essential difference between a medieval and a modern jury. A medieval jury was composed of individuals who were expected to be witnesses to the facts, in other words, to know all about the case in hand, and to be aware of the guilt or innocence of the accused. They were expected not merely to know all the facts, but to declare them.

But the members of this particular jury, being either themselves implicated, or related to those who were, refused to declare anything. Henry's blood was up. He was not to be defied with impunity by a few burghers and yeomen. He stormed at them, telling them he would hang them all if they refused to reveal the culprits. They remained obdurate, possibly realizing there would be hanging either way. Henry threw them into the dungeons of the castle, and summoned another jury. These, probably warned by what had happened to their predecessors, disclosed the facts. A number of the king's own retinue were found to be among the culprits. Restitution was made to the injured merchants, and a number of the culprits were hanged. It may have been this, and the de Gurdon incident, which helped to dictate the policy of Prince Edward, when he enacted that trees should be cleared for the space of a bowshot on each side of every main road, thus getting rid of robbers' harbourage. In this relation it may be recalled that it was the practice of the Bishop of Winchester, during the period of the annual Fair of St. Giles, to send a company of men-at-arms to guard "the pass at Alton."

The regular appearance of Henry III at Winchester had an effect upon the defences of the castle and the city. During Henry's long reign there was frequent expenditure upon the castle buildings, as is shown by entries in the Pipe Rolls. The castle was considerably enlarged, and the Great Hall was transformed from a Norman to an Early English building much as it stands to-day. For the first time it was fitted with "verrinae," or glazed frames for the windows, in 1236. The present West Gate of the city, and the King's Gate, date from this reign. The city walls were strengthened and kept in good order, the national exchequer sometimes assisting with the expense, when the "murage" tolls were insufficient for their purpose.

ST. JOHN'S CHURCH, WINCHESTER

As has been noted, Henry III was fond of doing everything himself. On one occasion he reversed the kingly role of listener to monkish oratory, and addressed a sermon to the monks in Winchester Cathedral. He had a reason. The bishopric of Winchester was vacant, and he wanted it for his half-brother Ethelmar (called also Audemar), the son of Queen Isabella who, after the death of King John, married Hugh, Lord of Lusignan and Valence, Count of La Marche. The Bishop of Winchester being *ex officio* abbot of the monastery, or the other way about, it was for the monks of Winchester to elect their new head. When the time came they were loth to accept the king's nominee. They had but recently had bitter experience of another royal nominee, Peter des Roches, the choice of King John, and they had no wish to have that experience repeated. Besides, Ethelmar was anything but suited to be a bishop, much less to be the holder of one of the greatest sees in the country. He was but twenty-three years of age. The Bishops of Winchester (save the odious Peter) had all been men who had upheld the great reputation of the monastery and the see. This boy was clearly unsuitable. The monks gave the king to understand that his nominee was unaccept-able, and could not be elected. Henry III was of the same kidney as the others of his name before and after. Opposition roused him to fury. He is said to have offered bodily violence to some of the monks in their cathedral, even at the altar rails. It was in this temper that he summoned them to listen to a sermon. The angry king thundered at the dour ecclesiastics, choosing with sardonic humour as text for his discourse Psalm lxxxv, 10: "Mercy and truth are met together; righteousness and peace have kissed each other." In his sermon he gave the monks some very broad hints concerning the kind of treatment they were to expect from him if they remained obdurate. His flaming vehemence overbore the opposition of the monks, and in due course Ethelmar was elected to the office.

But the private feelings of the monks evidently reached the Pope's ears, and there was some difficulty in getting the assent of the papal see to the election. The result was Ethelmar had to go to Rome to sue for the Pope's approval, which was given reluctantly. Ethelmar made a very indifferent bishop, indeed he soon tired of England. He went over to Paris, where he was more at home, and there in a short time he died, to the great relief of the Winchester monks.

Nevertheless, in his dying hours, the boy bishop, as he came to be called, bethought himself of his high office, and remembered the majestic cathedral of which he was the titular head. He begged that after his death his heart should be taken out of his body and, in a suitable casket, taken to Winchester to be interred in his own cathedral. His wishes were obeyed. Enclosed in a golden casket the heart was buried somewhere in the retro-choir, with an elaborate mural tablet of Purbeck marble to mark the recess in which the casket was placed. In the course of repeated building operations in the cathedral by Bishop Fox and others the tablet and casket were moved, and at some time the golden casket was replaced by one of lead. The two sections of the mural tablet became separated, and their identity lost. In 1912 the smaller section of the monument was found during repair works which were in progress then, and it was replaced in its original position above its fellow. Before this was done, however, an examination was made of the wall behind the tablet, then on the north-east wall of the retro-choir, and a leaden casket was found in a small recess. In the casket was found a small fragment resembling very old leather, which was thought to be the mummified heart. It was replaced in the recess, and covered by the mural tablet as before. The tablet shows a three-quarter length effigy of the bishop wearing his mitre, and holding in his hands a heart.

It may have been this Ethelmar, or perhaps his predecessor, des Roches, who built a castle on a pleasant hill some miles outside Paris, a castle which came to be named after its builder, Winchester.

Gallic pronunciation has softened the name to Bicêtre, and the area is now a suburb of the modern city. This castle of Winchester passed into the possession of the King of France, and, in the course of a long history, it has been successively monastery, prison, hospital, and is now a lunatic asylum.

Two years before the death of Henry III a famous trial took place in the Great Hall of the castle at Winchester. This was the trial of John Warren, or Warenne, Earl of Surrey, who had "cleft the skull" of the Chief Justice of Ireland at Westminster. He was convicted of murder, and fined one thousand five hundred marks, a heavy sum for those days, but doubtless a bagatelle to the proud earl.

In the last days of his father the young Prince Edward, satisfied that the realm was at peace, decided to go on a crusade to Palestine. He kept his vigil in Winchester Cathedral, and on the eve of his departure was consecrated in the chapter house of the monastery.

His successful campaign in Palestine was cut short by the news of his father's death. He hurried home and, with Queen Eleanor, attended service in Winchester Cathedral, giving thanks for his safe return. Shortly after he called his first Parliament at Winchester, the assembly taking place in the Great Hall of the Castle. At a later Parliament, held in the same hall in October 1285, was passed the celebrated "Statute of Winchester," one of the milestones in the progress of law and order in England.

To Edward I the city of Winchester owed the great seal which was regularly used by the civic authorities from his time down to the passing of the Municipal Corporations Act in 1834. The inscription around the seal was one of which the citizens were justifiably proud. It ran: "S. Edw. Reg. Angl. ad Recogn. debitor apud Winton."

Edward spent far less time at Winchester than his father had done. He was too busily occupied elsewhere. The steady growth of London meant the inevitable dwindling of Winchester as soon as royal favour was withdrawn, but even though her population diminished, so that houses fell empty in scores, and churches became derelict, there is no evidence that those of her citizens who remained did not prosper. On the contrary they would seem to have pursued their callings of woolstaplers, fullers, weavers, and the like, with considerable profit. And even during the great Fair of St. Giles each September, although it was with chagrin that the burgesses saw the bishop and his minions take control of all the trading organization, they managed to do good business amid their grumbling.

In the twelfth and thirteenth centuries there was a strong Jewish colony in Winchester, in the neighbourhood which still perpetuates their name, that is, Jewry Street. The Jews were useful to the king and to the community, for they lent money at interest in days when no Christian was allowed by his Church to do so, usury being reckoned a very heinous sin. The Jews prospered and, while many of their neighbours were living in poor houses of timber, or wattle and daub, with thatched roofs, they built themselves sumptuous dwellings of stone (brickmaking being then a lost art in England). The Jews in England would appear to have looked upon Winchester as their most favoured and beautiful centre. Thus one at the end of the twelfth century:

This is for the Jews the Jerusalem of these parts. Here, and here only, they enjoy perpetual peace. Here is the school of those who would live well, and prosper. Here men are men. Here there is bread in plenty, and wine for nothing. Here the monks are so full of pity and kindness, the clerks so wise and free, the citizens so civil and faithful, the women so beautiful and so pure, that I am tempted to become a Christian when I am with such Christians. Go thither, to the best of cities, the mother of all. Wintonians have but one failing, and that, after all, is only a matter of custom : like watchmen, they tell lies, but only in the inventing of stories. Nowhere under heaven are false rumours so easily concocted ; otherwise, they are all truthtellers.

But happy as were the Jews in Winchester, the time came when they had to depart the realm under the unreasonable edict for their expulsion made by Edward I in 1290. At three months' notice they had to sell their houses, collect their debts, and go overseas. They were not suffered to return for three hundred and sixty years.

In the next century, under Edward III, Winchester received a great fillip to its commerce, and it promised to rise once again to its former importance in the realm. It was made the premier wool staple of the kingdom. As wool was then the one great commodity for national export, and a business in which the Crown took the closest interest, because of the revenue to be derived therefrom, Winchester anticipated a vast increase in her prosperity. For a while this promise was in fair way to being fulfilled ; the population increased, and the guildsmen of Winchester began once again to put on airs befitting their importance in the state. Then came the terrible pestilence known as the "Death," the streams of commerce dried up and, when things began to be normal again, Winchester found she was no longer the centre of the wool export ; the staple was removed to Calais, and Winchester rapidly dwindled, so that in a short time it was said she had a thousand houses empty, and seventeen churches falling to decay for want of worshippers.

But, if she had lost the big profits and prestige of the wool staple, she still had left her importance as a base for the assembly of knights and men-at-arms for the wars in France. From all over the country men had gathered at Winchester in 1346 to help with a new invasion of France which was projected by Edward III, in prosecution of his flimsy claim to the throne of France. Eight years before Southampton had been sacked by the French as a reprisal for an ineffective invasion by Edward. He gave out that he would sail to Bordeaux and attack from there, but, gathering an army of nearly twenty thousand men, he slipped down to Southampton, crossed to Cherbourg, and went on to win the battle of Crécy. In the weeks before the move to Southampton Winchester must have been thronged with men-at-arms and longbow men, and the alehouse-keepers, of which there were a-plenty, would do a roaring trade if nobody else did. The company of shieldmakers, living then in Middle Brooks, and the armourers living in the south-east corner of the city, must also have found trade flourishing. This influx of troops for wars overseas must have recurred many times in the century following.

It was two years after Crécy that news came to Winchester of a terrible pestilence which was devastating the nations on the continent of Europe. All too soon it reached England. Weymouth had the ill fortune to see it first, but it was not long before Winchester, and the country round, fell under the dire plague. The city suffered terribly, the number of deaths of all classes being prodigious. Nothing like it had ever been known before. No city records remain to tell the number of victims among the citizens, but the ecclesiastical records tell an appalling tale. At the great Benedictine monastery of St. Swithun's the number of monks was reduced from sixty to thirty-five. Hyde Abbey, though aloof from the city itself, lost fifteen out of thirty-five of its number. Other institutions suffered in similar proportion, Dominicans, Carmelites, Franciscans, Augustinians, and Friars Minor, each having centres in Winchester, fell away in numbers.[1] The Nunnery of St. Mary lost half its members, while every religious institution was stricken with poverty by reason of the wholesale reduction of its revenues due to the deaths of so many tenants of holdings and farms.

The pestilence, apparently, did not visit the city for two or three months after its appearance in Dorset. But its ravages in the west were known, and there was open dread that it would come eastward and strike Winchester. It had been a summer made miserable by unprecedented rain, and the autumn was no better, so that, as always in a wet year, food scarcity threatened. The apprehension in the minds of the people who saw the calamity creeping nearer and nearer can be faintly imagined from the text of a letter addressed to his clergy by William of Edyngton, Bishop of Winchester, under date 24 October, 1348. He says:

William, by Divine providence, Bishop, to the Prior and Chapter of our Church of Winchester, health,

---

[1] The Dominicans had their abode near the East Gate; the Carmelites in Kingsgate Street; the Augustinians near the South Gate; and the Franciscans were in Wongar Street, or Middle Brooks, a terrace in which still preserves their memory by the style of "Greyfriars."

grace, and benediction. A voice in Rama has been heard; much weeping and crying has sounded throughout the various countries of the earth. Nations, deprived of their children in the abyss of an unheard-of plague, refuse to be consoled because, as it is terrible to hear of, cities, towns, castles, and villages, adorned with noble and handsome buildings, and wont up to the present to rejoice in an illustrious people, in their wisdom and counsel, in their strength, and in the beauty of their matrons and virgins, wherein too, every joy abounded, and whither multitudes of people flocked from afar for relief; all these have already been stripped of their population by the calamity of the said pestilence, more cruel than any two-edged sword. And into these said places now none dare enter, but fly far from them as from the dens of wild beasts. Every joy has ceased in them; pleasant sounds are hushed, and every note of gladness is banished. They have become abodes of horror and a very wilderness; fruitful country places, without the tillers, thus carried off, are deserts and abandoned to barrenness. And, news most grave, which we report with the deepest anxiety, as we have heard, has already begun to singularly afflict the various coasts of the realm of England. We are struck with the greatest fear lest, which God forbid, the fell disease ravage any part of our city and diocese. And although God, to prove our patience, and justly to punish our sins, often afflicts us, it is not in man's power to judge the Divine counsels. Still, it is much to be feared that man's sensuality, which, propagated by the tendency of the old sin of Adam, from youth inclines all to evil, has now fallen into deeper malice and justly provoked the Divine wrath by a multitude of sins to this chastisement.

But, because God is loving, and merciful, and patient, and above all hatred, we earnestly beg that by your devotion He may ward off from us the scourge we have so justly deserved, if we now turn to Him humbly with our whole heart. We exhort you in the Lord, and in virtue of obedience we strictly enjoin you to come before the face of God, with contrition and confession of all your sins, together with the consequent due satisfaction through the efficacious works of salutary penance. We order, further, that every Sunday and

WILLIAM OF WYKEHAM
(By permission of Warden and Fellows of Winchester College)
(Photo by F. A. Grant, Winchester)

Wednesday all of you, assembled together in the choir of your monastery, say the seven penitential psalms, and the fifteen gradual psalms, on your knees, humbly and devoutly. Also, on every Friday, together with these psalms, we direct that you chant the long litany, instituted against pestilences of this kind by the holy Fathers, through the market place of our city of Winchester, walking in procession, together with the clergy and people of the said city. We desire that all should be summoned to these solemn processions, and urged to make use of other devout exercises, and directed to follow these processions in such a way that during their course they walk with heads bent down, with feet bare, and fasting; whilst with pious hearts they repeat their prayers, and, putting away vain conversation, say, as often as possible, the Lord's Prayer, and Hail Mary.

The bishop ended his letter by promising the usual medieval "indulgences" to all who shall take their part in these religious exercises and pray that God "may cause the severity of the plague to be stayed."

But if the ecclesiastical authorities pinned their faith to prayers and fastings, there were some of the citizens who realized that something more was needed. When the disease at length struck the city, and the number of burials grew appalling, so that the normal burying places in the city became overcrowded, there rose a clamour that the pestilent corpses should be taken outside the city and buried where they could not contaminate the living by the effluvium of their decomposition. The biggest graveyard in the city was in the centre, to the south of the High Street, and some of the citizens did not view with favour the idea of hundreds of plague corpses being buried so near to the dwellings of the living.

But the Church attached the utmost importance to burial in consecrated ground. The tenet concerning the resurrection of the physical body was a

I

vital part of its creed, and it taught that there was scant hope for the resurrection of any body which was buried elsewhere than in consecrated ground. As burials in consecrated ground necessitated fees to the Church, it is plain that the mercenary-minded in the Church were directly interested in keeping the custom of consecrated burial vigorously alive.

Early in January 1349 the citizens came to a definite clash with the monastery over this matter of burial outside the city, and, as one of the monks of St. Swithun persisted in carrying through a burial in the great cemetery between the cathedral and the High Street, the citizens set upon him and gave him a vigorous trouncing; and, it may be, they took the body away and had it buried in a plague pit outside.

This stirred Bishop Edyngton to vigorous protest. Not only had a holy brother of one of the oldest monasteries in England been wickedly misused, and sorely wounded, but a vital tenet of the Church's doctrine had been assailed. Accordingly, on 21 January, 1349, by which time, of course, the plague must have gained a strong hold on the city, Bishop Edyngton addressed a letter to the prior of the Monastery of St. Swithun, and to the Abbot of Hyde Abbey, directing sentence of excommunication to be pronounced against all those who had "laid violent hands upon brother Ralph de Staunton, monk of Winchester," and ordering sermons to be preached immediately advancing the doctrine of the resurrection of the physical body.

The church [he says] believes in the resurrection of the bodies of the dead. These have been sanctified by the reception of the Sacraments, and are hence buried, not in profane places, but in specially enclosed and consecrated cemeteries, or churches, where, with due reverence, they are kept, like the relics of the saints, until the day of resurrection. Our city of Winchester should set an example to the whole diocese, and, above all other places, ought to reflect the brightness of the faith of the church. But some people there, not, thanks be to God, citizens, or even those born in the city, for they are wont to be conspicuous in their upright lives, and in their devotion to the faith, but low class strangers, and sons of the church who are degenerate, lately attacked brother Ralph de Staunton whilst burying in the appointed place, and, when by his habit and tonsure, they knew him to be a monk, beat him, and prevented him from continuing to bury the dead amongst those there waiting for the resurrection.

The monks of St. Swithun retaliated upon the citizens by laying claim to the whole area formerly occupied by the New Minster, lying between cathedral and High Street. This must have caused the city authorities great annoyance, because "the mayor, bailiffs and citizens had entered upon the usurped portions of the said land, and employed the site thereof to hold a market twice in the week, and a fair twice in the year," in consequence of which "the bodies of the dead have been iniquitously disturbed, for, owing to the great mortality and pestilence, and the smallness of the parochial burial-grounds, the bishop, in the exercise of his office, had consecrated the said ground, and many interments had taken place in it."

As a result of this claim by the monks the king ordered an inquiry to be held, and appointed the Abbot of Hyde and two others to hear and determine the matter. This was in February 1349. The commissioners duly sat, and determined in favour of the monks, and the city had to find another site for its market and fair, or pay regular toll to the monastery. It was never wise in those days to lay hands upon any cleric, much less a member of one of the old orders, for the arm of the Church was very long, and her power of reprisal very far-reaching.

Considerable discussion has taken place in recent years concerning the actual effect of the plague upon the population. The conservative opinion is that the mortality probably did not exceed a third of the whole population of the country. But it is extremely likely that cities had a higher percentage of deaths. During the year 1349 no less than two hundred and twenty-eight institutions were made to benefices in Hampshire and the Isle of Wight, ten times more than the average of the three previous years, apparently showing a very large mortality among beneficed clergy.[1] The prior of St. Swithun's, and the abbess of St. Mary's Nunnery were among the Winchester victims. No records whatever exist of the mortality among the citizens.

The great calamity had a noteworthy and unfortunate effect upon the fabric of the cathedral itself. Bishop Edyngton, with pious zeal, had a desire to emulate his great predecessor, De Lucy, by making extensive structural alterations to his cathedral. De Lucy had made a great change at the east end. Edyngton turned his attention to the west end. He probably had dreams of a magnificent west front which should excel the beauty of Wells; and he projected the transformation of the mighty nave from the Norman to the new style. He began the work by taking down the west front with its two substantial Norman towers. Then came the pestilence, and the great scheme had to be abandoned. A temporary west front was erected forty feet nearer the east than the

[1] Abbé Gasquet.

THE NAVE, WINCHESTER CATHEDRAL

original Norman front. It was in the plainest form, completely devoid of architectural ornament. No doubt it was hoped that at some time later, when the country had recovered from the effects of the terrible scourge, it would be possible to take down the temporary front and carry out the scheme for an ornate front. But that time never came, and Edyngton's west front still stands. And, if any should doubt that it was but a temporary expedient, let them look carefully just inside the great west door, and see how the front is merely butted up against the main building without any tie-bonds. All else that Edyngton was able to do was to transform the first two north windows of the nave, beginning from the west.

The effects of the great pestilence were still being felt in the days of Edyngton's successor, the great William of Wykeham, particularly in the difficulty in securing a sufficient number of capable young men for the offices of the Church and the professions. It was this which inspired him to project his great plan for twin colleges, at Oxford and Winchester, to secure "the cure of the common disease of the clerical army, which we have seen grievously wounded by lack of clerks, due to plagues, wars, and other miseries."

The name of Wykeham is one of the greatest which has ever been associated with Winchester, and it is the most fragrant to-day. The son of a small farmer, his rise to power and wealth was phenomenal, even for those days of kingly preference. He received a grammar-school education in "the primitive sciences" at a school in Winchester, no doubt the old High School in Minster or Symonds Street, where Henry Beauclerc also received his education. As a young man he was an under-notary to the Constable of

Winchester Castle, an office which brought him under the eye of the king. His gifts as an architect and builder were discovered, and, at the age of forty-two, he was acting for the king as overseer of extensive works at Windsor. The phrase "Hoc fecit Wykeham," which he inscribed there, was said later to have a double meaning; it had made him, as well as being made by him. The Black Death, and its second visitation in 1360–1, while it swept so many others away, actually helped Wykeham upwards. Preferments were heaped upon him by the king. Within five years of his taking holy orders in 1362 he was made bishop of the richest see in England, and was, moreover, Chancellor of the realm. His preferments, and the wealth which he had amassed hitherto, made him the richest subject in the kingdom. Small wonder that jealousies caused him to fall under the cloud of the king's displeasure. But his integrity won him through this trouble. He was restored to his preferments, and held them till his death.

His idea for the creation of twin colleges was, no doubt, in his mind almost as soon as he became Bishop of Winchester, for within two years he was buying land at Oxford for the purpose of founding a college there. Then he began to maintain a school at Winchester at his own expense, and, as soon as the cloud of the king's displeasure passed, Wykeham obtained a Bull from the Pope sanctioning the foundation of a college "of seventy poor scholars, clerks, to live college-wise and study grammar near the city of Winchester," and the appropriation of revenues of the church of Downton, near Salisbury, for the endowment of this new foundation. As soon as his college at Oxford was sufficiently advanced in its building he turned his attention to the creation of his school "near Winchester," so described because the site was outside the walls of the city, although within the Soke.

Having purchased some five acres of land and a messuage to the south of the city, as well as two other messuages which fell in the way of his scheme, Wykeham sealed the foundation charter of "Seinte Marie College of Wynchestre," on 20 October, 1382. The building of the college began on 26 March, 1387, the foundation stone being laid at nine o'clock in the morning. The construction of the original buildings occupied six years. The cost was £1,014 8s. 3d., possibly £40,000 or £50,000 in modern values. The quarry stone came partly from Quarr, in the Isle of Wight, and partly from Devonshire. The stone was landed on the banks of the Itchen just above Southampton, and was then carted the ten miles to Winchester. The thick stone roofing slabs, which are such a feature of the buildings, came from the Isle of Purbeck. For the walls of the lesser buildings, such as cloisters and brewhouse, flint, the native building material, was used.

Having regard to the perils of the time Wykeham built his college somewhat like a fortress, so that, if necessary, the inhabitants could withstand a siege. Where the ground was marshy he built upon piles. The porter's gate still shows how, while it was in building, subsidence took place, for the arch is considerably out of level. Huge buttresses were added, and the gate has stood securely ever since.

The opening ceremony took place on Saturday, 28 March, 1393. Early that morning Wykeham received the newly appointed warden and the seventy scholars at Wolvesey palace, and formally admitted them to the privileges of the institution. They then moved in procession from Wolvesey, and entered their new college at nine o'clock in the morning. Whether there were any curious citizens present to witness the momentous ceremony there is no record, but even if so, it is certain that they would not have realized that they were gazing at something which was to begin a new epoch in England, and which was to have beneficent effects upon the government of the realm for five centuries and more.

Wykeham's great conception began to bear fruit very speedily. For two generations Wykehamists were the rulers of State, Church, and education, and when the country settled down after the Wars of the Roses, they again came to the front as skilled rulers; and to-day, not only at home, but in many parts of the British Empire, Wykehamists are to be found as able administrators of the highest probity, and Wykeham's motto, "Manners Makyth Man," has been carried the world over by the invariable courtesy of his sons.

Winchester College was not a new invention, but it was the largest of its kind by a very long way. Moreover, it had a separate foundation, although it was linked to the older foundation of New College at Oxford. It was to be quite definitely a place for the teaching of grammar, and for a thorough preparation for wider study at Oxford. Its value in the building of the best in British character has been recognized all down the centuries since its foundation. It became the pioneer of a new school system, that which in modern days is termed, by a curious inversion of meaning, the English Public School System. So impressed was Henry VI with the type of scholar turned out of Winchester that he was persuaded that there must be something in the place itself which produced so remarkable a result. Hence it is not surprising that he made it the model upon which to found his great school at Eton. So determined was he that his school should have the spirit of Winchester that he not only framed the Eton constitution upon that so carefully drawn up by Wykeham, but he took the headmaster of Winchester to be the first headmaster of Eton. He also had some of the Winchester scholars removed to the new school in order that they might, by precept and example, impart the spirit of Winchester to the boys of Eton. And more even than this. In the manner of Naaman, who believed that the spirit of a place was enshrined in its very soil, Henry ordered that several cart-loads of earth should be dug up in Winchester College precincts, conveyed to Eton, and there spread abroad; a last master-stroke, in medieval belief, to ensure the transfer of the wonderful Winchester spirit to Eton.

Wykeham is honoured in Winchester for one other stupendous work, namely, the complete transformation of the great nave of Winchester Cathedral from the Norman style to the English Perpendicular Gothic. The edifice, until that time, had preserved the characteristics given to it by its builder Walkelyn, save for the east end where de Lucy, early in the thirteenth century, added some Early English work, and at the extreme west, where Edyngton had removed the Norman west front with its towers, and substituted a plain Perpendicular front. Wykeham began his great work in 1394, that is, as soon as he had seen the virtual completion of his college at Winchester, and what was left uncompleted at his death was finished by his successors according to the terms of his will. The marvel of the work is that it literally was a transformation, and not a rebuilding. As much as could be used of the Norman work was left intact, the Perpendicular being, as it were, grafted upon it with supreme skill. The Norman pier arches, triforium, and clerestory were removed, only the triforium arches being left in each bay. A Perpendicular clerestory window was built in the empty bay. A Perpendicular balcony, with panels above, covers the Norman triforium arches. At first the Norman piers were cut into to transform them into the desired moulding, but, after working on eight of them, on the south side, this method was abandoned. The other piers were skinned of their ashlar, new masonry being substituted. This was because the work of the Norman builders was too coarse, the stone too uneven, and the mortar joints too wide. No doubt this work of substitution of Perpendicular ashlar for the Norman was done piecemeal, for the Norman core would scarcely have stood complete exposure. The general appearance of the Norman nave before the transformation took place may be judged by the present appearance of the north transept, which is practically untouched, and as Walkelyn left it. It is claimed, and with sound reason, that Wykeham's transformation created the most beautiful Gothic nave in Europe.

The eastern end of the presbytery, which was originally apsidal, was altered earlier, and a polygonal end substituted in the Decorated style. After Wykeham's work had been completed a further addition was made at the east end of the cathedral about the end of the fifteenth century, and the beginning of the sixteenth; this was by carrying out the Lady Chapel beyond the line of de Lucy's work. It had the effect of making the cathedral the longest in England, or indeed in Europe, with the single exception of St. Peter's at Rome. Its extreme length is 556½ ft. The nave is 250 ft. in length, and 77 ft. in height. Bishop Fox completed the transformation of the choir and presbytery by setting up graceful stone side-screens in Renaissance style about 1525, the wooden vaulting in the presbytery roof having been put up some twenty years before. The beautiful carved choir-stalls of Norwegian oak date from the beginning of the fourteenth century. Prior Silkstede's pulpit, although in keeping with the woodwork of the stalls, was not put in until 1620. The seven chantries in the cathedral were probably erected in the lifetime of their occupants. The grill gates of wrought iron, on the south side of the choir, are probably the oldest of their kind in the country. It is thought they may be even as old as the cathedral itself.

Wykeham's successor was Cardinal Beaufort, a true prince-bishop, son of John of Gaunt with Catharine Swinford, arrogant and rich; so rich that he was able to assist the king with money and men-at-arms for his French wars. Like Wykeham, and other bishops of the see, he was Lord Chancellor of England. It was probably the contemplation of men of his kidney which stirred Holinshed to satirize them in these words:

And hereunto, if the old catalog of the bishops of this see be well considered of, and the acts of the greatest part of them indifferentlie weighed, you shall find the most egregious hypocrites, the stoutest warriours, the cruellest tyrants, the richest moni-mongers, and politike counsellors in temporal affairs to have (I wote not by what secret working of the Divine Providence) been placed here in Winchester since the foundation of the see.

Rich the Bishop of Winchester was bound to be. It has been calculated that the income of the see must have been something like £120,000 a year in present money value. He held lands in eight or more counties, and upwards of twenty manors in Hampshire. But sometimes a sumptuous life led to prickings of conscience as the end drew near. Whether for this reason or not may not certainly be determined, but Beaufort cast about for pious acts to perform. He decided upon the extension and improvement of the Hospital of St. Cross, with the grafting on to the old foundation of de Blois a new benefaction for those of the nobility who had fallen on evil days.

He rebuilt much of the place, and added a magnificent gateway and tower. The brothers who to-day share his benefaction in the "Order of Noble Poverty" wear on their gowns a silver replica of a cardinal's hat, as a reminder of the source of their charity.

Beaufort was one of the judges at the trial of Joan of Arc, and is said to have been present at her martyrdom, although he was unable to "sit it out" to the end. A spirit of ironic nemesis has decreed that her effigy in Winchester Cathedral shall gaze at the recumbent figure of the haughty cardinal housed in its magnificent chantry in the retro-choir.

It was during the episcopate of Beaufort that Winchester saw the coming of a French embassy to Henry V to seek peace. Henry received them at Wolvesey Castle. He listened awhile to what they had to urge, but at length he declared bluntly that he was the rightful King of France, and he meant to have the crown of Fleur de Lys. The Archbishop of Bourges, the head of the embassy, lost his temper, and roundly declared that not only had Henry no right to the crown of France, but that he had no right to the crown of England either, and that they really ought to be treating with the heirs of Richard II. Such a rejoinder provoked Henry to furious anger. Foaming with rage he bade the Frenchmen begone,

OLD CANAL WHARF AND BLACK BRIDGE

and vowed he would speedily follow them. Having delivered himself of this threat he left the room.

Beaufort remained behind, and informed the envoys of the full extent of Henry's demands. These were for the restoration to him of all the territory on the Continent held by Henry II. They were also told that Henry was prepared to go to any lengths in pursuit of his claims. The archbishop retorted that the French were not afraid; let Henry come over to France with an army or without, and he would speedily be driven back, or killed, or captured.

126

So the peace conference ended futilely in brag. The envoys, with their escort of mounted men, departed the way they had come, namely, by Canterbury and Dover. Had they gone by way of Southampton they might have seen Henry's fleet, and army of sixty thousand men, which had gathered at Southampton and Winchester, and which had been on the point of embarkation when news of the approach of the embassy induced the king to call a halt. But now the embassy had been sent away, as it were, with a flea in its ear, Henry was afire to pursue his adventure. Leaving Winchester in great haste he sallied to Southampton, where, having learnt of a conspiracy against his person, he had justice done upon the leaders, the Earl of Cambridge, Lord Scrope, and Sir Thomas Grey. Then he set sail for France, and soon followed the redoubtable victory of Agincourt. For nearly forty years after this Winchester was periodically stirred by the assembly and passage of men-at-arms and bowmen for the wars in France.

Although Henry VI is said to have spent more time at Winchester than at Westminster, the Wars of the Roses, which began in his reign, affected Winchester little, if at all. She saw none of the fighting, which perhaps was some recompense for her acute sufferings in the earlier civil disturbances.

Henry VII, after his triumph at Bosworth Field, set about the task of uniting the rival factions of Lancaster and York by wedding Elizabeth of York, eldest daughter of Edward IV. He brought her to Winchester, so that her first child might be born in the ancient capital of the realm. There, in the great castle overlooking the lush valley of the Itchen, was born in 1486 the son who united in his person the houses of York and Lancaster. Henry Tudor boasted a supposed descent from King Arthur of Britain, and he made much of this to bolster up his none too strong claim to the throne of England. Winchester was then considered to be the Camelot of the Arthurian legends, and Winchester Castle the birthplace of Arthur. Small wonder, therefore, that Henry Tudor should call his firstborn Arthur.

For weeks before the expected event Winchester was seething with excitement. Not for two hundred and eighty years had a royal prince been born within its borders. When the time came for the christening of the royal infant in the great black font of de Blois the city authorities surpassed themselves in their adulation of the royal couple and their son. The christening was one of the most elaborate ceremonies ever seen in the cathedral, and the revelry which followed outdid anything previously experienced. A minute report of the proceedings is preserved in the city archives. This sets out the elaborate adorning of the interior of the cathedral, as well as the order of the procession, giving the names of the many titled folk who took part, and the appurtenances necessary to the ceremony.

Then the earl of Derbye and the Lord Maltravers; after them the Basonns, then the Taper, then the Salte of Gold covered, and then a riche Cresome, which was pinnyde on the right Brest of my Lady Anna, Sister of the Quene, hanging on her left arm; Sir Richard Gilforde, Knight, Constable, on the right hand, and Sir John Turburvill, Knight Marshall, on the left hande, bearing the Staves of Office. After them my Lady Cecill, the Quene's eldest Sister, bare the Prince, wrapped in a mantell of Cremesyn Clothe of Gold furred with Ermyn, with a Trayne, which was borne by my Lady the Marquesse of Dorsett, and Sir John Cheyny supportede the middell of the same.

THE END OF A 6 FT. PARCHMENT ROLL IN THE POSSESSION OF THE CORPORATION OF WINCHESTER RECORDING THE ANCIENT USAGES OF WINCHESTER. THE JOKE OF A MEDIÆVAL SCRIBE

The Lorde Edward Widevill, the Lorde La Warre, the Sonne and Heire of the Lorde Audeley, and Sir John of Aroundell, bare the Canapye. The Marquesse of Dorcett and the Erle of Lincolln gave assistence to my Lady Cecill . . . and thus proceeded through the Closter of the Abbey unto a litill doore beside the Weest ende of the Chirche, in the South parte of the saide Chirche, wher was ordeyned a riche and a large Clothe of Estate; for the wether was too cowlde and too fowlle to have been at the West ende of the Chirche; and the Queen Elizabeth was in the Chirche abiding the comyng of the Prince. . . . Incontinent after the Prince was put into the Fonnt, the Officers of Arms put on their Coots, and all the Torches weren light. From the Font the Prince was had to his Travers, and above him a Cremesyn Cloth as byfore. From thens in faire order was he borne to the High Auter, and leide therupon by hys Godmoder. After certeyn ceremony, whan the Goospel was doon, Veni Creator Spiritus was begon, and solemnely songen by the King's Chapell, with Orgons, and Te Deum also. During which season the Erle of Oxynforde took the Prince in his right arme and the Bishop of Excester confirmed hym; and the Bisshop of Saresbury knytt the Bande of Lynene about his nek.

Then follow a list of the christening gifts, and a description of the conclusion of the proceedings, winding up with:

In the Chirche Yerde wer sette two Pipes of Wyne, that every Man myght drynke ynow.

Which, no doubt, he did, with gusto.

The same scribe took care to set down also a minute description of the prince's cradle, and its furnishings; and he ends by noting that there were

also appointed a Governess to the Nurses, and three Ladies to be Rocksters, who were on certain State occasions to be apparelled in Clothe of Gold.

It may be assumed that there was considerable competition for the important office of "rockster."

K   129

Despite so auspicious and sanctified a welcome to this world the young prince died when about sixteen years of age, and as a result the succession to the throne fell upon his brother Henry.

Henry VIII visited Winchester several times during his reign. In 1520 he spent a week at the castle in company with the Emperor Charles V.

The visit cost the city a great deal for entertainment and preparation. It was either at this time or during the stay of Henry VII that the famous Round Table of King Arthur received its present Tudor colouring and decoration, and had a massive iron bond put around its circumference, all at the expense of the city. It is believed that Henry and Charles, with a number of their retinue, used the table for dining in the Great Hall of the Castle, Henry himself sitting "in the place of King Arthur." It was at Marwell Hall, near Winchester, that Henry awaited the news of the execution of Anne Boleyn, and then hastened to wed Jane Seymour.

Turning from the subject of the connection of the Crown with Winchester, it will be of interest to look at the ordinary life of the city in the two or three centuries before the Reformation. Thanks to modern research a great deal is now known about the local government of the city and its customs. Three Anglo-French copies of *The Ancient Usages of Winchester* are in existence, two in the city archives, and one (the most accurate) in the possession of Winchester College. It is considered that these were made about the end of the fourteenth or the beginning of the fifteenth century from an earlier Latin original now lost. These *Usages* set out the government of Winchester by a mayor, elected annually, and twenty-four "jurats," otherwise burgesses. There were also two bailiffs, and four sergeants, elected from the general body of citizens as city officers whose duty it was to preserve law and order.

The life of the city was circumscribed by a multitude of petty laws and customs. There was very little personal freedom for a citizen, and no privacy. Everybody knew everybody's business, and everybody watched everybody else to see that they kept within the law. Trading was hemmed around with many restrictions. A baker might not begin to sell his bread until a certain hour in the day, and the weight for the penny must accord with that fixed at the Assize of Bread for the year; for the official weight of the loaf varied with the abundance or scarcity of corn. Brewsters, of which there were always a-plenty, beer being the universal drink, had to brew to a standard. Weaving, by far the largest industry in the city, had to be carried on under strict rules, and for every loom a fixed rate was paid to the city. Even the hours of labour at a loom were fixed, and there were summer and winter hours. The dyers were prohibited from emptying "wodegore" into the city streams during the hours of daylight, wodegore being the blue dye then still in use for colouring the woollen fabrics produced in the city. Perhaps the most heinous offence was for one to go outside the city early on a market day, intercepting the countryfolk as they came in with their produce, and buying it up with the intention of getting a bigger price for it later in the city market. The penalty was heavy for this offence, called forestalling; and it was equally bad to buy up large quantities of produce in the market itself to resell again at an enhanced price, otherwise regrating. Such practices were a great offence to the medieval sense of fairplay. The

Usages give a penalty of forty days in the king's prison, which was in the High Street, for regrating, but in practice a heavy fine was more usual. There was no profit to the city in imprisonment. Likewise, though the city had its stocks, the authorities preferred a fine, if there was a prospect of collecting it, than to order confinement to the stocks.

There were disputes between landlords and tenants then, as now, but the procedure for the recovery of a tenement in Winchester in the Middle Ages was a curious one. The aggrieved landlord had first to make formal complaint to the alderman of the ward. The alderman then called a jury of neighbours, and with them viewed the property. If he found no chattels upon which to distrain for the arrears of rent he reported to the city court, which thereupon gave leave to drive a stake in the ground in front of the door of the tenement. It was a sign that the house was under the control of authority. But the landlord could not yet take possession. He had, as it was said, to "sue the stake" twice at intervals of a week, and again after forty days. Then, if no one paid up the arrears in the interval, he could take possession after the lapse of a year and a day. Most of these suits appear to have been brought by monastic authorities and the like. In the middle of the twelfth century many Winchester houses were owned by religious bodies.

The citizens were not only liable to punishment for offences which they might commit, but they were also liable to be dealt with for offences of omission. Under the system of "frank-pledge" every burgess was bound, under severe penalty, not only to attend at every burgh-mote, but there to report any offence or crime any of his neighbours might have committed.

GOD BEGOT HOUSE FROM ROYAL OAK PASSAGE

In short, every citizen was *de facto* a policeman, and expected to assist the authorities by bringing offenders to court. The city court met twice or thrice a week, and notwithstanding the relative smallness of the population, possibly six thousand in the thirteenth century, there was a considerable amount of work to transact.

As has been indicated, the principal industry was weaving woollen cloth, "chalun" and "burel." The former was blanket cloth. There were four official sizes of chaluns, all other sizes being confiscated. This helped in the control of prices, and was a guide to the buyer. Burel was rough coarse cloth worked on a large loom. Burel looms paid five shillings yearly to the city, and chalun looms twelve and sixpence. It was an offence to put an apprentice on a loom without first paying toll to the city. It was also an offence to entice a journeyman away to other service before the regular day for hiring, St. Andrew's Day.

Wages were definitely fixed. At the end of the thirteenth century a weaver got eighteenpence a week in winter, and two shillings in summer, the difference being occasioned by the longer hours. The rate for a mason was fivepence a day, and for his unskilled mate one penny less, but then, living was unbelievably cheap by comparison with modern times. Shoes cost from fourpence to sevenpence per pair. Butcher's meat cost something like a farthing a pound, butter less than a penny a pound, with eggs twenty or thirty a penny, according to the time of year. Fish, a very necessary article of diet in the Middle Ages, by reason of the fast days of the Church, was expensive. It was generally brought from Southampton, and, if brought in by "fysshers"

134

who were "out of franchise," had to bear a charge (to the city) of twopence halfpenny per cart-load at the city gate, besides the charge (to the king) for the stall in the High Street on which it would be retailed to the citizens.

Reference to butcher's meat is a reminder that for a long period it was a city regulation that no bull's flesh should be exposed for sale unless the bull had been baited, i.e. worried by bulldogs. Bull-baiting would appear to have been one of the regular amusements of the citizens. The place of the "bullstake" was in the centre of the city, where all had an equal opportunity of witnessing the spectacle. One of the bitterest controversies between mayor and burgesses was brought on by one holder of the office of chief magistrate who had the bullstake moved from its wonted position to a spot immediately in front of his own house. The clamour of the citizens was so loud that he had to bow to the storm, and allow the bullstake to be replaced.

Much of the laundry work was done in the open at recognized public places on the streams running through the lower streets, as well as by the town pump, which stood near the City (or Butter) Cross (*temp.* Henry VI). What scavenging was done in the city was done individually, and not by the city authorities as under the modern system. Every householder had to clear away all rubbish and filth from before his house every Saturday, or incur a fine. He had also to keep the paving of the thoroughfare in repair to the middle of the street, and on dark nights he had to keep a light over his door. He had also from time to time to take his part as a member of the night watch of his ward, a very irksome service judging by the refusals and the fines for non-service.

The convivial character of the guild assemblies may be judged from the fact that such meetings are always referred to in city documents as "drinking the guild."

Between the merchant, the master man, and the craftsman or journeyman, was a gulf very difficult to bridge from the craftsman's side. To become an apprentice one needed the very large sum, for those days, of ten shillings to pay down. No craftsman could act as a merchant, or even buy the raw materials of his trade for working up for his own benefit, without incurring the penalty of confiscation of the materials so purchased. There is a record of a working tanner who bought a raw hide in the Soke, and as he was not a master man, the hide was confiscated. The purchases of yarn for weaving were watched very carefully by officials, not only to see that no un-authorized person bought yarn, but also to see that every master man had a fair deal, no one of them overbuying to the exclusion and detriment of any other, and also to see that the vendor of the yarn had not damped it to add to its weight. For a craftsman to become a member of the Merchant Guild he had to be able to show that he had at least £4 in chattels, and he had to pay an entry fee of half a mark (6s. 8d.), and sometimes more. In the latter half of the fourteenth century the average number of guild entrants per annum was not more than eight. Allowing that there was a regular supply of relatives of guild members who would look to be admitted as a matter of course, there would be very few of the lower order of workmen, if any, included in those entrants.

Not only was living cheap, but, compared with modern experience, taxes were light. There were the market dues, and the gate tolls; the duties on raw wool, and the "ulnage" or duty on manufactured cloth; as well as the "murage" for the upkeep of the city walls and three of the gates (west, east, and north), and an occasional levy for the repair of the buildings in the Staple, where was kept the "tron," or great wool-weighing machine, the proud possession of the city. It has been calculated that these burdens, direct and indirect, only amounted to about fivepence per head of the population, the equivalent of a day's pay of a skilled worker. The murage rate was rarely sufficient to keep the walls and gates in good repair, even though the city carried out the work by direct labour, buying the materials, and paying a supervisor a small wage for overlooking the work; so in many years the Crown made a grant towards the cost. Sometimes there was a special rate levied to pay the cost of sending burgesses to Parliament. The payment was generally so much per day, and, no attendance, no pay! Assessments for the payments of rates were made apparently not on the value of the tenements, but upon the capability of burgesses to pay. As everybody's financial position was well known, assessment would have been easy. The King's Tenths, i.e. special taxation sanctioned by Parliament for war or other special purposes, were not generally made every year. A tenth meant the payment by Winchester of a lump sum of £51 10s. in the fourteenth and fifteenth centuries, and the sum was apportioned among the citizens. It would have averaged about twopence and a halfpenny per head, but while the poorest families paid a few pence only, others paid as much as a mark.

Among the happenings which helped to enliven the yearly round in Winchester were the periodic processions which were carried out on certain saints' days. They were meticulously regulated, as the following extract from the city archives, dated 1435, shows:

At a Convocation holden at the cytie of Winchester the Frydaie next after of Corpus Christi, in the 13 yeare of the Raigne of King Harry the sixt, after the conquest, It was ordaynd by Richard Salter, Mayor of the cytie of Winchester, John Symer and Harry Putt, Bayliffs of the cytie aforesaid, and also by all the cytizens and comynaltie of the same cytie, It is accordid of a certain generall procesyon in the Feast of Corpus Christi, of diverse artyficers and crafts within the said cytie beinge, that is to saie, that Carpenters and Felters shall goo together First; Smythes and Barbars Second; Cooks and Bochars Third; Shomakers wh two lyghtes Fourthe; Tanners and Tapaners Fyvthe; Plummers and Silke men Sixt; Fyshers and Furryers Seventhe; Taverners Eight; Wevyres with two lyghtes Ningth; Fullars with two lyghtes Tenthe; Dyars with two lyghtes Eleventhe; Chandlers and Brewars Twelvth; Mercers with two lyghtes Thyrtenthe; the Wyves with one lyghte, and John Blake wh another lyghte Fourteenthe. And all these lyghtes shall be borne orderlie before the said procesyon before the Priste of the cytie, and foure lyghtes of the Bretheren of St. John's shall be borne abought the bodye of our Lord Jesus Christ the same daye in the prosession aforesaid. And if any of theis artificers aforesaid make any debate or stryffe, or els Do refuse herafter this ordynance or do absent himselffe from the prosession aforesaid that crafte wch soe dothe absente himselffe or refuse shall forfait to the cytie aforesaid 20d. accordinge to the Discression of the mayor and 24tie then there beinge, and shall have payne of imprisonment; and if any one crafte slander another he shall forfait 6s. 8d.

But although the Church feasts and holy days were honoured by cessation from work, some amount of work and commerce would appear to have been permitted on Sundays, at any rate during certain

138

hours. It was not unusual for the city court to sit for the hearing of causes on a Sunday, possibly to suit the convenience of one or other of the parties. But it may be taken for granted that the religious observances required by the Church would first have been paid by all and sundry.

WINCHESTER'S OLDEST HOUSE, FORMERLY ST. PETER CHESIL
RECTORY

The community living outside the walls in the Bishop's Soke, under the bishop's protection and rule, were despised by the proud burgesses within the city. They were looked upon by the insular citizens as worse than the guildsmen of other chartered cities. The Sokemen were the free-traders of the time, and there were continual quarrels between the city authorities and the Soke over matters of trade. An aggrieved city craftsman could go outside the city, and buy raw materials in the Soke, without

139

any limitation save the price; but if he tried to bring his purchases inside the gates his troubles would begin. Sokemen might commit offences against citizens, but they would refuse to come into the city court; they claimed to be tried in their own court, that of the bishop, which, until the second decade of the nineteenth century, was held at Cheyney Court, immediately inside the great gate of St. Swithun's monastery. The dwellers in the Soke were also free of many of the financial burdens which the citizens had to bear. They could build their tenements practically where they pleased. The general effect of this freedom can still be seen when walking round the district locally termed the "Wharf," and along the Weirs.

Besides the area of the Soke the ecclesiastical authority was exercised in the very centre of the city, in the Manor of Goodbegot or Godbiete. This was a little area having an abutment on the High Street of eight gyrda, or land-yards, equals 132 ft.; and on St. Peter Street of nine gyrda, equals 148 ft. 6 in. It was given by Æthelred to his wife Ælgyfa, as her marriage gift on their marriage in 1002. She bequeathed it to the monastery of St. Swithun, in which possession it remained until the Reformation. Shorn of its old privileges it was handed back to the new body, the Dean and Chapter of the Cathedral. The original privileges were jealously guarded by the monks. In the grant made by Æthelred, drawn up by a monk, the most awesome doom is called down upon whomsoever should seek to alienate any of the privileges from the little Manor.

This franchise embraced freedom from any payment for the "repairing of bridges, the repairing of walls, and the gathering of a host to make war."

Moreover, there was the right of sanctuary, a valuable privilege to wrongdoers in the Middle Ages, for the writ of the city officers stopped at the entrance to the Manor. Nevertheless, there were times when the zeal of the city officers overstepped the boundary, especially in the years immediately preceding the Reformation. When, in 1333, the city officers invaded the Manor to apprehend one William de Turry of Sussex, the Vicar-General of the bishop threatened the "Greater Excommunication" against "such presumptuous persons" who "without the will or permission of the prior or his officers did thereupon take, attach, withdraw; yea, and even remove the said William, and of their sacrilegious and rash emprise did detain, and do so detain him in prison, and it behoves us to proceed against them by all the lawful means in our power for the preserving of the rights and liberties of the said Church." In 1503 a sergeant of the city was fined for unlawful arrest in the Manor. Three such daring trespasses occurred in 1535, the citizens assisting in one of them, showing that the popular feeling was rising against the Manor's privileges. In 1541 those privileges were swept away, no doubt to the entire satisfaction of the mayor and citizens. The Manor in monastic days was a little community of dwellings, some with stalls for the sale of goods. These stalls paid toll, not as all other stalls in the city did, to the king, but to the Monastery of St. Swithun, and the rents of the dwellings of course went to the monastery also. Law and order within the tiny community was kept by a miniature manorial court, the records of which were kept as meticulously as were those of far bigger manors. In the fourteenth century a tapster who was proved to have broken the assize of ale was fined sixpence. In 1503 Stephen le

141

Fox, John Haywode, and Thomas Alayn, tapsters, convicted of breaking the assize of ale, were fined respectively sixpence, eighteenpence, and threepence. John Haywode apparently was an old offender. In the same year Joan Newport, another tapster, was accused of keeping in her house a woman of bad character (*male condicionis*) to the grave annoyance of her neighbours. She was ordered to remove the woman or be fined forty pence. At the end of the twelfth century the mayor and his jurats attempted to isolate the Manor and its inhabitants by the process of what is now known as boycott, but there is no evidence that the attempt was successful. The present God Begot House was built upon a part of the Manor site about 1558. The front is a restoration made in 1908.

The Middle Ages were sanguinary, and life was of little account. A political foe was considered safest dead. Hence when the aged Despenser, Earl of Winchester, was caught at Bristol by Mortimer's forces, in the struggle to depose Edward II, although ninety years of age, he was hanged, and his head was sent to Winchester to be hung out on a pike over one of the gates. The citizens would seem to have been proud of these ghastly souvenirs of internecine warfare, for, when David of Wales was executed at Shrewsbury, and his head sent to London to be stuck on London Bridge, the citizens of Winchester claimed one of the quarters, and were awarded the right shoulder, Winchester being next in importance to London.

The period of greatest excitement in the year for Winchester citizens was the sixteen days' Fair of St. Giles, held on the hill overlooking the city, and beginning on 31 August. At daybreak the mayor had to meet the bishop's justiciaries at one of the gates, and deliver up the keys of that gate where, immediately, the city guards and toll collectors were replaced by those of the bishop. Then followed a humiliating procession to the West Gate, the bishop's officers in front, and the supplanted city officials behind. At the West Gate proclamation was made of the opening of the Fair, and of the rule of the bishop over a seven-league radius, including the city of Winchester and the town of Southampton, during the sixteen days of the Fair. The procession continued to the other gates for similar proclamation, at length reaching the East Gate, and so out, and up the hill to the site of the Fair. More humiliating to the city even than the giving up of the keys of the gates was the handing over to the bishop's officers of the great wool-weighing machine, the "tron," which was taken up to the Fair ground, there to do the wool weighing for the bishop. All business ceased in Winchester and Southampton, and in the radius of the seven leagues allowed to the bishop. His officers were on every road and highway to take toll of those going to the Fair. No craftsmen might work in the city; they must go to the Fair to labour. The bakers alone were allowed to carry on their trade in their own ovens, for convenience, of course; but even then they had to submit samples of their wares to the bishop's officers at the Fair itself. And all wine and beer in store in the city had to pass the rigid test of the bishop's officers before it could be sold; and any found below standard would be spilled in the gutters, and the owners fined to boot. But if the city lost somewhat of its dignity during those sixteen days there is little doubt that it must have gained not a little commercially, not only as a result of so large a concourse passing through its midst and using its taverns, but also because in its booths in the Fair itself it would have been able to sell a great deal of its staple produce, the chaluns, and burels, and tanned hides.

There is little doubt that by the fourteenth century, when the Fair was in its heyday, the booths were to a large extent permanent. The site was laid out in orderly fashion, with streets named after the trades working in them, or the commodities sold there. It was circumscribed by a stockade, with entrance gates for the payment of toll. It must have been an extremely remunerative prerogative for the bishop, notwithstanding the fact that he had to keep a small army of men at work during the Fair collecting his dues. In the conduct of so vast a business it was inevitable that there would be disputes, therefore a regular court was set up for dealing with them, a court held in the bishop's pavilion, and termed in medieval phrase, the Court of Pie Powder, the English rendering of the Anglo-French *pie-poudré*, otherwise dusty foot. The court was one for settling the disputes of travellers, and travellers were individuals with dusty feet. The Fair, however, was not confined to business. A great amount of boisterous jollification enlivened the days, for it was a time when there were jongleurs, and dancers, minstrels, and acrobats, in plenty; and it is likely that never a Fair was held but there was at least one mystery play presented, and these medieval plays contained a deal of coarse humour suited to the outlook and taste of the time, generally travesties of Biblical stories, mixed up with English tradition and experience.

The ending of the Fair was a day of great rejoicing in Winchester. The great tron, and the keys, were

WINCHESTER LOOKING EAST FROM ST. GILES'S HILL.

(Photo by F. A. Grant, Winchester)

brought back in triumph, and the resumption of mayoral authority was celebrated in ale and much feasting. The city accounts contain a number of references to money spent in feasting the return of the tron.

Although outwardly a religious age, there was a vast amount of crude superstition, handed down, doubtless, from pre-Christian times. An instance of one pagan superstition came to light in 1918. About a quarter of a mile from the West Gate a skeleton was dug up in a garden. It had been buried surrounded by flint stones. It was an ancient superstition that flints would keep down an evil spirit as effectually as a stake through the middle of a corpse. The complete absence of the skull, and the presence of a pierced silver penny of Henry III, suggest that the skeleton may have been that of a felon who had worn around his neck a silver penny as a talisman.

It is noteworthy that the Peasants' Revolt of 1381, although it stirred Hampshire, in common with other southern counties, left Winchester undisturbed, so far as the records show. The rising was an agrarian one, to abrogate manorial rights, and to secure fixed rents for rural holdings. It found no echo in Winchester, which was not a manor, while its citizens had already obtained their freedom. Moreover, their loyalty to the young King Richard II was unimpeachable.

A tiny sidelight upon Winchester in the Middle Ages is afforded by a quatrain attributed to Robert of Gloucester:

In ye countrey of Canterbury most plenty of fish is,
And most chase of wilde beasts about Salisbury I wis,
And London shipps most, and wine at Winchester,
At Hartford sheep and ore, and fruit at Worcester.

L

CHAPTER V

Tudor Winchester

IN Tudor days Winchester had dwindled to a quiet country town, important within the county as the centre of shire administration, but being very little influenced by, and taking very little interest in, the doings of people outside. It was a typical example of an insular, self-satisfied, narrow English borough; very jealous of its privileges; meticulously careful of its many ancient customs; looking out upon the rest of the world with a pride wellnigh insolent, counting itself still as the first city in the kingdom.

The momentous changes which came with the Reformation no doubt pleased the greater number of the citizens. They had long resented the arrogance of the monastic authorities in their midst, so it is certain they did not regret the breaking of the power of the great monastery of St. Swithun, nor of the lesser establishment at Hyde. They certainly rejoiced at the suppression of the little Manor of God Begot, which had for centuries been a thorn in the side of the city authorities; it was a place where their jurisdiction had not run, and, therefore, a refuge into which malefactors could escape, and defy the officers of the "Mayor and 24tie." They had, however, a good word to say for Nunnaminster, but their prayers to the king for "tolleracon of the said monastery" were of no avail.

Whether or not the citizens were glad that the

GATEWAY AND CHAMBER COURT, WINCHESTER COLLEGE

GATEWAY AND CHAMBER COURT, WINCHESTER COLLEGE.

"College of St. Marye, near Wynton" escaped the general destruction is not very clear. It is to be suspected that they troubled very little what happened to this and the other bodies in and near the city. There is, however, definite evidence that they were very much alive to their own interests, and were on the watch to see what scraps they might secure for themselves in the general scramble.

Shadows of the approaching change in ecclesiastical polity in England were perceived by the discerning long before Henry VIII finally broke with the Pope. It is, however, doubtful whether many realized even a tithe of what it was in Henry's mind to do with the monastic houses and their properties. There was a presage of his intentions given in the course of one of his visits to Winchester. Chapuys, a certain foreign envoy, records that one autumn Henry had gone down to Winchester to reside. When at the cathedral he cast his eyes covetously upon the surpassing rich treasures there, and he "caused an inventory to be made of the treasures of the Church, from which he took certain fine rich unicorn's horns (licornes), and a large silver cross adorned with jewels." Henry salved his conscience for this theft by giving the monastery several mills. But these he had previously, with sardonic humour, taken from the Bishop of Winchester.

Henry knew there was a strong feeling in the country against the monastic houses. They represented in many cases a foreign element; they held large tracts of land, the revenues of which flowed away from the general well-being of the country; and the inmates of most of the monasteries were considered to be useless encumbrances upon the nation.

Wyclif's doctrines had found their way into Hampshire in an earlier generation, so that William of Wykeham had felt constrained to take action against those who were "tainted" with Lollardry. Nevertheless, a hundred years later the spirit of Wyclif was still operating in the county, for, in the last decade of the fifteenth century a man from Woodhay, named Richard the Sawyer, was accused at the bishop's court at Winchester of heresy. He admitted that he had been "buying and conceiling of Englyshe bokes," and that he had said:

the Blessed Sacrament was but a pece of dowe bakyn and prentyd betwyxt Irones, and that I cowde make 30 of theym within a owyr if I hyd such prentyng Irones.

Being aware that such beliefs were abroad, and even spreading within the realm, Henry felt himself safe in flouting the Pope, placing himself at the head of the English Church, and then suppressing the monastic houses, the smaller ones in 1536, and the larger ones in 1539.

In order to justify, on the surface, the seizure of the monasteries and their possessions, Thomas Cromwell, the king's minister, sent round "visitors" to inquire into the state of the houses which were marked for suppression. The report they made represented many of the places to be dens of wickedness and vice. There is no record that any such charges were brought against either of the foundations at Winchester. The most that could be said against them was that they were elaborate and enormous husks housing insignificant and useless kernels, and that neither served much useful purpose to the community.

There was the notable exception, already mentioned,

of Nunnaminster. This was a useful school for the daughters of gentle folk, and at the time of the visitation there were some twenty-five girls receiving education there. The report of the "Visitors" was unusually praiseworthy. They declare that the nuns at St. Mary's, Winchester

have been and are of very clene, vertuous, honest and charitable conversation, order, and rule synce the first profession of thym, which is also reported not only by the Mayor and Comynaltye of the Citye of Winchester, butt also by the most worshipfull and honest persons of the Countre adjoynynge thereunto, which have dayly made a contynuell sute unto the said Commissioners to be suetors unto the kinges highness for tolleracon of the said monastery . . . around the house are many poor householders which have theyr only lyvynge of the said monastery.

The heads of the several Winchester houses made haste to prepare themselves for the storm which was imminent. The Prior of St. Swithun's sent a present of something over £300 to Cromwell, the Vicar-General, in the hope of averting spoliation, or, alternatively, preserving the prior in his office, or a similar one. Documents show that there was a definite bargain arrived at between Cromwell's agent and the prior, for the payment of £500. It did not save the monastery, but it probably had some effect in safeguarding the prior's welfare.

Winchester College authorities also distributed a few valuable presents with discretion. To Cromwell they sent a silver salt-cellar, and to the king they dispatched a couple of fat oxen, ten sheep, and a dozen plump capons. These gifts, or perchance personal influence rightly exerted, proved of value, for the college escaped the net, and, moreover, under a statute of 1536, it was exempted from the payment to the Crown of those dues which had formerly been paid to the Pope.

As for Hyde Abbey, Salcote the Abbot signified his willingness to acquiesce in the suppression of his house. The smaller houses, and friaries, lacking any influence, had no chance; they were suppressed without mercy.

In 1538 there was a general dispatch of officers to destroy every noted shrine in the country. Their instructions were to take away "shrine and bones with all the ornaments of the said shrine belonging, and all other relics, silver, gold, and all jewels belonging to the said shrine," and they were further enjoined to "see them safely and surely conveyed unto our Tower of London," meanwhile taking extreme care "to see that both the shrine and the place where it was kept be destroyed even to the ground."

The officers came to Winchester to destroy the famous shrine of St. Swithun. Whatever the citizens thought about it there can be no doubt that the prior and monks were grievously dismayed, and appalled at the unheard-of sacrilege. But they could do nothing more than they had done. The substantial bribe to Cromwell had failed in its purpose. Pollard, one of Cromwell's officers charged with the destruction of the shrine, in a letter to his principal described what he and his fellows did. The work was not done in a moment, it occupied many hours, and went on into the small hours of the morning. Assisting in the work was the Mayor of Winchester, with eight or nine of his brethren, as well as the bishop's chancellor, "Mr. Doctor Crawford, with a good appearance of honest personages besides." Pollard says: "About three o'clock in the morning we made an end of the shrine here," and he adds, "the prior and convent were very conformable." They had not very much choice.

There was some disappointment in store for the spoliators, for they found in the shrine no gold, nor any "ring or true stone, but all great counterfeits." There was, however, a great quantity of silver, amounting, it was estimated, to nearly two thousand marks. On the same early morning Pollard took possession of the cross called "Hierusalem," a cross of emeralds, a cross of gold, and two gold chalices, as well as some silver plate. Then he went into the choir (the shrine having been in the retro-choir, probably midway between the chantries of Beaufort and Waynflete), and there he marked the reredos and altar.

We viewed the altar, which we purpose to bring with us. It will be worth the taking down, and nothing thereof seen; but such a piece of work it is that we think we shall not rid it, doing our best, before Monday night or Tuesday morning. This done, we intend, both at Hyde and Saint Mary's, to sweep away all the rotten bones that be called relics, which we may not omit lest it should be thought we care more for the treasure than for avoiding of the abomination of idolatry.

The royal treasurer acknowledged the receipt of 1,035½ oz. of gold, 13,886 oz. of silver gilt, 300 oz. of silver and parcel gilt, and one mitre, from Winchester. Where most of the jewels went, and who had them, is a mystery, for no mention is made of their being received by the king. Probably they were intercepted by Cromwell. But the prior managed to secrete a "gylt pax of Saint Swithun, with hangings of the Carnalles hat, and the golde ringe of Saint Silvester," for, when he died, he bequeathed them in his will, the ring to "Mr. Chaunceler," i.e. the chancellor of the diocese.

As Pollard indicated, the Prior of St. Swithun's Monastery, William Kingsmyll, formerly known as William Basyng, was not of the same timber as Whiting of Glastonbury, Cook of Reading, and Marshall of Colchester, each of whom was executed because he would not surrender his house and its treasures to the king. No doubt Kingsmyll had been given a hint of favours to come if he were sufficiently complaisant in the matter of the surrender. So it proved. He assented to all that was proposed or done by the king, and his vicar-general. His reward came in March 1541, when Letters Patent came from the king, establishing, in place of the old monastery, a dean and chapter, and appointing "Prior Basynge" as "Willelmum Kyngesmyll the first original and modern Dean." Moreover, places in the new establishment were found for most of the monks. After an existence of seven or eight centuries the Benedictine foundation ceased to be. Two months later Henry restored to the new body most of the manors which had belonged to the monastery, and he added some others which had been taken from other suppressed houses. This property remained in the possession of the dean and chapter until the nineteenth century, when it was all handed over to the Ecclesiastical Commissioners in exchange for a fixed income.

As for the form of worship in the cathedral, practically no change was made in the lifetime of Henry. The Mass was celebrated, and the services were sung in Latin as they always had been. Protestant changes, organized by Cranmer, were made in the next reign. Orders were then received for the

Scriptures to be read in English, for the choristers to allow their hair to grow, and sermons were directed to be preached.

Abbot Salcot of Hyde was, if anything, more complaisant than Kingsmyll. He had been, so to speak, bought off several years before by his preferment to the see of Bangor, being allowed to retain his abbacy at the same time. When, in 1539, he was called upon to surrender the Abbey of Hyde, he did so without the least demur, and his reward was to be made Bishop of Salisbury. He was the "Vicar of Bray" of the period, for he was a zealous reformer under Henry VIII and Edward VI, while under Mary Tudor he was one of the court which condemned Latimer and Ridley.

The Abbey of Hyde fell into the hands of Thomas Wriothesley, one of the king's most active supporters in his policy of spoliation. A great part of the stone of the abbey church and monastic buildings was carted away to Titchfield where Wriothesley used it in the building of a stately mansion. Even then much stone remained on the site, and for many years local builders used the place as a quarry, paying the Wriothesley estate so much a cart-load. Many houses in Winchester, especially on the north side, show in their walls stone obtained at Hyde, while not a few garden walls, still standing, show scores of fragments of ashlar, once parts of the sacred fane, and now put to baser use. A beautiful chartulary of the abbey, made in 1354, is now in the library of the Earl of Macclesfield.

When, in the last quarter of the eighteenth century, the site of the abbey was purchased by the magistrates of Hampshire, for the building of a county bridewell, all that then remained of the monastic buildings was swept away, leaving only the porter's gateway, an uninteresting erection of the fifteenth century, and two old stone bridges, one of which has an appearance of great antiquity, spanning the abbey lockburn. It was at this time that the remains of the great Alfred, and his son, Edward the Elder, were scattered.

A century later, the county bridewell in its turn having disappeared, a row of modern cottages was built on the foundations of the nave of the abbey church.

In the later suppression fell the College of St. Elizabeth, a foundation of Bishop Pontissara, situated just to the south of Wykeham's College of St. Mary. Like the Abbey of Hyde it fell into the clutches of Wriothesley. He sold it to Winchester College, the authorities of which pulled it down, and with the stone built a fine wall to enclose a pleasaunce which was for many years a resort for the Fellows only, but since early in the nineteenth century, a playing-field for the scholars.

The destruction of so many buildings in and near Winchester provided much building stone for houses and walls. In the district formerly termed the Soke much of this stone can still be seen.

The citizens of Winchester, as has already been noted, were very much alive to their own material interests. In the reign of the boy king, Edward VI, the city authorities petitioned for the reduction of the fee-farm of one hundred marks, annually paid to the Crown in quittance of the king's dues from the city. The ground of the petition was that the population had dwindled, so that the civic revenues had been severely diminished, many houses were empty, and a number of churches, formerly in regular use, were derelict and falling to ruin. They implored the king to reduce the fee-farm to fifty marks, and they also begged to be allowed to have those tenements and rents within the city which had belonged to the suppressed Abbey of Hyde. These were reckoned as being worth £16 a year. They also petitioned that all broadcloths, kerseys, and clothing made in the city might pass out of the country through Southampton without paying any custom dues; and further, that they might have a lease of the farm of the ulnage (cloth duty) on all the cloth made in the county of Hampshire, that is, to be allowed to pay the Crown a fixed amount per annum, and then collect all the duties. It was an impudent request, but the king assented to it. But before the grant had been officially sealed the young king died, and it became inoperative.

The spoliation of the churches which went on in the reigns of Henry VIII and his weakly son was not confined to those attached to monasteries, although those seemed to suffer most because they had most to lose. The parish churches were ordered to surrender their sacramental vessels, and, in most cases in Winchester, the incumbents seem to have obeyed the command, and to have surrendered their silver chalices and patens, as well as silver candlesticks if they had any. One notable exception was the little Norman church of Weeke Without, now within the city, but then a mile outside the city walls. This church still possesses a silver paten which is claimed to be the oldest pre-Reformation paten in the country. It is reckoned by numismatists to have been wrought in the reign of King John, probably about 1215. The reason why it escaped the general confiscation, and resultant melting-down, is probably because in

Reformation times it was the custom to refer to the sacramental vessels as the "Challice," and when, in the great spoliation, the "Challice" was called for, it was understood that both chalice and paten were meant. But a few astute incumbents chose to read the order literally, and surrendered only the chalice, retaining the paten.

Winchester Cathedral lost not only its shrine of St. Swithun, which for centuries had been a source of substantial income from pilgrims who came to visit it, and also every article of value which adorned the place, but, what was infinitely more precious, very many illuminated manuscripts, centuries old, as well as much coloured glass. The cathedral was denuded of its monasterial regime, and placed under a new system, with some of the land of the old monastery as its endowment. The rest of the land went into private hands. In the reign of Edward VI a set of rules was drawn up to govern the services in the cathedral. One of these rules directed that "all maner of coristars of this sayde chirche shall from hensforthe suffer ther crownes to growe and be no more shaven butt onely ther hear to be rowndede and clypped short."

But with the death of the young king, and the accession of Mary, his sour-faced half-sister, came a reversion to the old order of religion. This was to the mind of most of the citizens of Winchester, who, while they had welcomed the fall of the monks, had not taken kindly to the reformed religion, although, like the first Marquis of Winchester, who boasted that he was "a willow, not an oak," most of them had professed a superficial acquiescence in the changes which had been ordered by the authorities in London. Bishop Gardiner, who had been removed from the bishopric in the reign of Edward VI, because of his Romanist tendencies, was restored to the see of Winchester by Mary, and he thereafter became her favourite prelate, so much so that she chose Winchester as the place of her marriage with Philip of Spain, and Gardiner as her marriage priest.

It was a highly unpopular marriage, but it brought Winchester once again into the forefront of happenings in England, and filled her with regal pomp, now, alas, all too rare within her walls. Whatever the rest of England thought of the nuptials, the citizens of Winchester were prepared to regard them as the most desirable that had ever taken place. The honour of a royal marriage in their midst sent them into ecstasies of delight, and their scribes into a state of maudlin imbecility. The contemporary descriptions of the queen and the ceremonial of the marriage are slobbered over with the most fulsome adulation. One writer set it down that the queen was so beautiful and so adorned with jewels that eyes were blinded as they gazed upon her, and even her attendant ladies looked like celestial angels!

Philip arrived at Southampton in July 1554, escorted by a fleet of about one hundred and sixty vessels, some of which were English. He remained at Southampton four days, the while Mary, having heard of his safe arrival on her shores, made the journey from Windsor to Winchester. On 23 July Philip travelled from Southampton to Winchester, "accompanied by many marquises, dukes, earls, and other lords and gentlemen, besides those from Spain, and having with him upwards of a thousand of horse." It is possible that he had a suspicion that his welcome might be a mixed one, and so was prepared with a strong bodyguard.

He was received at the city gates by the mayor and leading citizens, the mayor holding the keys of the city on a velvet cushion for the haughty Spaniard to use as a sign of his welcome to the former capital of the realm. Before arriving at the gates it is recorded that Philip had arrayed himself in a white velvet suit trimmed with gold bugles, and a surcoat of black velvet.

Philip was received at the cathedral by no fewer than six bishops who had come to Winchester to assist in the marriage ceremony. Apparently it was determined that there should be a plenitude of episcopal blessing to ensure the blissful union of the ill-assorted couple. But, as history tells, it was all unavailing. The very elements were unpromising, for Philip arrived at Winchester in a downpour of rain. Up to this time he had not seen his bride, who was eleven years his senior. He was housed at the deanery, while Mary was the guest of Gardiner at his palace of Wolvesey.

The marriage took place in the cathedral on the 25 July, in the presence of a vast concourse. Among the dons who came over with Philip was the Duke of Alva, later execrated in history as the scourge of the Netherlands. Mary sat in a chair which is still preserved in the cathedral, and exhibited to the curious. Immediately after the ceremony the pair were pompously proclaimed in Latin, English, and French, thus: "Philip and Mary, by the grace of God, king and queen of England, France, Naples, Jerusalem, and Ireland; defenders of the faith; princes of Spain and Sicily; archdukes of Austria; dukes of Milan, Burgundy and Brabant; counts of Hapsburg, Flanders, and Tyrol."

Winchester was wild with excitement. Not since

the visit of Henry VIII and the Emperor Charles had there been such display of regal splendour. The citizens vied with each other in shouting their adulations of Mary and her dark-visaged husband. There was an ulterior reason. Philip had brought over with him a vast treasure, some of which was destined to be distributed among the people. Ninety-seven chests, each over a yard long, contained this Spanish bribe, and twenty carts were needed for their transport. There is little doubt that Winchester got some of it. Certainly the elder scholars of Winchester College benefited a little, for, besides giving a large sum as an offering to college on their visit there, the royal pair gave money to the masters, and a sum to be distributed among the elder scholars as a reward for the verses which they had composed in honour of the marriage.

As far as she could, Mary restored to the cathedral, and other churches of the city, the property and movable treasures of which they had been despoiled, but in large measure the passage of time defeated this endeavour. Most of the landed property which had got into secular hands remained there, and there were few silver vessels which had not been melted down.

As for the burnings of Protestants which have made the reign of Mary infamous, Winchester had little experience of them. Two inhabitants only fell under ecclesiastical displeasure, and of them one only suffered in Winchester. He, Sir John Philpot, a native of Twyford, three miles to the south of Winchester, and a Wykehamist, was accused of heresy, tried in London, and was burnt at Smithfield.

The other was Thomas Bembridge, or Benbridge, a man of some standing both in the city and

M

neighbourhood. He was accused of heresy under nine heads and was examined by Dr. White, the bishop who had succeeded Gardiner in the episcopate. His answers not being satisfactory he was adjudged guilty, and was handed over to the Sheriff of Hampshire for execution.

It is recorded that Bembridge maintained his determination until the flames began to lick his naked legs. He then exclaimed, "I recant, I recant." His friends, hearing this, eagerly pulled away the burning faggots. The sheriff, Sir Richard Pecksall, had the unfortunate man released from the stake, and then conveyed back to prison. While at the stake he was with some difficulty induced to sign a written form of recantation which had been hurriedly drawn up on the spot. But when he got back to prison Bembridge repented of his weakness, and wrote a letter denouncing his recantation.

This, of course, made Mary and her advisers the more determined, and a fortnight later Bembridge was burnt to death in Winchester market-square. Nor was that the end of the business. The Privy Council summoned the sheriff peremptorily to London, where they upbraided him for his leniency, and for having, without authority, stopped the execution in the first instance. He was then ordered to prison himself, and kept in durance for a considerable time. But Mary died in the November of that year, and the burning of Protestants ceased.

With the coming of Queen Elizabeth it was the adherents of the "ancient religion" who suffered. For many years, that is, throughout the reign of Elizabeth and for a part of the reign of James I, Winchester and the neighbourhood continued to be agitated by the obstinacy, as it was termed, of the recusants; those who refused to acknowledge Elizabeth as supreme head of the English Church. There were some in Winchester who did not take kindly to the idea of the daughter of Anne Boleyn being Queen of England. They thought of her as illegitimate, and they feared she would follow the lead of her imperious father and insist on being recognized as head of the Church. The idea of a woman presuming to pose as the head of the Church was revolting to many.

At first all the leaders of the Church in the city declined to acknowledge Elizabeth. The dean and canons of the cathedral, the warden and fellows of college, and the master of the Hospital of St. Cross, all refused to take the oath of supremacy on her accession. But very soon they saw the imminent danger of refusal, and most of them abandoned their rigid position, and subscribed.

There were, however, some lay men and women, as well as priests, who refused absolutely to conform to the new order of things as directed by Elizabeth. Their determination cost them fine and imprisonment, the fines being large enough to reduce them to penury, and the imprisonment being often "unto death."

Elizabeth was really as devoid of real religion as her father had been. But she considered it was essential to good government that there should be one form of religion in the realm, and one only. She decided that that form should be one in which the sovereign was recognized as head of the Church. She ordained that the services should be those which had been drawn up by Cranmer, and she insisted that every subject should attend church service regularly. She did not care in the least what people believed privately, as long as they conformed outwardly, and she said as much. All she was determined to have was outward observance, and she was prepared to "leave opinion free." The Act of Uniformity, passed two months after her succession, prohibited the use of any liturgy save the Anglican, and imposed a fine of one shilling upon all who should absent themselves from Church on Sundays and holidays. Immediately began a regime of persecution of Roman Catholics, which lasted for more than sixty years. At first the recusants in Winchester and the neighbourhood were allowed to compound their recusancy by regular payment of fixed fines, calculated upon the number of attendances missed from services of the Established Church.

No doubt Elizabeth calculated that conformity would soon be general, and recusancy a dwindling phenomenon. The Hampshire recusants proved dourly obstinate. They showed that they were prepared to suffer loss of money or goods rather than conform. This obstinacy roused the imperious daughter of Henry to sterner action. Orders were issued for more zealous dealing with those who would not obey the queen's will. Nor were the conforming relatives of recusants left unscathed, as witness the following letter from a Bishop of Winchester in 1580 to Her Majesty's Privy Council:

Touching the last letter we received from your honours containing an order how such women are to be dealt with as are relapsed in this diocese, whose husbands come to church and hear sermons, and do according to Her Majesty's laws in these points: we have called before us many of the husbands, and mean to deal with the rest towards the latter end of this week, and hope we shall do some good therein. But at the beginning they thought it strange that they

164

shall be punished for their wives' faults. But . . . we have taken bonds . . . of them to keep their wives from conference, all manner of ways, with such as are backward in matters of religion, and also have imposed a mulct upon every of them weekly, till their wives shall come to church.

With the translation of Thomas Cooper to the see of Winchester in 1583 the persecution of recusants became still more rigorous. Cooper was a zealot in supporting the new order. The ecclesiastical machine gathered speed and force under his direction. There was much more diligence shown in the search for those who held by the "old religion." Fines were increased. People were forbidden to harbour any whom they knew to be recusant in temper. This order was aimed at landowners who were in the habit of keeping a priest as a regular member of their household. Immediately, in a number of houses in the county, hiding-places for the family priest were constructed. Some of these can still be seen.

But if the priests were often successfully hidden, and clandestine services held from time to time, the refusal to attend service in the Established Church brought its inevitable and regular fine. Many Hampshire landowners paid large sums to the queen's treasury each year as recusancy fines. In some instances the arrears of fines became so large that entire properties were taken by the Crown and farmed out to tenants. The original owners meanwhile languished in prison, some even dying there.

Very early in his episcopate Bishop Cooper was instrumental in securing the execution of two recusants, one at Winchester and one at Andover. The first was a certain John Slade, a native of Dorset. After studying abroad he returned to England, and settled in Winchester as a schoolmaster. Apprehended by the zeal of the bishop, Slade was challenged to take the oath of supremacy, acknowledging Queen Elizabeth as head of the Church. He refused. His refusal was reckoned as high treason, and, in consequence, himself worthy of death as a traitor. He was executed in Winchester on 30 October, 1583, according to the barbarous sentence of hanging, drawing, and quartering. After hanging, the body was cut down from the gibbet, disembowelled, the head severed from the body, and the body then cut in quarters. These were thrown into boiling pitch to preserve them, and they were then displayed on poles at the several gates of the city. When at length they were buried the authorities took care that none of the pieces fell into the hands of their friends, and Roman rites said over them. There is, however, a story told of a Catholic girl who, in a spirit of religious zeal, and at great risk to herself, was successful in retrieving one of the quarters of a priest named Roger Dickenson, and it was no doubt buried reverently.

Three days after the execution of Slade at Winchester, one John Body, or Bodie, a native of Wells, Somerset, a Wykehamist, who had been carrying on a school somewhere between Winchester and Andover, was executed in the market-place at Andover for refusing to take the oath of supremacy.

At the Lent Assizes at Winchester in 1586 appeared two priests who had set out from Douai to come to England as Roman missionaries. They landed in the Isle of Wight, and were promptly arrested and charged with being Roman priests. At their trial at Winchester the judge, with a kindly sympathy, suggested that they might say that they were on their way to Scotland, but had been driven by bad weather to take shelter in the Isle of Wight. They refused the well-meant suggestion, and declared that from the first it had been their intention to come to England to work as Roman priests. "The Lord have mercy on you," said the judge, "for by the laws you are dead men." And indeed they were, for they were taken back to the Isle of Wight and there executed.

The priest, Roger Dickenson, already referred to, was caught exercising his office near Winchester in 1591. He was promptly arraigned, found guilty of high treason (as recusancy was reckoned), and executed with all the horrid barbarity which then followed that sentence. In the same year two laymen suffered a similar fate. One was a mere boy, Laurence Humphreys, barely twenty-one years of age. He was said to have vilified the queen, and called her a heretic, while he was "in the delirium of a violent fever." The other was a poor man named Ralph Milner, who had a wife and seven children. He was accused of having assisted the priest Dickenson in the exercise of his office. At his trial the judge urged him to save his life by attending one service of the Established Church, but he resolutely refused. A last effort was made to break down his resolution at the place of execution (probably the market-place) by bringing his seven children to see him in the executioner's hands, but he still refused to conform. He gave his children his last blessing, and assured them he could wish them no greater happiness than to die in the same cause as he was about to do.

In 1593 the citizens of Winchester saw yet one more execution of a recusant. This was a man of gentle birth named James Bird. He was the youngest of all the recusants who suffered, for, when executed, he was but nineteen years of age. He had been abroad, studying in a Roman Catholic College in Rheims. When he returned to his native city he was apprehended and charged with "making himself a Catholic." He was kept a long while in prison, being repeatedly harassed to conform. His father besought him to attend a Protestant service but once so that his life might be spared, but he refused, and the authorities, losing patience, had him executed, his head being set on a pole over one of the city gates.

During these years Winchester prison was kept well furnished with recusant prisoners. Bishop Cooper, writing on one occasion to the Privy Council, remarked, "the gaol hath so many backward people," i.e. people who harked backward to the ancient religion. The Clerk of the Peace for Hampshire in an official report makes complaint of the great increase in work which has fallen to him as a result of the obstinacy of recusants. In one list of prisoners are included the names of four widows who are recusants, and the record adds, "their husbands have died in prison." A notable prisoner was Nicholas Tichborne, of the notable Hampshire family of that name. He died in Winchester prison in 1589, after having been there nine years, stripped of all his property, and being dependent, even in prison, upon the charity of his friends. When at length he died, Bishop Cooper declared that "his conscience would not permit him to suffer a papist to be buried in any of his churches or cemeteries." But it so happened that there was an ancient burial-ground on the western downs, a quarter of a mile outside the West Gate. It was the churchyard of St. James, a place then derelict. It had been transferred by Cardinal Beaufort to the Hospital of St. Cross, the authorities of which allowed it to fall into disuse. When the Catholic friends of Nicholas Tichborne applied for permission to bury his body in this old churchyard, the then Master of St. Cross, more Christian than his bishop, gave consent. The place has ever since been used as the Roman Catholic cemetery of Winchester.

But, as usual in religious persecutions, all this failed of its purpose. There always remained some who would not conform. Fifty years later Laud finds, in a visitation to Winchester, there were still some who held to the old religion. He noted:

> One Polwhele, dwelling in Winchester, is a dangerous Papist. He teacheth music, and his son, of the age of 17 or 18 yeares, teacheth grammar in his father's house, and many who come to school there are infected by them. Likewise one Agnes Francis, in St. Michael's parish, in Winchester, is a dangerous schoolmistress in that kind. I have inhibited all these.

Uniformity, so zealously pursued by Elizabeth and her ministers, did not secure that ready and constant church attendance of the people generally which was usual in pre-Reformation times. In the reign of Henry VIII, and in the reign of Elizabeth, the mayor and the 24tie of Winchester had to make a solemn resolution calling upon all their body, as well as the citizens at large, to attend church on every Sunday, "and every holydaye not beinge a market daye," under pain of a fine of eightpence, with the alternative of imprisonment for a day and a night. But church support was not as in the old days. A perfunctory conformity was enough. The result was some of the parish churches became neglected and derelict. Even the cathedral began to show neglect, so much so that, rather than go to the expense of re-pairing the cloisters and chapter house, the cathedral chapter, with the consent of the bishop, Dr. Horne, pulled them down.

But if there was a falling off in church-going, except such as would satisfy the law, there was probably good support given to the several companies of players who were licensed to present plays in the provinces.

EARLY NORMAN ARCHES AND REMAINS OF INTERNAL ARCADING OF CHAPTER HOUSE

Such companies visited Winchester from time to time in the last two decades of the sixteenth century. No doubt the plays were presented in the yards of the great hostelries, the Chequers, the George, the "Sterre," and others. These inn yards made excellent places for play-acting. The public, such as could not pay, could be shut out by closing the entrance from the street; and the galleries round, which gave entrance to the bedrooms, provided an admirable auditorium for the spectators. There is no record that Shakespeare ever came on tour in Hampshire, but it is certain he must have known many of the players in some of the famous companies which visited Winchester. In 1581 the city coffers pay out sixteen shillings to the "players of the Earl of Derbie." In the following year payments are made to the players of the Earl of Leicester, and the players of "My Lord Ambrose Dudley." In 1594 the players of the Earl of Sussex are welcomed, and in the same year the players of the Countess of Derby have two grants, while another company entitling themselves "The Players of a Nobleman in the Partes of the North," are also in receipt of money from the city funds. In 1595 appear the Queen's Players, and they have a larger grant than any of the foregoing, equal perhaps to £15 in modern money.

It was a day when municipal gifts were expected. The visit of royalty always called for a substantial gift from the city, generally of plate. Each visit of the Judges of Assize meant gifts to the judges of sugar loaves, or expensive salmon, or a fat sheep. Nobility visiting the city would also be similarly honoured, for their interest might be valuable in London. The city archives contain a number of references to gifts of sack and claret, sometimes expressively referred to as "bellycheer."

In the spring of 1582, by an Order in Council, there was a round-up of "all rogues, vagabonds, and sturdy and mighty valiant beggars" in Winchester, so that very soon the House of Correction was full. Funds were raised for the correction and employment of these people, and it was especially directed that "due punyshment with the whyppe shall be ministered unto every rogue." The money raised was spent in buying yarn, and the individuals who were to be "corrected" were taught the spooling and carding of wool, weaving, making hats and gloves, and those who could not be taught these crafts were to be set to the grinding of wheat. Women might also be set to the knitting of hose, and the dressing of flax. All unskilled workers were to be treated somewhat as apprentices, and they were to work three years learning a trade, and then to work two more years to pay the community for having taught them. It was a plausible scheme, but the objection of the freemen of the city to this influx of new labour into their ranks brought the experiment to an end.

The Bishop of Winchester of this period, the zealous Thomas Cooper, just before the year of the Spanish Armada menace, made a strong attempt to abolish the medieval practice of raising money for the upkeep of the churches by means of "Church Ales." These, the forerunners of the modern church "social," were nothing less than occasions for un-ashamed carousing. Ale or money was contributed by the parishioners, and, on a given day, the wardens, having used the contributed money to buy ale to add to that which had been sent in, sold the lot for the benefit of the church funds. It was a day of jollification, and it was argued that the church was the gainer. But the bishop was rightly indignant, and expressed his mind to his incumbents thus:

Whereas a heathenish and ungodly custom hath bene used before time in many partes of this lande about this season of the yeare to have Church Ales, may games, morish Dannces, and other vaine pastimes upon the Sabath Dayes, and other Dayes appointed for comon prayer, which they have pretended to be for the relief of theire Churches, but indeede hath bene only a meanes to feed the mindes of the people, and specially of the youth with vaine sight . . . which is a strange perswasion among Christians, that they cannot by any other means of contribution repaire theire Churches, but must first do Sacrifice to the

172

Devil, with Drunkennes and Dancing, and other ungodly wantonnes. These are therefore to charge all Ministers and Churchwardens, and Other like Officers . . . that they suffer not any such Church Ales, Morish Dannces, or Riflings within theire parishes. And if any . . . will not obey this order . . . put them in bands to appear before me, or before the Justice of the Peace at the next Sessions of the Peace, there to receive further order . . . you will answere to the contrary att your peril. This 13th of Maye, 1585. Thomas Winton.

Judging by the city archives, and their many references to drinking, it is to be feared that the bishop had no easy task in enforcing obedience in his diocese. It was a time when most of its citizens were lovers of what the city archives term "bellycheer."

When the threat of a Spanish invasion of England was made by Philip II, Elizabeth made ready to meet it. She sent to a number of counties, calling for funds to help her in the task of resisting the invader. Hampshire was one of the counties called upon, and the response was not inconsiderable. A number of gentlemen and wealthy traders put themselves down for sums of £25 and £50, and in the case of Robert Kinglake, a gentleman of Southampton, £100. Five citizens of Winchester appeared in the list, namely, William Badger, £50; William Burton, £25; Edward Cole, £25; William Hobson, £25; and William Symonds, £50. One striking fact emerges from a perusal of the complete list, and that is, it must have been open more than four months, for the earliest contribution is dated 23 February, and the latest 5 July, so that there was a fair period for preparation to meet the menace. And, as history tells, the Armada entered the English Channel on 19 July, coming, not as a fighting fleet in the usual sense, but as a floating transport of an army which expected to be able to land without much opposition.

Except for the monetary help subscribed by her five citizens, Winchester was able to give little assistance in the task of repelling the invader. She had fallen on evil days. Her population and trade had dwindled indeed. At this time less than a hundred men were found among her citizens fit to bear arms, whereas Southampton was able to produce nearly five times that number. The Mayor of Winchester received a letter from Queen Elizabeth's chief baker complaining in strong terms of his worship's "slack diligence" in providing bakers for the fleet. Thus the "Master Backer":

Whereas affore you said you had bowt one backer in the holle citie, but it is a great deal more the shame for your having so many women backers in that citie that after a whele we shall be faine to have them serve the Quine.

But perhaps a few young men from the city found their way into the queen's ships, which set out from Southampton and helped in the great drive up the Channel. And those citizens who stayed at home must have been stirred by the sight of the beacon fires on Old Winchester Hill and other high points in the county, intimating that the enemy was at hand.

Elizabeth visited Winchester four, possibly five times during her reign. There is a tradition that once she was welcomed by a mayor who was more loyal than literate. "Yours is a very ancient city, Mr. Mayor," said the queen. "It have-a-been, your Majesty, it have-a-been," was the reply.

If the city was not particular about the grammar used by its mayor in Tudor times, it was very careful that the dress of the chief magistrate should be fitting to the dignity of so exalted an office. The mayor and the mayoress were supplied with scarlet robes which were to be worn at all important functions under a penalty of six shillings and eightpence. If the mayor went to Southampton to purchase things to sell in his shop or stall, he had to have with him a servant who would carry home the goods for him; he must not carry them himself. Neither the mayor, ex-mayor, nor either of the aldermen might walk in the streets, nor go to the market, in their jerkins or coats; they had to wear their official gowns and so uphold the dignity of their respective offices. Nor might they wear gaily coloured hose, nor at Sessions or Sermons, Sundays or holydays, wear any white, green or yellow doublet, under pain of a fine of six shillings and eightpence; but they might do business in their shops, or before their own doors, clad in jerkins.

The following transcript of the will of a Rector of Winnal, dated 1550, throws some light upon domestic chattels and clothing of the time. Winnal was then in the Bishop's Soke, but is now in the city.

I geve and bequethe to every howseholder in Wynnall a quarteryn of wood & ij busseles of cole. Item, to Grangers wyffe a quarteryn of wode and ij bussels of cole. Item, to John Scole a quarteryn of wood and ij bussels of cole, and the same quantity of each to John Taylor and to Sanders wyffe. Item, to Alice Kynge half a lode of wode and a quarter of cole, & a lyttel tabell with iiij legges and my tawney gowne lyned with cottyn. Item, to Kateryne my mayde a flocke bed that I lye on, with the blanketes and the schettes, and pellow and bolster longing thereunto, and the tester, a cauderyn with the broadest bond, and a brasse pott brokyn yn one egge, a frying pann & a gryddyern, a stone morter, a platter, a potynger with ij sawsers, ij candelstykes & a saltseller, a coverlet that lyethe on her owne bedde, & my beddestede in the parlor, my lytyll kover, & a coffer. Item, to Thomas Waller my best clothe jaket. To Nycholas Waller my second jaket and a cauderyn with a lyteyl bonde. Item, I geve to the mausters of the College xv^s and to the chyldren vj^s viij^d. Item, I geve to Syr Vole my best gowne & my chamlet frock, my cappo presso & my sylken gyrdle.

It was a period when some of the citizens began to have a suspicion that there might be a connection between civic cleanliness and the public health. There were visitations of the bubonic plague from time to time, analogous, probably, in incidence, to the epidemics of influenza in modern times. In the summer of 1577 the area of Staple Garden, now thickly populated, but then probably an open space in the north-west of the city, was paled around by the authorities, and used thereafter as a common dumping place for all manner of filth, an accompanying ordinance imposing a fine of sixpence upon any citizen who deposited any "filthe, dust, or donge in anye strete or Lane of the cyty without their own houses or groundes."

Seven years later another ordinance decreed that "noe pson or psons wth this citie shall keepe any hogs or hogsties within the boundes of the High Streete, or within one hundred yardes of the same boundes," the penalty being a fine of ten shillings. About the same period an order was decided upon by the mayor and the 24tie "to avoid the infections of the Plague," that:

It is agreed that evry Inhabitant of this cytie shall rid, make cleane, and carry away all the Rubbish, duste, and filthe before evry of their doores, both back-doores and fore-doores before Wednesday next,

THE BEAUFORT TOWER, ST. CROSS HOSPITAL

upon paine for every Inhabitant making default therein to lose 6s. 8d. . . . .

Itm. That evry Inhabitant of the saide cytie shall cause evry morning before 6 of the Clocke, and every Evening between 8 and 9 of the Clocke, . . . five buckets of water to be drawne, and the same to be caste downe in the cannoll, and shall rake out and carry away the filthe of the cannoll upon paine for every default to lose 6s. 8d.

Itm. That every Inhabitant of this cytie shall pave before his door according to the Ordinance of the city, within convenient time, and in the meantime to keep every decayed place of the Street before his door cleane and sweet upon paine to lose 6s. 8d. for every week.

If a house happened to be infected with the plague there was an ordinance which required the inmates to keep their dogs from wandering outside. And, as nurses to attend any who might fall sick of the plague, the mayor was directed to appoint eight women of the city. It was not until the year 1601 that a public scavenger was appointed and paid by the community. But long before this time there was an ordinance directed against butchers who threw their offal into the city streams; they were forbidden to do so, unless they had first cut it into lengths of not more than four inches, the penalty being three shillings and fourpence.

It was an outbreak of the plague which drove James I out of London and down to Winchester in September 1603. The visit cost the city two large silver cups to begin with, and a great deal of upset besides in the months following. The officials of the London law courts were brought down in the November, and the trials of Sir Walter Raleigh and several others were held either at Wolvesey or at the Castle of Winchester, the charges being of conspiracy against the new king. The city was crowded with officials and witnesses. The warden, fellows, and scholars of Winchester College were made to quit their apartments to make room for the judges and other officials whom the king directed to lodge there. No doubt the "typlers" (publicans) did good business. At any rate Winchester, for a brief while, tasted again the flavour of royal patronage.

THE DEANERY, WINCHESTER

179

CHAPTER VI

Winchester under the Stuarts

IT is likely that one of the reasons which determined James upon a sojourn at Winchester so early in his reign was the fact that it was at Winchester that he had been first proclaimed King of England. The zealous sheriff of the county, Sir Benjamin Tichborne, whose family claimed to be the oldest in the whole of Wessex, hurried over from Tichborne to Winchester the moment he heard of the death of Queen Elizabeth, and without waiting for the fiat of the Privy Council, on his own responsibility he proclaimed James of Scotland King of England. It was a daring act, done in a perilous time, but events justified the worthy knight, and James at once showed his appreciation of this early act of loyalty by conferring upon him and his heirs for ever, the governorship of the royal castle of Winchester, together with a pension of one hundred pounds a year for himself and his eldest son.

The trial of Sir Walter Raleigh and his fellows on a supposititious charge of conspiracy took place in the Great Hall of the castle. There is little doubt that the whole matter was based upon fabrications made by some leading officials of state for their own purposes, to ingratiate themselves with James; and James was so fearful a simpleton that he was ready to believe even the most preposterous charges. Moreover, he had a personal dislike of Sir Walter Raleigh, no doubt that of a small-minded person

180

for a great. The royal zeal of the citizens caused them to pelt Raleigh with tobacco pipes as he was being brought into the city, but after the trial there was a revulsion of feeling in his favour.

After a great deal of elaborate ceremonial all the prisoners were found guilty save one, Sir Edward Parham. Those condemned to death were Sir Walter Raleigh, the Hon. and Rev. George Brooke, brother to Lord Cobham who was also convicted, Lord Grey de Wilton, Sir Griffin Markham, Antony Copley, Bartholomew Brooksby, and two priests, named William Watson and William Clark. These two priests were executed in the usual barbarous style reserved for traitors, that is, by hanging, disembowelling, and quartering. The Rev. George Brooke was beheaded on the Castle Green. As he had complained of having been deprived of the mastership of St. Cross, his executioners, with a brutal irony, placed him so that he might view the distant tower of St. Cross, just before his head was struck off.

Then James, who had gone to Wilton near Salisbury, intervened with what he conceived to be a divine display of magnanimity. Openly he had sent the orders for the execution of Lord Grey de Wilton, Lord Cobham, and Sir Griffin Markham, but secretly he had arranged for a last-moment reprieve in each case. The farce of bringing each to the block separately, and then, without reason given, taking him away again to a cell, was gone through. At length all three were brought out together and informed of His Majesty's clemency. It was just such a childish parade as only a mind like James's could conceive. Probably it achieved its purpose in holding up the new sovereign to the populace as the very embodiment of kindness and generosity even to his supposed enemies. As for Sir Walter, he was conveyed from Winchester Castle to the Tower of London, where he was beheaded fifteen years later on the same charge.

There is a little poem of Sir Walter Raleigh's which is thought to have been written while he was in confinement at Winchester Castle, inspired, it may be, by the view across the valley of the Itchen, and having for its subject the immanence of death:

> Give me my scallop shell of quiet,
>   My staff of faith to walk upon,
> My scrip of joy, immortal diet,
>   My bottle of salvation;
> My gown of glory, Hope's true gage,
> And thus I 'll take my pilgrimage.
>
> Blood must be my body's balmer,
>   No other balm will here be given,
> Whilst my soul, like quiet palmer,
>   Travels to the land of heaven,
> Over all the silver mountains,
> Where do spring those nectar fountains.
>
> And I there will sweetly kiss
> The happy bowl of peaceful bliss,
> Drinking mine eternal fill
> Flowing on each milky hill.
> My soul will be a-dry before,
> But, after, it will thirst no more.

The brief visit of the Court during the Raleigh Plot trials had little influence upon the fortunes of Winchester, which continued steadily to decline. In the closing years of James's reign John Taylor, the Water Poet, in *A New Discovery by Sea with a Wherry from London to Salisbury*, writes thus:

On Thursday, the 21st of August, I took Winchester in my way homewards, where I saw an ancient city, like a body without a soule; and I know not the reason of it, but for ought which I perceived, there were

almost as many parishes as people. I lodged at the
signe of the Cock, being recommended to the host of
the house by a token from Salisbury; but mine host
dyed the night before I came, and I, being weary,
had more mind to goe to bed than to follow him so
long a journey, to doe my message or deliver any

THE SICK-HOUSE, WINCHESTER COLLEGE

commendations. But the whole city seemed almost as
dead as mine host, and it may bee they were all at
harvest worke. But I am sure I walked from one end
of it to the other, and saw not thirty people of all sorts.
So that I think if a man should go to Winchester for a
goose, he might lose his labour, for a Trader cannot live
there by vending such commodities. On Friday I
gallop'd a foot pace one and twenty miles from Winchester to Farnham; where I and one of my company
hired a couple of Hampshire Jenets, with seven legges
and three eyes betwixt them, upon whom we hobbled
seventeene miles to Stanes, whence on Saturday the
23 of August we footed to Brenford and Boated
to London.

183

Charles I visited Winchester, with his queen, Henrietta Maria, at least once during the peaceful part of his reign. They stayed at the Deanery, and there their arms in stained glass were set up in the hall in commemoration of their visit. This was probably about 1637. A few years earlier, thanks to the zeal of Laud, and the ready co-operation of Bishop Curle and Dean Young, a great improvement was made, not only in the services of the cathedral, but also by abolishing much rubbish at the south-west corner of the edifice, and cutting through a passage from the churchyard to the Close. Previously the citizens who wished to enter the Close without troubling to traverse Symonds and St. Swithun's streets went through the cathedral. Laud disapproved of this practice of making the cathedral a highway. The Slype remains as a monument to his zeal. On the south-west corner of the building a curious anagram was cut, indicating one way for prayer and another for the wayfarer. Over an arch, which at first spanned the new passage at its east end but at a subsequent enlargement of the passage was placed in the south wall, a similar anagram was cut.

About 1630 two bronze figures representing King James I and King Charles I, the work of the French sculptor Hubert le Sueur, came into the possession of the cathedral, and were set up within. During the Commonwealth they were sold to a Mr. Newland of the Isle of Wight for the sum of £10. He had them conveyed to the island, and there buried them in his garden for safety. At the Restoration they were dug up and purchased from him for the sum of £100. The sculptor saved himself labour by carving only the heads differently; the bodies were cast in the same mould.

Another mark of the visit of Charles and his queen to Winchester may be seen in the wooden vaulting of the tower of the cathedral, their faces being painted on medallions. It is somewhat of a wonder that these escaped defacement during the Civil War.

Hampshire's assessment for the Ship Money was £6,000, and while Portsmouth's share was set at £70. Winchester's quota was £190. Even before the disruption between the king and his Parliament the Ship Money caused dissension between the city authorities and the dean and chapter. Apparently neither party wished to be disloyal to the king and, like Hampden, refuse to pay, but the dean and chapter appealed to the Privy Council that the city authorities were assessing them too highly in the matter. The king sided with the cathedral body, and not only ordered the city to repay to them the money alleged to have been paid in excess, but ordering also that the £20 paid by the dean and chapter for Ship Money should "be taken off from the Citty," i.e. that the city should pay the cathedral quota as well as their own; and in order to make sure that his mandate was obeyed, Charles directed "Mr. Attorney Generall be required to take care that the Charter for the said Citty shall not be renewed till the Charter for the said Church be passed the Great Seale."

The dispute between the two bodies took another form shortly afterwards. This time it was over the right of the mayor and the 24tie to carry their maces into the cathedral at divine service when they attended in state. The dean sought to deter the citizens from indulging in such pomp, but the mayor and his colleagues insisted upon their age-old rights, and appealed to the Star Chamber on the matter. The cathedral body appear to have won the first round, but the city won the second, the king reversing the first decision, "since when the maces have been carried into the church."

The quietude into which Winchester had sunk was rudely broken by the quarrel between Charles I and his Parliament. Very early in the war it became evident that Winchester was a key position, and again and again the conflict surged round the old city. In 1642, when Portsmouth had fallen into the hands of Parliamentary troops, Winchester became of great importance because by its position it blocked the road from the west to London. Being occupied by Royalist troops under Lord Grandison, who had had to retreat from the west, it was seen by the Parliamentarian commander, Sir William Waller, to be such an obstacle in his path that he must take it. There was also obstinate Royalist resistance being shown at Basing House about twenty miles to the north.

Waller chased Grandison to Winchester from Marlborough, but failed to prevent him entering the city, which, according to a Parliamentary scribe, was "a place more like to give him kind entertainment, being full of malignant spirits, who indeed were not a little glad at his coming, thinking themselves now secure from danger, being under the wings of a bird of their own feather."

There is some disparity among the authorities concerning the strength of Lord Grandison's force. In any event he was greatly outnumbered by Waller's troops, and moreover, the city itself was ill prepared for a siege, although in the previous month, November 1642, the city authority had voted money for "swords, bullets, and providing for the Citie armes," they evidently having foreseen the possibility of conflict near home. They had also expended money upon the repair of the city walls.

Grandison decided to make a sortie in the direction of Salisbury. The skirmishing began somewhere near Wherwell, and in less than an hour the Royalists were overcome. Some retreated upon Winchester, but Lord Grandison and many of his subordinates were captured. One account says the captured included nearly fifty officers of good standing in Hampshire, a thousand foot, two hundred dragoons, six hundred horse, and their accoutrements.

Repulsed at the city gates Waller resolved to take the place by assault. A point was selected to the north of the West Gate, and although the approach was exceedingly steep, so that the attackers "had no other way to get up but of necessity to creep up upon their hands and knees from the bottom to the top, which was as high as most houses, the enemy playing on them all the while with their muskets, and yet slew but three men in this their getting up, so at last (though with much danger and difficulty) our soldiers got up and plied their business so hotly and closely that they had quickly made a great breach in the wall . . . and drove the cavaliers before them into the midst of the town; who, having no place else of shelter, fled apace into the castle, which yet was not so considerable a sanctuary, or place of sanctuary to defend them long, especially it being destitute of ordnance, so our men beset the castle round with musqueteers and horse, and lay per-dues [i.e. in hiding] under the wall, so that not a man of them could stir."

It would appear that the capture of the city was effected in less than three hours. The attack on the wall began at noon (one account says it was on 12 December, while others put the date as 17 December), and entrance was secured between two and three o'clock. It must have been a grievous time for the citizens who, according to a soldier who took part in the attack, offered the greatest opposition to the besiegers. When the Parliamentarians were in possession the mayor and his fellows sued for terms to save the city being given up to loot. Waller demanded £1,000, and this sum was agreed upon and paid by the hapless citizens. But it did not save the city from considerable pillage, for, despite the bargain made between their commander and the mayor, the troops entered many houses, "taking whatsoever they liked best out of them, but chiefly some Papists' houses there, and the sweet cathedralists, in whose houses and studies they found great store of Popish books, pictures, and crucifixes which the soldiers carried up and down the streets and market-place in triumph to make themselves merry." There was also much despoiling of prisoners even of their very clothes, while well-to-do cavaliers endeavoured to save themselves by handing "gold in handsful" to the victorious troopers. Waller later expressed publicly his regret for having allowed this plundering of the citizens. But throughout the war Hampshire troops had an unenviable record for unwarrantable looting.

The morning following the successful assault on the city Waller prepared to attack the castle. Tar barrels and faggots were brought up in great quantity for the purpose of burning down the great gate, but the besieged surrendered incontinently. The prisoners were sent to Portsmouth to be kept in safety, but on the road Lord Grandison and several other officers, who were said to have given their parole, made their escape, and joined the king at Oxford. Grandison

ST. CATHERINE'S HILL AND WINCHESTER COLLEGE FROM CATHEDRAL TOWER
(Jane Austen's house extreme right-hand bottom corner

was wounded at the siege of Bristol in the following July, and died two months later of his wounds at Oxford, whither he had been conveyed in the hope of saving his life.

After the surrender of the castle the Parliamentarian troops ranged the city and cathedral buildings in search of loot. A very circumstantial account (*Mercurius Rusticus*) tells of wholesale spoliation in the cathedral itself:

The doors being open as if they meant to invade God Himself, as well as His profession, they enter the Church with colours flying, their drums beating, their matches fired, and that all might have their part in so horrid an attempt, some of their troops of horse also accompanied them in their march, and rode up through the body of the Church and quire until they came to the altar. There they begin their work, they rudely pluck down the table, and break the rail, and afterwards carrying it to an alehouse they set it on fire, and in that fire burnt the books of Common Prayer, and all the singing books belonging to the quire; they throw down the organ, and break the stones of the Old and New Testament, curiously cut out in carved work, beautified with colours, and set round about the top of the stalls of the quire. From hence they turn to the monuments of the dead, some they utterly demolish, others they deface.

The account gives details of the destruction wrought upon particular tombs and chantries, but there is reason to doubt its accuracy. It is probably somewhat over-coloured by the partisan zeal of the time. It is certain that very soon after the events of those troublous days there grew up a confusion in the minds of people concerning the destruction wrought by Parliamentary troops, and that done by the agents of Henry VIII and the ministers of Edward VI. In other words, Oliver Cromwell has been unfairly burdened with much of the obloquy which properly belongs to Thomas Cromwell, Wolsey's successor. Nevertheless, it is certain that in December 1642 much wanton destruction was done by Waller's troops. Bishop Fox had not long before reverently collected the relics of Saxon kings and bishops, and had them placed in leaden chests upon the two screen walls which he had built to enclose the choir of the cathedral. According to the account of *Mercurius Rusticus* the troops even pulled down these leaden caskets and threw the bones about the church.

These monsters of men, to whom nothing is holy, nothing is sacred, did not stick to profane and violate these cabinets of the dead, and to scatter their bones all over the pavement of the church; for, on the north side of the quire they threw down the chests wherein were deposited the bones of the bishops; the like they did to the bones of William Rufus, of Queen Emma, of Hardicanutus, and of Edward the Confessor, and were going on to practise the like impiety on the bones of all the rest of the West Saxon kings, but the outcry of the people, detesting so great inhumanity, caused some of their commanders (more compassionate to these ancient monuments of the dead than the rest) to come in amongst them and to restrain their madness.

Many windows of coloured glass, the account goes on, were destroyed by throwing bones through them. Endeavours were made to deface the bronze statues of King James and King Charles. The swords were broken off and making a particular assault on the crown of King Charles, the soldiers "hacked and hewed the crown on the head of it, swearing they would bring him back to his Parliament." They also broke into "the Muniment House and took away the common seal of the church, supposing it to be silver, and a fair piece of gilt plate, given by Bishop

Cotton. . . . In a word, whatever they found in the church of any value and portable they take it with them, what was neither they either deface or destroy it."

That much destruction was done to the cathedral at this time is proved in a negative fashion by the fact that William of Wykeham's chantry was untouched. This was because a certain Captain Nicholas Fiennes, brother of Lord Saye and Sele, was in command of the 36th Troop of Parliamentarian Horse. His family then, as now, claim the much prized rights of "Founder's Kin" at Winchester College. He had been a scholar at that renowned school, and being thus a zealous Wykehamist he made it his business to protect all Wykeham relics from destruction or defacement. It is said that he himself stood with drawn sword at the door of Wykeham's chantry, daring the reckless troopers to touch it, and he is also reputed to have posted a guard at Winchester College to prevent destruction there. Certain it is that both Wykeham's chantry and college escaped injury, even the fourteenth-century effigy of the Virgin and Child over the Porter's Gate at the college being untouched.

Perhaps the worst disaster to the cathedral, even surpassing the defacement of the windows and the sacred monuments, was the destruction wrought in the cathedral library, which had been one of the finest in Europe of its kind. Priceless manuscripts were thrown out into the streets to be swept down the gutters as worthless rubbish. Others were sold to "grocers and sope sellers, and sent overseas in whole ship's full" (Fuller). Some found their way to London, and then by the good offices of one, Nicholas Love, they came back to Winchester, but

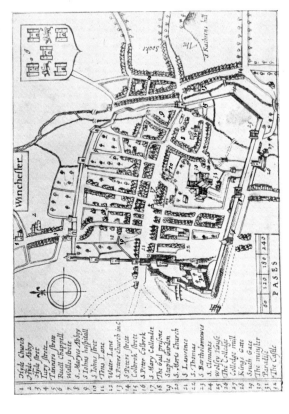

1	Hyde Church
2	Hyde Abbey
3	Hyde ſtreet
4	Iury ſtreet
5	Tanners ſtreat
6	Rudll Chappell
7	Wallis ſtreit
8	S. Maryes Abbey
9	S Iohns hoſpitall
10	S Iohns ſtreet
11	Tous Lane
12	Watr Lane
13	S.Peters church in C
14	S.Peters ſtreit
15	Colbrok ſtreit
16	S.Peter Colbrok
17	S.Mary Callender
18	The Gul priſone
19	Staple garden
20	S.Mary Church
21	S.Lawrence
22	S.Thomas
23	S Bartholomews
24	S.Clements
25	wolſey Ringe
26	The Colledge
27	Colledge mill
28	Kings Gate
29	South Gate
30	The minſter
31	Paradiſe
32	The Caſtle

SPEED'S MAP: SEVENTEENTH-CENTURY WINCHESTER

to college, and not to the cathedral. Perhaps the greatest loss of all was the masterpiece of ancient art, the famous Benedictionary of St. Æthelwold, a product of the Winchester school of illuminating upon vellum at its zenith. This, as previously stated, is now in the library of the Duke of Devonshire.

John Chase, the zealous librarian of the cathedral, was in despair at the dispersal of his beloved manuscripts, but he set to work with energy to retrieve what he could as soon as the soldiers had gone. He was aided by many townsfolk, who viewed the wanton spoliation with horror, and at length he succeeded in getting back a large number of documents. But a subsequent visit of Parliamentary troops brought about a second dispersal of his treasures, and Chase had all his work to do again. Some of the documents found their way to the Bodleian Library at Oxford, where they may now be seen. The manuscripts which were for long in the possession of Winchester College have been returned to the cathedral.

To return to the story of the Civil War. The news of the capture of Winchester was taken to London, the emissary, Theodore Jennings, for his welcome news receiving £20 from the delighted Parliament. Public thanksgivings were held on the following Sunday in London, Southwark, and Westminster, and Waller was thanked "for his care and vigilancy at Winchester."

Waller now turned his attention to Sussex, and took Arundel and Chichester, at the latter city similar destruction taking place in the cathedral as at Winchester; organ, windows, monuments, etc., being defaced or destroyed. After working into Surrey and capturing Farnham, Waller moved west, and in

o

March again entered Winchester. He departed the following day, but left behind him a sergeant-major and troop of horse to collect the sum of £600 which he levied upon the city to help him in his campaign, "a most unreasonable sum to be imposed upon a town so lately and so miserably plundered. But, say what they could in their own behalf, no less than £500 would be accepted, and that accordingly was raised, namely £350 out of the inhabitants of the city, and £150 on one, Sir Henry Clerke, a neighbouring gentleman."

Waller was sorely in need of horses, as well as of money; the price having doubled since the war broke out. Formerly a horse could be bought for about 40s., but now £4 and more was asked. There is a story told of the attempts of Waller to get possession of two horses which belonged to the son of a prebendary of the cathedral, named Saye. The horses had been hidden, and Waller, being unable to get Saye to disclose their whereabouts, handed him over to the tender mercies of his provost-marshal. This individual took the unfortunate Saye to the stable of the George Inn, and there suspended him by the neck until he was nearly strangled. He was then released and further questioned, but getting no satisfaction his persecutor hung him up again. The story goes that although this torture was repeated several times, it was unsuccessful in its object, and the discomfited trooper dismissed the unfortunate Saye with kicks and blows. The story ends with the remark that Saye was dangerously ill for many days afterwards.

It was on this latter visit of Waller's troops that the second destruction of the cathedral library took place. John Chase himself set it down that on

194

10 March, 1643, "the Muniment House was the second time by the army and soldiery broken up, and all my ledgers and register books taken away; the records, charters, deeds, writings, and muniments lost, divers of them burnt, divers of them thrown into the river. . . . Divers large parchments they made kytes withal to flie in the air, and many of the old books lost, to the utter spoiling and destruction of the same muniment and charter house." Chase also records that some of the valuable documents were retrieved for him by one of the brethren of St. Cross Hospital as they were floating down the Itchen.

Waller passed on through Romsey to Salisbury, and for some months the Parliament cause lost ground in Hampshire. The king's successes in the west were an encouragement to the Royalists. In September 1643 both Houses of Parliament were informed that Hampshire was in great danger of being taken by the enemy unless strong measures of defence were speedily put forward. Waller was given power to impress five thousand men, any between the ages of eighteen and fifty, with the following exceptions: widows' sons, clergy, scholars, trained-band soldiers, servants of peers, and attendants and assistants of Parliament.

Meanwhile Sir William Ogle, the Royalist member for Winchester, had, with a few Royalist friends, taken possession of Winchester and the castle for the king. He set about repairing the defences, and digging trenches on the west, so that it might be a rallying place for the king's forces in southern England.

In November Waller was attacking Basing House, which had continued a persistent obstacle to Parliamentary success in Hampshire, but his assaults were in vain. About the same time as this assault was taking place Lord Hopton arrived at Winchester from the west with an army of some three thousand foot and one thousand five hundred horse, a portion, it is said, of the garrison of Bristol.

The presence of so large a force in Winchester, even of friendly troops, must have been no small burden to the citizens, for the adult population of the city was almost certainly less than that of the army gathered there. A little sidelight upon this is afforded by a pitiful appeal which was made to Lord Hopton by the master and almspeople of the Hospital of St. Mary Magdalen, which at that time stood on the eastern downs about half a mile out of the city. The appeal was for help because the Royalist troopers quartered on the east of the city had eaten up all the seed corn belonging to the hospital, and they had broken up and burnt for firewood all the seats and benches in the hospital chapel. Lord Hopton promised the petitioners relief, but whether they got any is doubtful.

Hopton, regarding Winchester as a key position, set about making field works on the east and west, those which he made at Oram's Arbour being traceable until the nineteenth century. He also had earthworks thrown up on a high point of the chalk downs to the south-west, about a mile from the city. He was never able to use this eminence, but, later in the war, Cromwell occupied the defences constructed by his adversary, so that ever since the place has borne the name of Oliver's Battery.

At this time, the winter of 1643, the hopes of the Royalists were in the ascendant. The Parliamentary forces in the neighbourhood of Farnham were restive, and some of the leaders in London were becoming very apprehensive of the result of the conflict. The king was encouraged by his successes in the west, and by the seemingly strong positions held by his generals in the north, and in Hampshire. Plymouth and Hull alone held out in the west and north. But these two places ultimately led to the king's undoing, because they prevented whole-hearted support from those areas. Winchester and Basing House on the other hand were centres of encouragement, together, of course, with Oxford, where the king was planning a threefold advance on London in the spring.

The presence of so many Royalist troops in and around Winchester no doubt encouraged the Royalist supporters there, so that when the king called upon the city for help in the shape of money or plate for the maintenance of the royal army the mayor and 24tie were not slow in responding. They chose out several pieces of plate, and by a minute dated 30 December, 1643, they resolved to hand them to Mr. Jasper Cornelius, the individual charged to convey money or valuables to the king. They set their value at £58 16s. 3d., there being two hundred and twenty-five ounces at 5s. per ounce. Yet within a very short time the king sent a sharp reprimand to the city because of the number of his enemies there, the reprimand ending with a promise to punish the city when occasion permitted. The occasion never came.

In the last week of 1643 Lord Hopton sallied from Winchester to the relief of Arundel, but he was unsuccessful in his object. While he was absent on this enterprise Colonel Norton, a native of Alresford, who was the Parliamentary commander in charge of Southampton, moved with some of the Southampton garrison on a foray in the neighbourhood of Winchester. He came nearly into St. Cross, and succeeded in capturing and carrying off more than fifty fat cattle.

The leaders of the Parliamentary cause in London becoming alarmed at the king's success, resolved to strengthen Waller's forces in the four counties of Hants, Surrey, Sussex, and Wilts. He was made Major-General of these forces, and given more material aid for a campaign against the Royalists. In a skirmish near Petersfield some of Waller's troopers defeated those of Lord Hopton with severe loss, and then came a severe set-back for the Royalists by the extermination of a contingent under Colonel John Bolles at Alton. Bolles was surprised by a much larger force of Parliamentarians, but sooner than ask for quarter he endeavoured to hold out in the parish church, hoping to be relieved. Bolles was shot down after a stubborn resistance. The king, when he heard the news of Bolles's death, was greatly disturbed, called for "a moorning scarffe," and declared that he had lost one of the best commanders in his kingdom. A brass tablet in Winchester Cathedral commemorates Bolles's death. It is affixed to the pillar at the north-west corner of the dais.[1]

[1] The inscription on the tablet runs:

A memoriall

for this renowned martialist Richard Boles of yᵉ Right Worshipfull family of yᵉ Boles in Linckhorne Sheire Colonell of a Ridgment of foot of 1300 who for his gratious King Charles yᵉ First did wounders at yᵉ Battel of Edge Hill. His last action to omitt all others was at Alton in this county of Soughampton was surprized by five or six thousand of the Rebells which caused him there quartered to fly to the church with neare four score of his men who there fought them six or seven houers and then the Rebells breaking in

Another disaster befell Lord Hopton about this time. A battalion of men, marching from the west to join him at Winchester, mutinied on the way, and took service with the Parliament. Baffled by his first effort to relieve Arundel, Hopton laid siege to Warblington House, but he was attacked by Waller and driven hotfoot back to Winchester.

Despite the reverses which they were sustaining as a result of Waller's renewed activity, the Royalists got ready for a movement on London. As early as possible in the spring three forces were to advance on the capital: from the north, from Oxford, and from Winchester.

Lord Hopton had summoned all Hampshire men between the ages of sixteen and sixty to appear in arms for the king at Winchester. As that summons did not bring in as many as he wanted, he resorted to impressment. But many of these "pressed" men deserted at the first opportunity, and those who stayed were mostly lukewarm, while almost all were badly armed.

At length some substantial reinforcements from the king at Oxford gave Hopton considerable encouragement, and he began to think of trying conclusions with Waller in the open country. If he could

upon him he slew with his sword six or seven of them & then was Slayne himfelfe with sixty of his men aboute him.

1641

His Gratious Souveraigne hearing of his death gave him his high Comendation in his patronale exprefsion Bring me a moorning Scarffe i haue Lost one of the beft Comanders in this Kingdome.

Ricardus Boles Wiltoniensis in Art. Mag. Composuit Posuitique Dolens.

1689.

overcome Waller in Hampshire it would clear the way for the Royalist march into Surrey. Moreover, there were several reverses to avenge, so, in the words of a chronicler, Hopton was "filled with the desire of a battle with Waller to make even all accounts."

But Lord Ogle, who was then in charge of the defences of Winchester Castle, when summoned to a conference at Hopton's lodgings in Eastgate Street, gave some sage advice to the hotheaded Royalist leader. It was, he said, a mistake to "seek a well-formed army, and well commanded, with raw men new raised." "If Waller were near the city," he said, "a sortie of a mile or two might be tried, but in extreme hot weather soldiers would be wearied to carry stores" for a conflict at a distance.

Ogle's wise advice was disregarded, and Hopton resolved on a battle with Waller. Ogle was asked to supply a quantity of stores from the castle, and with some reluctance he agreed to let some go. Hopton pushed on with his preparations for meeting Waller. He moved out to a position near Bramdean and Cheriton, and on a fateful day in March 1644 the battle took place. This battle, sometimes referred to as Cheriton Fight, is looked upon by modern military strategists as nothing more than a skirmish. Waller was as eager for the conflict as Hopton, and as Ogle had said, he was much better prepared. In point of sheer numbers it has been calculated that there was not much difference between the opposing forces; but in efficiency Waller's was much the better. Yet, such was the reckless valour of many of the Royalists, especially those of the better class, that the issue of the fight hung in the balance for a while, and it is recorded that at one point only Waller's personal resource and encouragement saved the situation.

But in the end the Royalist forces were routed. Two
regiments of Irish, brought over from Dublin to assist
the king, were said to have been the first to break
and run; and their bad example set many English
Royalists running also. The defeat became a rout,
and soon fugitives were pouring into Winchester

THE CLOISTERS, WINCHESTER COLLEGE

crying out: "The kingdom's lost. The kingdom's
lost."

This was literally true. Cheriton Fight, in the light
of modern warfare, may seem but a poor affair, but it
proved to be the turning-point of the king's fortunes.
It made impossible his grand scheme of a threefold
advance upon London. Instead of a widespread
offensive he now had to act upon the defensive, losing
all along the line, until at length came his surrender
to the Scots, his imprisonment, and death.

The losses at Cheriton have been computed at

UNIVERSITY
COLLEGE
LIBRARY
NOTTINGHAM

about nine hundred on the Parliamentarian side, and one thousand four hundred on the side of the king. It is said that over a hundred loads of provisions were captured by Waller, and quite half of the stores which Lord Ogle had so grudgingly handed over to Hopton fell into the hands of the victors. Hopton retreated to Basing with most of his cannon, but some of his army hastened to Winchester, and some to Alton and Basing, the latter setting fire to the little town of Alresford as they passed through.

The comment of Clarendon is to the point: "This battle was fought on 29 March, which was a very doleful entring into the beginning of the year 1644, and broke all the measures, and alter'd the whole scheme of the King's Counsels." He goes on that the king had meant to take the offensive about Easter, but that now he "discerned he was wholly to be on the defensive, and that was like to be a very hard part too."

Waller moved on to Winchester, but did not stay there. He left a small force of about a hundred men in charge of the city. The castle, with its Royalist garrison, he did not attempt to take. The result was that when he had gone elsewhere, pursuing his campaign to break up any organized opposition by Royalist forces in the county, a number of zealous loyalist citizens, loth to believe that the king's arms would not at length prevail in the land, set upon the small force Waller had left, and disarmed them. But the Parliamentary general soon returned, and although the city gates were barred against him, he blew one down, and once more took possession of the place, severely punishing all he could find who had set upon his guard.

But the stress of the wider campaign in the county,

and especially the urgent need of capturing Basing House, which had held out so long against the Parliamentarian attacks, compelled Waller to leave Winchester again without assaulting the castle. It was not until much later in the campaign, when the Parliamentary cause had advanced in the counties, that Oliver Cromwell was spared to deal summarily with Winchester and reduce the castle so that it should cease to be a Royalist rallying-place. He arrived on the high ground to the south-west of the city, and occupied the earthwork which Hopton had thrown up. He had with him three foot regiments and two thousand horse troopers. There is a tradition that his field-pieces were used to drop balls from the earthwork through the great west window of the cathedral, but as the distance is over a mile this feat was manifestly impossible with such artillery as existed at that date. It is, however, not improbable that Cromwell's artillerymen trundled their pieces down the hill towards the city, and fired from a short distance outside the walls; taking the cannon back to the earthwork at the end of the day's cannonade. They would do this to avoid a mishap which had befallen them in another part of the country, when camping with their field-pieces outside a place they were besieging. During the night the besieged made a sortie, and captured a number of the cannon which had been annoying them during the day. Thereafter the habit was to withdraw the artillery to a safe distance before nightfall.

According to his dispatches to Fairfax, Cromwell arrived at Winchester on 28 September, 1645, just eighteen months after Cheriton Fight. Cromwell's letter to Mr. William Longland, mayor of the city, is interesting both in contents and phraseology:

SIR, I come not to this city but with a full resolution to save it and the Inhabitants thereof from ruine. I have commaunded the Souldyers upon payne of death that noe wrong bee done, wch I shall strictly observe, only I expect you give me entrance into the City, without necessitateing mee to force my way, wich yf I doe, then it will not be in my power to save you or it. I expect yor answeare wth in halfe an houre and rest,

Your servant,

OLIVER CROMWELL.

Sept. 28th, 1645.
    Five o'clock at night.

The mayor replied with circumspection:

SIR, I have received yor Letter by yor Trumpett, and in behalf of the Citizens and Inhabitants return you hearty thanks for yor favourable expression therein. But wth all I am to signifie unto you that the delivry up of the City is not in my power, it being under the comand of the right hoble. the Lord Ogle, who hath the military Govermt. thereof. In the mean tyme I shall use my best endeavour with the Lord Ogle to perform the contents of yor letter concerning the City, and rest

Your most humble servant,

WM. LONGLAND, Mayor.

WINTON, *Sept. 28, 1645.*

Nevertheless the city (probably by direction of Lord Ogle) offered some resistance to Cromwell, but, in the words of a Parliamentary correspondent, "the gate being fired our men entered." The resistance by the citizens could have been but half-hearted, for the besiegers got into the city on the morning of 29 September. Another chronicler comments: "with the townsmen's consent we have cooped up in the castle one hundred and twenty horse and four hundred foot, and all the malignant gentry and clergy of this Hampshire and Sussex, with many Papists

204

and Jesuits. It is hoped the Parliament will order these great delinquents shall trouble them no more."

It was now the turn of the garrison to defend their position, or surrender. Being in hope of getting some relief from the king Lord Ogle decided to fight, and he set up a red flag in a turret in token of his defiance of Cromwell. The Bishop of Winchester, Dr. Curle, was in the city when it surrendered, but so sure was he of the security of the castle and its resources for resistance, that he refused Cromwell's offer of a safe-conduct out of the city, and fled into the castle. When his lordship heard the thundering of Cromwell's cannon outside the castle walls he altered his mind, and sent to say he was "sorry he had not accepted of Lieut.-General Cromwell's former proffer, and being better advised, did now desire the benefit thereof." He was told it was too late to change his mind; if taken in the castle he would be esteemed a prisoner of war. And surely enough he was. He was eventually allowed to retire into private life, losing all his income, so that he was dependent upon the charity of his friends until his death at his sister's house at Soberton five years later.

Winchester must have been a parlous place in which to be abroad during the siege of the castle. "The chiefest street of the town the enemy played upon, whereby divers passengers were wounded and some killed." Thus a Parliamentary recorder, and he adds: "In this street my quarters being, I have that cause to bless God for my preservation."

The attack began on Saturday, 4 October, and was carried on all that day and the next. The defenders on one occasion made a sally and beat the besiegers from their guns, but reserves were hurried up, and

Ogle's men had to beat a hasty retreat into the castle. Cromwell kept on battering at one spot (the Black Tower) with his cannon, and on the Sunday evening he reported: "We . . . made a breach in the wall near the Black Tower, which after about two hundred shot we thought stormable, and purposed on Monday morning to attempt it. On Sunday night about ten of the clock the governor beat a parley, desiring to treat."

Cromwell treated the garrison generously. Lord Ogle and all his commissioned officers were given safe-conduct, with horses, as far as Woodstock, and they were allowed to leave the castle "with colers flying and drums beating." All the arms, ordnance, and ammunition fell to Cromwell, while the castle itself was handed over to Sir William Waller according to the terms of surrender. Waller had made a claim to it at the very outset of the war, as also had his sister, the wife of Lord Ogle. It may be noted that during or prior to the final siege she had been given free passage from the castle and city by Cromwell, but she died on the journey.

It has been thought that the Black Tower, at which Cromwell directed his attack, stood a little to the south-west of the West Gate, and that his batteries were placed upon the site now known as Oram's Arbour. Ogle would probably have continued his resistance longer, but he was dispirited by the news of the death of his wife, and moreover, many of his garrison clamoured for surrender, while some "thirty or forty ran away over the works in one night." Some of his officers actually drew up a request for a treaty and handed it to Ogle. The governor put it in his pocket as if dismissing the matter, whereupon Sir John Pawlet exclaimed: "My Lord, you are too hard on us." Ogle's reply was: "I am in sadness both for the treaty, and for my lady's death."

A Parliamentarian, reporting upon the surrender, declared that the final yielding up of the fortress was delayed by the carousing of the vanquished Royalists. "Our men . . . could not take possession until two in the afternoon by reason the governor and some of the officers being unwilling to leave any wine behind them, had made themselves drunk." He goes on: "seven hundred men marched out of the castle, and Viscount Ogle as drunk as a beggar." But, as this chronicler was the notorious Hugh Peters, "the ecclesiastical newsmonger," this story may perhaps be discounted. He was chaplain to Cromwell's army, and after the surrender of Winchester Castle Cromwell sent him, and Mr. Spavin his private secretary, with dispatches to London. The Commons gave £50 for the good news. Peters addressed the House of Commons immediately after his arrival thus: "Mr. Speaker, I came from Winchester the last night late, but I had come sooner had not my Lord Ogle and his company been so unwilling to part with their sack and strong beer, of which they drank so liberally at their farewell that few of them, as is their manner, could get up their horses without help, for the agreement was for their marching out at three o'clock, but it proved late through their debauchery."

Cromwell's own report of the surrender, sent to Fairfax, was as follows:

SIR, This is the addition of another mercy. You see God is not weary in doing you good. I confess, Sir, His favour to you is as visible when he comes by His power upon the hearts of your enemies, making them quit places of strength to you, as when he gives courage to your soldiers to attempt hard things. His goodness in this is much to be acknowledged, for the

Castle was well manned with 680 horse and foot, there being near 200 gentlemen, officers and their servants, well victualled with 15 hundredweight of cheese, very great store of wheat and beer, near 20 barrels of powder, seven pieces of cannon. The works were exceeding good and strong. It's very likely it would have cost much blood to have gained it by storm. We have not lost 10 men. This is repeated to you that God may have all the praise, for it's all His due. Sir, I rest your most humble servant,

OLIVER CROMWELL.

WINCHESTER, *6th October*, 1645.

Cromwell went on to Basing, that stubborn fortress which had held out against Parliamentary attacks for so long, and eight days after Winchester it also fell. The gallant Marquis of Winchester was committed to the Tower of London where he endured much privation. Orders were at once issued for the demolition of both these troublesome strongholds. Basing was levelled to the ground and never rebuilt. The work of "slighting" Winchester Castle dallied, possibly because it was a prodigious task. Repeated Orders of State were issued during 1649, 1650, and 1651, but it was not until the spring of 1651 that the work of destruction was actually begun. It was probably effected for the most part by mining. The archives of the Corporation of Winchester contain the following entry made date 2 May, 1656: "Taken then out of the cofers to pay Sir William Waller for the purchase of the castle, with the appurtenances and other material thereunto belonging, the sum of two hundred and three score pounds." This did not include the Great Hall, which was sold to the Quarter Sessions of Hampshire for £100. There being some difficulty in raising the money it was advanced by Sir Thomas Jervoise, who borrowed half the sum from

CHARLES II BY SIR PETER LELY
(In the possession of the Corporation of Winchester.
Photo by F. A. Grant, Winchester)

his cousin, the regicide, Sir Robert Wallop. This
sum was repaid to the latter after the Restoration, while he was a prisoner in the Tower (where
he died).

ANCIENT SUNDIAL ON BEAUFORT TOWER, ST. CROSS

King Charles himself must have seen the desolation
of his famous Castle of Winchester, for, after his
confinement at Carisbrooke, while on his final doleful
journey to London he spent one night in the empty
fortress. The route of his journey was through
Lyndhurst, Romsey, Winchester, Alresford, Farnham,
Bagshot, and Windsor. Some months before he

P

went upon this journey a brave but reckless Royalist, one Captain Burleigh, had attempted to foment a rebellion in the Isle of Wight with the object of rescuing the king from Carisbrooke Castle. The attempt was ruthlessly crushed. Burleigh was tried at Winchester on a charge of high treason, and, being convicted, he was hanged, drawn, and quartered. No Hampshire man could be found to carry out the sentence, so the Parliamentary leaders sent down a man from London.

The king's progress through Hampshire was watched by many villagers and townsfolk. Some were merely curious to see him, but others prayed aloud for his liberty. "As he approached Winchester the mayor and aldermen came to meet him, and presenting him, according to custom, the keys and mace of the city, addressed to him a speech full of affection. But Cobbett (the colonel in charge of the guard) rudely pushing his way towards him, asked if they had forgotten that the House had declared all who should address the king traitors. Whereupon, seized with terror, the functionaries poured forth humble excuses, protesting they were ignorant of the will of the House, and conjuring Cobbett to obtain their pardon." The recollection of the execution of Burleigh would have been vivid in their minds, and would have damped their loyalist ardour. There is a tradition that a sufferer from scrofula besought the king to "touch" him, after the superstition of that time, and that the king's response brought recovery.

Cromwell did not visit Winchester again, but his son Richard, "Tumble-Down-Dick" as he came to be called, was squire of Hursley, four miles away, for many years, and on his death in 1712 he was buried in the chancel of Hursley Church, famous in later years as the church of the Rev. John Keble.

During the Commonwealth there was a rumour in Winchester that the Parliament purposed to destroy the cathedral, as they had already destroyed the castle. The citizens were in great perturbation, and a petition was sent to London protesting against the proposal for "destroyinge and pullinge downe of Trinitie church theare scituate, an auncient and most beautifull structure, the most convenient and spatious place of assemblinge for the hearinge of God's word wheare many thousands of soules may be served and satisfied."

If there was any basis for the rumour that the cathedral was marked for destruction (and there was all too much reason for the citizens to fear that the vindictive vandalism of many fanatic puritans would have fastened upon such an object if they could have had their way), the danger passed, and in the following year there was a town subscription of funds to put the place in some sort of repair. Even though the canny citizens only lent their money (they would not give it outright), barely enough was contributed to defray the cost of repairing the roof, which was very ruinous, thanks to the depredations of Bishop Horne two generations before, that prelate having, amongst other things, stripped much lead from the roof.

A similar spirit of religious intolerance prevailed during the Commonwealth in Winchester to that which characterized the time of Elizabeth, only now it was an intolerance of the Anglican form of worship as well as a burning hatred of anything savouring of papistry. The narrow intolerance of Scottish presbyterianism, which had gained a footing in England as a result of a bargain between Scottish leaders and the Parliament, even reached as far south as Winchester, for Bishop Curle, after his capture in Winchester Castle, was not allowed to compound for his private estate because he refused to take the Covenant. Many others of the clergy of Hampshire were deprived under the Cromwellian regime. In Winchester itself the Rev. Dr. William Lewis, D.D., Master of St. Cross, was deprived of that position, and in his place was put the puritan member for Winchester, Mr. John Lisle, the husband of Dame Alice Lisle, of Moyles Court, near Ringwood. And when Cromwell called Lisle to sit in the Upper House of Parliament, the office of Master was given to John Cooke, the Solicitor-General. Cooke was one of the Parliamentarian leaders who were executed after the Restoration, while Dr. Lewis was restored to the office in 1660, and died at St. Cross seven years later.

It is said that most of the cathedral clergy "were plundered." The Rev. John Oliver, a prebend of Winchester, and President of Magdalen College, Oxford, had his Oxford house ransacked, and he was so stripped that he "wanted himself what he had before bestowed on others." At the Restoration he was made Dean of Winchester, but enjoyed his preferment only a year. The Rector of Chilcomb, the Rev. John Hagar, was ejected from his benefice and kept out for thirteen years. Of him it has been recorded that "during that time he was reduced to such extremity that as he hath walked the streets of London, if he hath seen a cast piece of bread in the streets, he hath dropt his glove upon it, took it up, and eaten it with greediness."

The Rector of Old Alresford, the Rev. Dr. Peter Heylyn, appears to have been an especial object of

Parliamentarian hatred, no doubt because of his zealous advocacy of King Charles. He escaped to the king at Oxford while the Parliamentarian troops were eagerly searching for him, "resolving if they could have took him he should have followed his good lord of Canterbury to another world than that described in his cosmography; but since they could not light upon his person they secured his estate, sending down an order for the sequestration of all his goods and chattels." Colonel Norton, himself an Alresford man, was credited with having taken to himself the best of the reverend doctor's belongings. The books were carried away to Portsmouth, a worthy library valued at a thousand pounds, yet many of the volumes were sold by the way, "good folios for a flagon of ale apiece." But, as for the doctor, some supplies of money coming in, and the Royalist cause strengthening in Hampshire, "he settled himself, his wife and eldest daughter at Winchester, then a strong garrison of the king's, where for a while he had some halcyon days, but they endured not long, for this place, thought invincible, was cowardly yielded up in three days' time, so that the Doctor was now in more danger than ever, had not Mr. Lizard, in whose house he boarded, secured him in a private room, so cunningly contrived that there was no door to be seen nor entrance into it, supposed to be formerly made for the hiding of seminary priests and Jesuits, the house heretofore belonging to a papist family. Here did he abide in safety while the soldiers hunted about for him. But, desirous of liberty, while the soldiers were gaming and rioting, he took his opportunity on the market day . . . and so walked out of the town confidently with the country crowd, leaving his wife and daughter to the care of his faithful friend, Mr. Lizard." After this it was a small thing that he should have been robbed of a ring, and a small sum of money, by some Parliamentarian soldiers, for he escaped bodily harm. His chronicler adds: "And thus did the Doctor run through many dangers for his loyalty, never secure from their rage and malice, which was so inveterate that, could they have catcht him, nought had satisfied but his blood."

As in the case of St. Cross, many of the sequestered livings were given to laymen, chosen in some cases after the Independent custom, by the community assembling in the church. Some, like John Bunyan of Bedford, were artisans; indeed, at Over Wallop the puritan incumbent was of the same profession as the Immortal Dreamer. A saddler was the parson at Hound, and in another parish one of the same trade was rector. Time brought its reverses, for after the Restoration, and the passing of the Act of Uniformity, many of these puritan preachers gave up their livings rather than conform. The puritan incumbent of Crawley, five miles from Winchester, one Samuel Tomlyns, who had been presented to that living in 1655, was one of those who "came out" in 1662. He founded an Independent community in Winchester which, despite many vicissitudes, has continued to the present day. Another non-conformist was John Hicks of Portsmouth, who later was allied with Monmouth at Sedgemoor.

But, while the puritan regime endured, the non-covenanting clergy suffered greatly, not merely in deprivation of their livings, but in many cases by actual bodily insult and injury. It is recorded that "Portsmouth was made a sort of convict settlement for the clergy who refused submission to Parliament.

ST. CROSS CHURCH FROM THE BROTHERS' BOWLING-GREEN
AT DUSK

They were put on board ship, and there hooted and even pelted as they were at prayers, being called 'Baal's Priests.' Whipping was the puritan punishment for Quakers, but Roman Catholics were hanged. In Hampshire during the Civil War and up till the summer of 1654 twenty-one priests were hanged!

But the intolerance of the Parliamentarian, or rather, the Army rule, in time turned the nation against it, and people began to wish for a return to the old order. It is said that one of those who plotted with Fairfax and Monk for the return of Charles II was Colonel Clobery, of Clobery House, situated in Parchment Street, Winchester. The proclamation of Charles in Winchester was on 12 May, 1660. The city was overjoyed, and spent no less than £34 2s. 6d. upon revelry to commemorate the occasion.

According to a petition which the citizens presented to "the county, the bishop, and all other pious and charitable harts" in the same year, it would appear that they could ill afford such expenditure. They had been sadly despoiled for close upon twenty years, and their fortunes were at a very low ebb. This petition was for "help in making navigation from Winchester to Southampton, and so to give labour to the poor and revive trade in the future." The reason given is "that the Revenue hereof is not sufficient to releeve our Poore who consist of above 200 famylyes, and the sayde citie not being able to undertake any manufacture to set them on worke, and here being no road or thoroughfare Trading is altogether decayed." After some delay the petition bore fruit, the navigation being considerably improved. But in the next century it became a monopoly in the hands of a greedy individual whose rapacity had to be curtailed by an Act of Parliament obtained by several citizens.

The translation from Worcester to Winchester of Bishop Morley, the companion of Charles II on his travels, marked the beginning of better times for Winchester. He brought with him to Winchester his friend, Izaak Walton, and very soon after, the saintly Wykehamist Thomas Ken was made his chaplain. No doubt Morley had great influence with Charles, and consequently it was not surprising that the king at length came to Winchester with his court. Charles was delighted with the place, and with the country round, which just suited his habit of taking long walks. There were therefore times when Winchester was full of notabilities, not merely courtiers, but men whose names are enshrined in English literature and poetry, architecture, music. Morley set to work energetically to rebuild the houses of the Close, and also to rear on the ruins of Wolvesey a stately episcopal palace. In this work he enlisted Christopher Wren, who spent much time in the city, and who is thought to have designed several of the houses still standing, as well as the present Wolvesey Palace. There is a doubt whether he, or one of his pupils, designed School at Winchester College.

Besides arranging for the rebuilding of the Close, Morley had the sum of £420 set aside for the provision of a new organ in the cathedral. In 1665 a contract was made with Thomas Thamer of Cambridge University for "a double organ," that is, a great and a choir organ. Such an organ was probably built. The records show that in 1693 the great Renatus Harris was working on it.

The year 1666 was a disastrous one for Winchester,

for in that summer the place was devastated by the plague. Very many citizens died, and their bodies were carted out of the city and buried in pits dug on the south of St. Catherine's Hill. The country folk would not enter the place with their wares, but placed them on a flat stone just outside the West Gate, the citizens placing their purchase money in basins of vinegar so that the infection might be destroyed. Years later, when societies had been formed for the purpose of alleviating the families of those who had died in this pestilence, one society being formed to help the natives of Winchester, and another to help the aliens (for in those days the cleavage between those born in the city and all others was very definite indeed), a monument was erected on the site where this exchange of commodities took place, and the actual stone which served for a counter was built into the monument where it is still to be seen at the south-west corner.

King Charles became more and more interested in Winchester, and towards the close of his reign he conceived the idea, or it was suggested to him, of building a magnificent palace on the lines of Versailles on the site of the now ruined castle. The city authorities were nothing loth, and although they were the owners of the major part of the site, they eagerly agreed to sell it to the king. They had given Waller's son £260 for it, but so enchanting was the prospect of Winchester becoming once again a royal city that they sold their interest in the castle to Charles for five shillings! Wren was commissioned to design a palace unhampered by any considerations of existing houses or ownerships; and that the king might be able to develop to the full his idea of a spacious park, ranging possibly for miles to the south and west,

Wren and Lord Rochester wrote to the cathedral chapter (who held much of the land surrounding the city) forbidding the leasing of any land to the south of the city "till the king's pleasure is known."

The work was begun in 1682, and the site was cleared of the ruins left by the Parliamentarian engineers. Wren's plan was for a lengthy building, with a façade to the east, with the centre aligning with the west front of the cathedral, the new building being linked with the old by a magnificent drive, bordered with trees and statues. This would have had the effect of opening up a splendid aspect of the ancient west front of the cathedral. Above a central portico of the new palace was to have been a lofty cupola, carried to such a height that the king might there stand and see his ships of war, or his private yacht, riding at anchor in the Solent. Unfortunately for the completion of the scheme, and incidentally for the prosperity of Winchester, Charles died when things had gone but a little way, and the work was immediately dropped, James II being interested in other things. Something like £25,000 had been expended upon the work.

Charles got on very well with his loyal subjects in Winchester, but they were no more successful than others in getting money out of him. The city coffers were low, but in vain did they hint, albeit quite delicately, concerning the money that had been taken from the city by the Parliamentarians as punishment for its loyalty. In vain did they remind him that they had given their plate to his father to help with the prosecution of the war against the Parliament. They reckoned the Crown was indebted to the city to the tune of several thousands of pounds. Charles admitted it all, and then generously repaid the citizens by handing to the mayor a full-length painting of himself, the work of Sir Peter Lely. Their chagrin may be imagined, for in the impoverished state of the city's finances, a piece of painted canvas was but a

NELL GWYNNE'S DOOR, WATER CLOSE

poor substitute for the hard cash they were so sorely in need of. But Charles's gift has, by the passage of years, "grown into money," so that it is now worth more than the amount which the city lent to Charles I.

Shortly before his death the Merry Monarch, being pressed for money, had resort to the trick of calling upon chartered towns to surrender their charters, and returning them only after a heavy fine had been paid for their renewal. Winchester had to come into line with the rest, notwithstanding a cautious remonstrance from the mayor and his fellows. They had to dip into the city coffers to the extent of nine pounds to pay for the hire of a coach to take the mayor and charter to London. It cost them more than eighty pounds to get a new charter, although Charles had already assured them that he was "very well satisfyed of the Loyalty of my antient city of Winchester." He was more generous to the cathedral. One of his gifts is the pair of service books still kept on the altar.

On the occasions when the king and his court stayed in Winchester the several families were housed in different places. Charles himself was often entertained at the Deanery, the occupant of the office being as obsequious as an old-time butler, and ready to do anything to oblige the king. Not so little Thomas Ken, the bishop's chaplain, for when Charles suggested that Nell Gwynne should be housed by Ken at his residence then standing in the Deanery gardens, Ken bluntly refused, to the amazed horror of the sycophantic dean. Ken said it was not fitting that a woman of such character should come into the house of God's priest. Charles remembered this incident later when the see of Bath and Wells became vacant. Several names were suggested to him for the office, but he waved them all aside. "Who shall have it," said he, "but that ugly little man who would not give poor Nelly a lodging." For all his faults Charles knew a man when he saw one, and he ever admired courage, so for his resolution Ken got a bishopric, and Meggott, "the bowing dean," for all his obsequiousness, was passed over.

The queen, Catherine of Braganza, used to stay at a house which still stands at the south-west corner of Canon Street and Southgate Street. James, the king's brother, stayed at a house in St. Swithun Street, facing St. Thomas Street; Nell Gwynne is said to have lived in a house which she bought in St. Peter Street, at its junction with St. George's Street on the east side, but there is a tradition that she often stayed in a house in Colebrook Street, long since destroyed, and that the king used to visit her, passing from the Close through a low brick arch a few yards to the west of Water Close Gate. This archway is now closed in, but it is plainly visible.

There were several petty squabbles among the city rulers during Charles's reign, the records of which take up considerable space in the city archives. Very soon after the Restoration, the mayor and certain of his fellows were imprisoned and kept under restraint by one Captain Edmund Clerke, much to their indignation. The outraged mayor appealed to the king, who, in his Privy Council, issued the following order:

Whereas the Mayor of Winchester was upon Sunday last the 21st present made Prisoner in the Guard there by Captain Edmond Clerke, and is still, with divers of the Aldermen of that city, kept under restraint by the said Captain, these are to will and command the said Edmond Clerke and all others whom it doth concern, forthwith upon sight hereof to set the said Mayor, Aldermen, and all others by him committed, at full liberty, And hereof they may not fail as they will answer the contrary at their utmost perils.

What it was that had caused trouble between the mayor and this petty martinet does not appear from the records, but it is clear that the mayor and his fellows secured a speedy release. The Privy Council ordered Clerke to make a public apology, but it was not until he had been himself imprisoned that he thought fit to obey the order.

About the time when the king had resolved to build a palace in Winchester, the Corporation were convulsed by a most determined attempt to impose a certain individual upon the freedom of the city and guild of merchants, contrary to the customs of the place, and much ink was spilt, and parchment wasted, in the matter. The individual was a certain Edward Harfell, "of this citie, gent.," who had induced the then mayor to propose his election. The election was turned down by the majority of the aldermen. Harfell threatened the Corporation that he would petition the king. He did so, and persuaded the mayor to support him. Hearing only one side of the matter the king issued an order that Harfell should be admitted; but the others of the Corporation, resenting any interference with their ancient privileges, although seemingly trivial to outsiders, went to the king with their side of the matter, and the order was reversed. The end of the business was that Harfell failed to gain his desired freedom of the city, and the mayor was himself removed from his office as Justice of the Peace, and ordered to be suspended until he should have paid the whole of "the greate charge and expence of the Stocke of the citie" caused by the "irregular proceedings of Mr. Thomas Coward . . . against the antient ordinances of the citie."

Later in that year the grateful Corporation made the king himself a freeman of their body. The Duke of York, his brother, also accepted the honour on the same day, 1 September, 1682.

The death of Charles, barely two years after he

had laid the foundation of his new palace at Winchester, was an unmitigated disaster to the citizens. James II had no love for the place, and even had his reign been free from disturbance he would never have continued the building of the palace his brother had begun with such zest. But his reign produced an event which is indelibly inscribed in the history of Winchester: that is the trial and execution of Dame Alice Lisle, widow of John Lisle, the regicide, Parliamentarian M.P. for Winchester, and erstwhile Master of St. Cross. Lady Lisle was over seventy years of age, but neither her age nor her gentle birth, nor her benevolent character, served to save her from the savage vengeance of James. She was the Edith Cavell of the seventeenth century.

At the battle of Sedgemoor, when the Duke of Monmouth made his fatal bid for the crown of England, there was among his army the zealot puritan, John Hickes of Portsmouth. Incidentally it may be recorded that on the other side was the Bishop of Winchester, Dr. Mews, aged seventy years, leading a contingent of Hampshire loyalists. Mews had been an officer in Charles I's army before taking Orders. In the flight after the disaster John Hickes, like Monmouth, fled eastwards into Hampshire, and, with a companion named Nelthorpe, sought shelter at Moyles Court, near Ringwood, the residence of Lady Lisle. In the kindness of her heart the lady gave them shelter, no doubt without realizing to what she was exposing herself. The king's soldiers found Monmouth in a ditch not far away, and Hickes and another fugitive they found at Moyles Court. As a consequence Lady Lisle was charged with high treason in that she had harboured the king's enemies.

She was brought to trial in the Great Hall of

Winchester Castle, her judge being the infamous Justice Jeffreys. The trial is outstanding as the first and the most shocking of all the incidents of that appalling judicial slaughter known to history as the Bloody Assizes, and which has left such a terrible memory in the western counties. The jury at Winchester was "packed," but even so the judge at first found it was not going to be easy to secure a verdict of guilty. They were reluctant to condemn so gentle a lady for so humane an act as giving shelter to men in distress. Moreover Hickes himself had not as yet been formally convicted of treason. But the scruples of the jury were overborne by the ferocious judge, who, in his own picturesque phrase, "gave them a lick with the rough side of his tongue." After he had stormed at them for some time they reluctantly found a verdict of guilty. It might very accurately have been described as "by direction." But they must soon have been appalled at the result of their weakness in yielding to Jeffreys, for, with Satanic savagery, he ordered his frail prisoner to be burnt alive in the Winchester market-place that very afternoon.

Instantly the city was in an uproar of protest. Lady Lisle was well known in the place as a kindly gentlewoman, and the fiendish sentence sent a thrill of horror everywhere. The dean and chapter and the chief citizens united in an appeal to the brutal judge for mercy, or at the very least for a respite giving time for an appeal to the king. No doubt knowing full well what the royal decision would be, Jeffreys, with a sardonic show of graciousness, consented to a respite of five days.

The appeal reached the ears of James, but he was as hard and as inhuman as his tool Jeffreys. With the crass blindness of his race he failed to see that to

Q

refuse clemency in such a case was to harden the nation's heart against him. The execution of Lady Lisle and her fellow sufferers in the Bloody Assize had no little part in ending the Stuart dynasty in England. James, despite every argument urged by

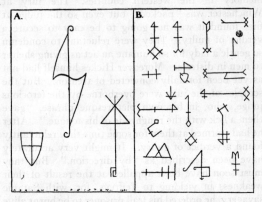

MASONS' MARKS IN THE CATHEDRAL

the Winchester emissaries, coldly declined to abate the sentence of death, but he consented to change the mode from burning (the punishment for treason in women) to beheading. And to the general grief, and the eternal infamy of James, the aged lady was beheaded in the market-place at Winchester on 2 September, 1685. The site of her martyrdom is either where the present Winchester Museum stands, or within a few yards of it. Her body is interred in Ellingham churchyard, near her old home. On the 14th of the same month James was in Winchester attending service at the cathedral and hobnobbing with Bishop Mews at Wolvesey.

The hapless Monmouth had already been beheaded at the Tower, and with him in his last moments was the saintly Bishop Ken. Three years later the "little ugly man," as Charles II had called him, became one of the leaders of popular sentiment against James II. As one of the seven bishops who had refused to obey James in the publication of the Declaration of Indulgence, and one, moreover, who had dared to give James a face-to-face refusal, Ken was confined in the Tower. But the famous trial ended in an acquittal which sent the whole nation into uproarious rejoicings. Trelawney, another of the famous "seven," in 1707 became Bishop of Winchester, and completed the work of rebuilding the episcopal palace at Wolvesey which Bishop Morley had begun. It is noteworthy that Ken had another Wykehamist with him as fellow prisoner, Bishop Turner of Ely, while one of the judges who tried them was also a Wykehamist.

The blind obstinacy of James was again exhibited in an interview which he had with Lord Churchill in the Deanery garden at Winchester in August 1687, not long before his ignominious flight. Churchill urged that the king's measures for advancing Catholics in the State were alarming the people, nine-tenths of whom were Protestant. James replied haughtily:

I tell you, Churchill, I will exercise my own religion in such a manner as I think fitting. I will show favour to my Catholic subjects, and be a common father to all my Protestant subjects of what religion soever, but I am to remember that I am king, and I am to be obeyed by them. As for the consequences, I shall leave them to Providence, and make use of the power God has put into my hands to prevent anything that shall be injurious to my honour, or derogatory to the duty that is owing to me.

227

Queen Anne visited Winchester in company with her Consort, during her reign, and, contemplating what had been constructed of "The King's House," as Charles's palace was called, she gave directions for an estimate to be prepared of the cost of completing it as a royal residence. But the expense of wars on the Continent effectually prevented anything being done. Thus died all hope of Winchester becoming again a royal city. Wren's incomplete building fell from its purposed high estate, and became a receptacle for prisoners of war, then after the French Revolution a haven for French priests, and during the nineteenth century a barracks for soldiers, the depot for the Rifle Brigade and the King's Royal Rifle Corps, and depot for the county regiment. Fire destroyed a considerable part of it in 1894, and new buildings were erected, but a portion of Wren's original work may still be seen in the small house fronting on Southgate Street, and used as the Hampshire Depot Sergeants' mess. This particular building was in use in the latter part of the nineteenth century as a lodging for the Judges of Assize. A very modern attempt to carry out Wren's design for a wide walk from this building to the west front of the cathedral, as a Hampshire memorial of the Great War, was frustrated by strong opposition on the part of some leading citizens.

CHAPTER VII

Modern Winchester

THE Georgian period in Winchester was marked mainly by destruction. Ancient buildings were swept away, being replaced by others more in keeping with the debased architectural taste of the time, while others were hidden from view by stucco and white-wash. Even the superb fluted pillars of Purbeck marble which support the roof of the Great Hall of Winchester Castle were covered with plaster. Four of the six gates of the city were destroyed on the plea of public convenience. Their narrowness was said to be "detrimental to the public in general," for it was said that there was danger in foot-passengers passing through at the same time as wheeled traffic, and moreover, it was urged that "a tun of hay and a load of straw cannot be brought in or out of the city through the said gates without a great diminution thereof." About the middle of the century the North Gate apparently was in bad repair. The gate-keeper invited a number of neighbours to celebrate the christening of his latest born, and while the party was engaged in dancing the floor collapsed, causing the death of twenty-six of those present, besides injuring others. The baby is said to have escaped unhurt. The ruined Hospital of St. Mary Magdalen on the eastern downs was completely razed on the plea that it was become a refuge for tramps and wastrels. Much stone from the ruined Castle of de Blois at Wolvesey was sold by the Bishop of Winchester for making up the roads, and, rather than repair the front of Morley's palace, Bishop Brownlow North swept a considerable portion away. Even the ancient Butter Cross, standing by St. Lawrence Church, was marked for removal, for the Corporation sold it to a landowner in the county who wished to erect it in his park; but a furious outcry by the citizens against this vandalism caused the city fathers to withdraw from their bargain. Towards the end of the century the city prison and some dilapidated buildings which stood with it in the eastern part of the High Street were pulled down, a wise piece of demolition, for it created the "Broadway."

During the eighteenth century Winchester again became a military centre, as in the days of the Plantagenet and Angevin kings. In the Seven Years' War five thousand Hessian mercenaries were encamped on the downs outside the city, and as the prisoners began to come into the ports of Southampton and Portsmouth from the Continent they were confined in "The King's House." A similar state of things prevailed in 1778 and the years following. In 1779 a terrible epidemic raged among the prisoners in "The King's House," the infection being brought by the inmates of a French hospital ship captured in the Channel. Credit is given to an officer of the Gloucester Regiment, which was quartered at this time on St. Catherine's Hill, for planting on its summit the clump of trees which makes it so conspicuous a landmark. When the danger of an invasion by the French became imminent the county magistrates and leading gentlemen met at Winchester, and organized a strong militia for defence. In 1794 the county subscribed more than £11,000, and, as the menace grew, so the activity of the authorities in the county became more keen until, in 1801, the volunteer forces totalled about 1,500 foot, 1,200 horse, and 800 artillery. Much of this military preparation operated from Winchester, the county town.

Reference to Winchester as the county town is a reminder that it is, and has been since the earliest days, the place of criminal administration for the county. The barbarous punishments common to medieval times persisted in Winchester until the nineteenth century had run two decades. The crime of petit treason in woman, that is, husband murder, was visited by burning in the Middle Ages, and that was the sentence carried out upon women in Winchester in 1784 and in 1819. The first was Mary Bayley who, with her paramour, a man named Quinn, was convicted of the murder of her husband. She was ordered to be burned with fire until she should be dead, and Quinn was ordered to be hanged near her. The sentences were duly carried out on the high ground about half a mile out on the Andover road. The second woman was a Mrs. Huntingford, who had murdered her husband at Portsmouth. She was similarly executed, but there was such a huge concourse of people, many of them coming from Portsmouth to witness the barbarous ritual, and the scenes around the fatal spot were so disorderly, that the magistrates came to a resolution that any similar execution should be carried out in the precincts of the gaol. Fortunately the awakening of a more humane spirit in the nation put a stop to such brutality.

Nevertheless it was many years before the sanguinary criminal code under the Hanoverian kings was ameliorated. Its savage character may be gauged from the fact that 190 executions took place at Winchester between 1771 and 1820, and that in a population far smaller than now. In the ten years following 1771 the total executed was 18, but in each of the succeeding decades, during which time the criminal code had been made progressively more severe, under the mistaken idea of those in power that the more severe the code the less would be the crime, the numbers were respectively 45, 39, 43, and 45.[1] Severity had increased crime, or, at least, it had increased bloodshed in the name of the law. A very much greater number were transported overseas, for periods of seven or fourteen years, or not infrequently for life, often for what would in these days be considered very venial offences, such as rabbit snaring.[2] This was a period when Winchester was a pocket borough, returning two members to Parliament, the interest being shared by the Dukes of Chandos and Bolton.

Howard of Bedford, the prison philanthropist, in his itinerary of the gaols of England, visited the Winchester prisons, and according to his reports found them neither better nor worse than others in the kingdom. On the whole they would seem to have been rather above the average in some respects, although here, as in every other case at that time, the

[1] Hanging in chains was common; and there exists in Winchester West Gate a set of "chains" made for a felon who was fortunately reprieved. The condemned were measured for the "suit" during life.

[2] In 1768 William Stigant was fined 40s. at Winchester Assizes for unlawfully following the trade of a baker, he not having served an apprenticeship thereto. Half the fine went to the Sheriff, and half to a common informer.

office of governor was farmed out to the highest bidder, there being no salary attaching to the office, the holder getting his money out of the unfortunate inhabitants of the prison. Those were days when even an acquitted prisoner had to pay fees to get out of prison, and there are records of innocent individuals, acquitted by a jury, being thereafter held in prison for months for no other reason than that they could not find the fees for the gaoler, or for the clerk of the peace. Even his food, except for the barest subsistence of bread and water, had to be paid for by the unfortunate prisoner or his friends. Hence it was counted a humane act among well-to-do people to contribute to the sustenance of prisoners. The unfortunate debtors, confined at one period in the West Gate, were wont to hold a collecting-box out through the bars of the window looking on the thoroughfare for the alms of those passing in and out through the gate. The Hospital of St. Cross allowed a penny loaf to each prisoner in the Winchester gaols six times a year, a beggarly allowance for so rich a foundation. Winchester College was far more liberal. Their allowance to felons was once a week an ox head, four sheep's heads and pluck hinges, seventeen pints of oatmeal, three pints of salt, and twelve twopenny loaves; while a twenty-gallon cask of table beer was allowed three times a week, together with broken victuals left from the tables in the college dining-hall. The hygiene of the gaols must have been very bad, for not long before Howard's visit more than twenty prisoners had died of gaol fever within a year. Gaol-breaking was by no means uncommon. It was made the more easy because there was less rigorous surveillance over the visits of friends and relations than now. The following advertisement, which appeared in the

Hampshire Chronicle on 11 November, 1776, is interesting:

ESCAPE

Broke out of the County Bridewell at the City of Winchester on the night of the 28th of October last, by cutting away the rafters, and making a hole through the top of the house, from whence they let themselves down into the street, the three several undermentioned prisoners charged with several misdemeanours. 1. Adrian Butler, of Monk Sherborne, labourer, a thin man, aged 41 years; William Goodall, otherwise Webb, of Lower Clatford, labourer; and James Morrise, late of Fareham, pock fretten. . . .

Nor were escaping prisoners the only individuals sought for in this way. In the same journal, in the same year, appeared this advertisement from an aggrieved master four miles from Winchester:

Whereas John Warren, apprentice to Mr. James Comely of Otterbourne, Blacksmith and Farrier, did on Wednesday the 21st of August last run away from his said master, hath upwards of two years to serve, and is supposed to have gone towards Portsmouth or London. He was born at Hursley, and is about nineteen years of age, of a fair complexion, black eyes, about 5 feet 9 inches high, slim grown, small long legs and thighs, a little bending in at his knees, short brown hair, sometimes a little curled, hath a small scar on the upper part of his face near his hair, occasioned by a cut, can neither write nor read, is very apt to swear and draw his words a little; had on when he went away a light coloured cloth coat with white metal buttons, striped breeches, and a little hat with a buckle and band. Whoever will secure him and bring him back to his said master within one month shall receive a reward of Five Guineas, and all persons are cautioned against harbouring or employing him, but are desired to give immediate notice to the said Mr. J. Comely at Otterburn on pain of being prosecuted as the law directs.

With so rigorous a spirit prevailing among the governing classes in the latter half of the eighteenth century it is not surprising that gaol building was carried out with some zeal. In 1788 the county built a new bridewell on the site of the church of Hyde Abbey, clearing the ruins for the purpose. The number of prisoners at the county assizes was increasing. Whereas the average for many years had been about eight or ten, the numbers went up by leaps and bounds as the century drew to a close, and at the Lent Assizes two years after Waterloo there were no fewer than one hundred and eighteen prisoners for trial. Convictions were secured in rather more than half the cases, and of these thirty-five were sentenced to death, and four were actually executed. In the next year, out of one hundred and nine put up for trial forty-one received capital sentences, and eight were hanged. All these hangings took place on the spot which came to be known as "Gallows Hill," on the Andover road. They attracted vast crowds from all parts of the county. It is on record that one schoolmaster, the proprietor of a very popular academy in Hyde Street, used to order some of his elder pupils to go and witness a hanging, it being in his view a desirable part of their education.

This gentleman's idea of education was apparently shared by the fellows of Winchester College during these years, for the college records show a sad neglect of the scholars by those who were receiving the fat revenues, both in the education provided and the provender served in the dining-hall. Sydney Smith, who was there from 1782 to 1787, in later years described the system at Winchester as one of "abuse, neglect, and vice." There had been three rebellions of scholars before his time, but the most serious occurred after he had left. This was in 1793, by which time, perchance, the boys had caught the overturning spirit of the time, wafted from Paris.

The trouble began because a prefect had disobeyed the order of the warden, Dr. Huntingford, and had gone to hear the band of the Buckinghamshire Militia playing in the Cathedral Close. Huntingford was furious, and stopped the whole school their Easter leave-out. Such a drastic punishment called for drastic reprisal. The senior boys, forty in number, swore fealty to each other, and then, taking the college keys from the porter, they locked the warden in his own house, together with the second master. The warden in desperation sent an urgent message for help to the High Sheriff of Hampshire. That official came, with his *posse comitatus*, but, when he saw that the boys had prepared themselves to receive him, like de Blois on an earlier occasion with Stephen, he thought discretion the better part of valour, and drew off his forces. The scholars had put Outer Gate to its original purpose of defence; they had carried a number of heavy paving stones to the top of the gate ready to throw them down upon any who might attack them, and if those should not prove enough they had loosened the parapet stones to use for the same purpose. In the end the sheriff tried peaceful mediation, and succeeded, but Huntingford proved perfidious, and by a trick secured the resignations of some thirty-five of the malcontents.

Winchester was a coaching centre of moderate importance, being on the London-Southampton route and the Oxford-Newbury-Portsmouth route. But the main roads were blocked by turnpikes, so that it was impossible to get in or out of the city on either of the principal roads without the payment of toll.

In early Victorian times the toll at the Winchester "pikes" was fourpence halfpenny. The journey to Portsmouth cost about two shillings and tenpence, and if the return journey was not effected in the same twenty-four hours, reckoning from midnight to

FOURTEENTH-CENTURY TILES, ST. CROSS CHURCH

midnight, the cost was considerably increased; so that it was the practice of higglers and people attending markets at long distances from their homes, to set out immediately after midnight, and strive to return within the day. The business of toll collection was let yearly to the highest bidder. The trustees of the turnpikes had power to prosecute drivers who took side roads to evade the turnpikes, and in the early years of the nineteenth century there were

237

several prosecutions of people who slipped round the "pike" on Magdalen Hill, entering the city on the south side of St. Giles's Hill. Drovers took their cattle and sheep along drift-ways over the downs, and the deep scars made in the chalk by the passing animals can still be seen in places, especially on the old Portsmouth road to the east of St. Catherine's Hill. The turnpike trustees were generally short of money, and they were often unable to keep the main roads in decent condition. The by-roads got little, if any, attention, save perhaps at long intervals the dumping of a few cart-loads of farm flints into the ruts when they became too bad even for the farmers to put up with. These flints would be left for the wheeled traffic to grind in as best it might. It was ironically called "wheel rolling" in the early days of the steam roller.

Two old turnpike cottages still remain on the outskirts of the city as a reminder of days long past. One of these is on the Worthy road, at Abbots Barton, and the other is on the Andover road, very close to the site of the old gallows tree.

Deacon Hill, on the south-east ridge of the Chilcomb Downs, is the site where for many years stood one of the Admiralty semaphores and the house of the signalling staff. It was one of a string of semaphores from Portsmouth to London, along which news of the progress of the French wars was passed with surprising rapidity.

Winchester is proud of the fact that Jane Austen spent her last days in a house in College Street, dying there in June 1817. Her remains were interred in the north aisle of the nave of the cathedral, close to the grave of Dr. Warton, friend of Dr. Johnson, and for a long period Headmaster of Winchester. Inscribed

238

slabs mark their resting-places. In the nearest window a stained-glass memorial commemorates the novelist's genius, and on the south wall of the nave a statue of Warton sits for ever in the attitude of teaching.

In the early years of the eighteenth century what education existed for the children of the workers was of a very indifferent type. A self-styled schoolmaster of Winchester, in 1728, is reputed to have given the following receipt to a parent in return for money paid for alleged teaching:

Recefed of Jon Godwin ye som of sefenten shillings & forpense for 4 children skolen from Eastear to this day Nof ye 19. In ol is 5 skor & 4 weaks.

Then came the founding of a "free school" by one William Over. This was a great boon to the children of the poor in Winchester. It survives even yet in the form of scholarship grants. Over vested the choice of the head teacher in the mayor for the time being, who, by the terms of the trust, was forbidden to choose either an Irishman, a Scotsman, a Welshman, or a man from the north, or a foreigner from overseas. The reason for this embargo was in order that the scholars might not acquire a bad pronunciation!

Two years after the death of Jane Austen there came to Winchester another immortal in search of bodily healing. This was John Keats, already stricken with fell consumption. His letters give a delightful picture of the sleepy old town, and of some of its inhabitants. He was mildly interested in the ceremony of electing Earl Temple as mayor of the city. He revelled in the downs around. They filled him with delight, and he described the air as being "worth sixpence a pint." It is certain that in his walks in and around Winchester he got the inspiration for his *Ode to Autumn*, for he wrote it during his stay there. One letter, in which he speaks of his lodging near the cathedral, has piqued the curiosity of many Winchester people. They would like to know the house in which Keats stayed. But, alas, there is no clue but the letter itself, and that is too vague for certainty.

I go out the back gate, across one street into the cathedral yard, which is always interesting; there I pass under the trees along a paved path, pass the beautiful front of the cathedral, turn to the left under a stone doorway, then I am on the other side of the building.

In another letter to his friend Reynolds Keats set down his impressions of the place:

The side streets here are excessively maiden-lady-like, the doorsteps always fresh from the flannel. The knockers have a staid, serious, nay, almost awful quietness [1] about them. I never saw so quiet a collection of Lions' and Rams' heads.

In the same letter he speaks of the season of the year, and of the "warmth" of a stubble field, which had so impressed him that he had "composed upon it." Appreciating the loveliness of autumn in what was to be the autumn of his own life, he sang its glories in undying verse.

For all the beauty of the surrounding country, and the staid cleanliness of the dwelling-houses, the streets of Winchester at this time were only good in

[1] But for all its quietness some of the citizens made themselves prosperous. One of these, being asked how he had made himself so affluent, replied, "Well, you see, I charges very high, and I bows very low." Sycophancy was a Winchester characteristic then.

WINCHESTER IN 1805

parts. Down each of the three "Brook" streets flowed an open stream, often tainted with refuse, and even the High Street was seamed with an open gutter. It was not until 1901 that the streams in the Brooks were piped. Perhaps that is not surprising when it is recalled that the Corporation did not instal a system of sewerage for the city until 1880.

Winchester, and the district around, was greatly excited by the agricultural revolt of 1830, when what were termed the "Swing Riots" were in progress. A formidable rising had taken place in Kent among the land workers. They demanded a living wage, in place of a pittance eked out by parish relief. They saw in the newly invented thrashing machine a grave menace to their livelihood, and they smashed machines and burnt ricks where their demands were treated with contumely. By November the movement had spread through Sussex into Hampshire, and on the 22nd of that month the Duke of Buckingham wrote from his seat at Avington (five miles from Winchester) to the Duke of Wellington, the Lord Lieutenant of Hampshire, in these terms:

Nothing can be worse than the state of this neighbourhood. I may say that this part of the country is wholly in the hands of the rebels. . . . Fifteen hundred rioters are to assemble to-morrow morning, and will attack any farmhouses where there are thrashing machines. They go about levying contributions on every gentleman's house. There are very few magistrates, and what there are are completely cowed. In short, something decisive must instantly be done.

Agricultural wages in Hampshire at that time were generally eight shillings per week. The demand was for two shillings per working day, twelve shillings per week. The clamant labourers, driven desperate by the degradation of their lot, declared they could

R

not possibly live on less. The outbreak did not last long. The energy displayed by the authorities, directed by the victor of Waterloo, soon put an end to the disturbances, and by Christmas 1830 the Winchester gaols were overflowing with prisoners. The landlord Parliament had passed a law making thrashing-machine breaking and the demanding of money by an assembly of people capital offences. Mobs had smashed machinery at many places in Hampshire, and many of the ringleaders in this work were laid by the heels on the capital charge. The bitter hatred of the workers against the poor law found its vent in the eastern part of the county in the destruction of the workhouses at Selborne and at Headley. A certain Robert Holdaway was the leader in these latter exploits. At Fordingbridge, where much machinery was destroyed, the leader was a man named Cooper. Both were haled to Winchester. At Northington, the seat of a branch of the wealthy Baring family, Bingham Baring, a Hampshire justice, while ordering the labourers to disperse from outside his house, had his hat knocked off by a Micheldever labourer named Henry Cook, a youth of nineteen. Cook was seized and charged with attempted murder.

A Special Commission of Assize was ordered for the trial of the army of prisoners at Winchester. Three judges were sent down to conduct the trials, Baron Vaughan, and Justices Parke and Alderson. The trials took place in the Great Hall of the castle, and the Duke of Wellington as Lord Lieutenant of the county also sat on the Bench. The attitude and temper of the judges toward the ignorant and down-trodden culprits may be seen from the retort of Alderson, when an attempt was made on behalf of

the prisoners to urge in their favour the grievances
under which they had lived and laboured for so long,
and which had been the root cause of the rising.
"We do not come here to inquire into grievances.
We come here to decide law." It was just such a
retort as might have been made by Jeffreys a century
and a half before. And indeed they did apply the
law with vigour, so that by the time they had concluded their labours at Winchester they had secured
over 200 convictions, 101 of them for capital offences
as the law then stood. Only 67 out of 269 were
acquitted. Six of the capitally convicted were
"left for execution," in Voltaire's caustic phrase,
pour encourager les autres.

The consternation and dismay of the poor labourers
and their relatives was terrible. Even the citizens
of Winchester, many of whom had sided with the
authorities against the labourers, were constrained
to sympathy with those who were condemned to
death, or what in those days was almost as bad,
transportation from the country and the sight of
their relatives for the rest of their lives. The correspondent of *The Times* wrote thus on 7 January, 1830:

The scenes of distress in and about the jail are most
terrible. The number of men who are to be torn from
their homes and connexions is so great that there is
scarcely a hamlet in the county into which anguish
and tribulation have not entered. Wives, sisters,
mothers, children, beset the gates daily, and the
governor of the jail informs me that the scenes he is
obliged to witness at the time of locking up the prison
are truly heartbreaking.

A petition was got up praying for a reprieve for
the six men who lay under sentence of death. It was
signed in Winchester "by the clergy of the Low
Church, some of the bankers, and every tradesman

in the town without exception." The clergy of the cathedral were asked to sign, but they refused unless the county magistrates signed first. *The Times* correspondent waxed sarcastic about this, saying they were daily preaching mercy to their flocks, yet they refused their consent to a practical application of their own doctrines.

Nevertheless the appeal from all parts of the county, as well as from Winchester, saved the lives of four of the men. But two—Cooper, who had led the crowd in the destruction of machinery at Fording-bridge; and Henry Cook, the nineteen - year - old labourer from Micheldever, who had aimed a blow at Bingham Baring and knocked his hat off—were both hanged at Winchester. A few days later Baring himself, in the heat of temper, struck with his stick a farmer who was being conveyed to Winchester handcuffed. The farmer later sued Baring for assault, and the latter had to pay £50 damages. Those were times when justice was heavily weighted in favour of the landowning class.

A special convict ship was commissioned to convey these poor wretches from Hampshire and Wiltshire. No fewer than one hundred and thirty-seven were transported from Winchester to Australia with little if any hope of ever seeing England and their families again. On 17 January, immediately before they were drafted to Portsmouth for embarkation, *The Times* correspondent visited Winchester gaol, and there "saw many of the convicts weeping bitterly, some burying their faces in their smock frocks, others wringing their hands convulsively, and others leaning for support against the wall of the yard, and unable to cast their eyes upwards." It is a sad page in Winchester's long story.

One big change occurred in 1835 which was probably not to the taste of some of the old rulers of the city. By the provisions of the Municipal Corporations Act of 1835 a system of town government, which had endured from the time of Edward I, if not earlier, was swept away, and a new order instituted. The old narrow franchise was abolished, and the townsfolk had more voice in the election of those who had the welfare of the place in their hands.

As the nineteenth century progressed modern invention began to awaken the moribund city, despite the conservatism of centuries. In the eighteenth century the city had been content with six public "oyle" lamps, but, twenty years after London had been lighted by gas, Winchester ventured upon the expensive business of lighting its streets by this new invention. The coming of the railway in 1839 was regarded with great suspicion by many of the citizens. It was something new, and would therefore destroy ancient customs. This anticipation was fulfilled in that it destroyed the cherished "navigation," the canal between Winchester and Southampton. But it initiated a period of new prosperity for the city. The line between Southampton and London was not completed until 1840, the eighteen miles between Winchester and Basingstoke necessitating much cutting and tunnelling.

Awakening prosperity and increasing population led to some useful public building. On the hill to the west of the city a new hospital was erected in the sixties. Miss Florence Nightingale, rightly counted the leading authority on nursing and hospital planning at that time, gave much thought to the plans. The hospital, which until then had been housed in Parchment Street, is claimed to be the oldest provincial hospital, having been founded in 1737 by a prebendary of Winchester Cathedral.

Some seven parish churches were built in the Victorian period, and six or seven free churches. The cathedral chapter also showed activity in improving the cathedral, both inside and out. A large space on the north, which had been neglected, was levelled and planted with trees. Soon after the Great Exhibition of 1851 Samuel Sebastian Wesley, then the organist of the cathedral, was sent by the chapter to inspect the great organ which Willis had exhibited there. The result was the chapter purchased half the organ. The other half went to America. The purchase then made forms the nucleus of the present organ. Several substantial additions have been made in recent years. Wesley lived in Kingsgate Street, and there composed several of his greatest anthems, as well as the popular tune "Aurelia." About the same time was living at Winchester College as master of the quiristers William Whiting, composer of the hymn, "For those in peril on the sea."

One piece of "improvement" carried out by a Victorian dean had very unexpected results. He initiated a system of drainage of the streams which flow through the close, and beneath the cathedral. This caused a gradual shrinkage of the peat upon which rested the huge timber baulks used by the early builders as their foundations. The result was that early in the present century signs of movement appeared in the walls and the stone groining, especially at the east end. The movements were found to be progressive, and soon huge masses of stone fell in the retro-choir. The work of making the cathedral safe occupied seven years, and cost nearly £120,000. The method applied was unique. Walkelyn's timber baulks were taken out piecemeal from beneath the foundations, and were replaced by concrete and masonry. This was done in a series of excavations, technically termed headings. Because of the depth of water in the headings a diver was employed to remove the timber, and lay a bed of concrete in each heading. This done, the water was pumped out, and masons completed the work up to the base of the old foundations.

Before this a carved wooden screen was placed at the west end of the choir. This was as a memorial to Bishop Samuel Wilberforce and to Dean Garnier. A little later a still more elaborate work was undertaken in the restoration of the great stone reredos, which, dating from the time of Cardinal Beaufort, had remained with its niches empty of effigies since the Reformation. An elaborate Renaissance screen, the work of Inigo Jones, presented to the cathedral by Charles II, was at last, and very properly, swept away. Fanny Burney, generations before, had had the good sense to satirize a taste which had erected such a thing in a Gothic edifice.

In 1873 the City Corporation built a new Guildhall at the lower end of the High Street. This took the place of the one built in the reign of Queen Anne at the corner of High Street and St. Thomas Street. The clock hanging from the latter building, as well as the leaden statue of Queen Anne facing the High Street, were presented to the city in 1713.

In 1885 the Didcot and Newbury Railway Company linked Winchester with the Great Western Railway at Didcot, but it was not until 1891 that this line was connected with that of the South Western Company at Shawford, thus permitting its trains to run into Southampton.

247

Since the Great War a considerable growth of the old city has taken place, particularly to the south, the garden suburb of Stanmore comprising nearly a thousand houses.

The most remarkable addition which has been made to the buildings of Winchester in modern times is the New Cloister set up by Winchester College as part of its memorial to the five hundred Wykehamists who gave their lives in the Great War, 1914–18. It lies just behind Commoners' Gate, the South African War Memorial, sometimes referred to by Wyke-hamists as Boer Gate. Some uninteresting buildings were cleared to make room for the cloister, which was in large measure the idea of the then headmaster, Dr. Rendall. It contains a profusion of emblem, linking with every unit of the British forces, land, sea, and air; it has reference to every part of the British Empire, to every one of the Allies in the War, and to every important centre in the county of Hampshire. A dedication, in superb English prose, runs along each of the four walls, the letters being picked out in black Hampshire flint let into light stone. In its area and in one or two of its broad features, reminiscent of Wykeham's fourteenth-century cloister, this new erection is a creation worthy of its object, and a superb addition to the many fine buildings of the college.

As has been noted, in the past the temporary vagaries of taste have done much to destroy or spoil things of beauty which the old city once possessed; quaint old shop fronts have given way to modern erections not always in keeping with the ancient architecture of the place. Fortunately, the advent of the Town Planning Acts, and more especially, a new spirit among those who govern the city, is likely to ensure that the changes which take place in the future will not alter too severely the general appearance of the city. A realization of the value of old and irreplaceable things has grown up, and there is a desire to conserve all that is worth conserving. So it may be that, while moving with the times, Winchester will keep its ancient beauty, its hoary buildings, its emerald garths, its limpid streams, its spacious downs, unscarred, unimpaired, for the delight of many generations yet to come.

PART II.—THE CITY

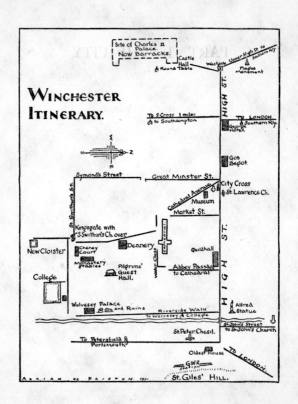

Winchester Itinerary.

Site of Charles II Palace. Now Barracks.

Castle Hall & Round Table

Westgate Upper High St to Southern Rly.

Plague monument

HIGH ST.

To S. Cross 1 mile & to Southampton

To LONDON & Southern Rly.

George Hotel.

God Begot.

Symond's Street

Great Minster St.

City Cross & St. Lawrence Ch.

Cathedral Avenue

Museum

Market St.

St. Swithun's St.

Kingsgate with S. Swithun's Ch. over

Cheney Court

Deanery

Cathedral

Guildhall

New Cloister

Monastery Stables

Pilgrims' Guest Hall.

Water Close

Abbey Passage to Cathedral

College

Wolvesey Palace and Ruins

Riverside Walk to Wolvesey & College

Alfred Statue

St. John's Street to St. John's Church

HIGH ST.

To Ptersfield & Portsmouth

St. Peter: Chesil.

Oldest House

To LONDON

G.W.R. Stn.

St. Giles' Hill.

ADRIAN DE ERISTON. 1921.

SECTION I

TRAVELLING to Winchester from London by motor-car there is a choice of two roads: (a) through Guildford, Farnham, and Alton; or (b) through Chiswick, Bagshot, and Basingstoke. The former route, which traverses in parts the medieval Pilgrims' Way from Winchester to Canterbury, is to be preferred for its more picturesque scenery and because, in its approach to Winchester over the eastern downs, it affords a magnificent prospect of the city and the Itchen valley.

Hempage (or Hampinges) Wood will be passed (R) about five miles from Winchester. It was here that Bishop Walkelyn cut the timber for the roof of his new cathedral in Winchester, clearing the wood in three days, and in so doing incurred the wrath of his cousin, William the Conqueror.

Nearing Winchester, on either side of the road, will be seen the residuum of the camps which housed many thousands of British and Colonial troops during the Great War.

About a mile outside the city (R) will be seen the ragged slopes of Winnal Down where, in the fall of 1914, were quartered, in atrocious weather conditions, that glorious harbinger of the rising might of the Colonies, the first battalion of Princess Patricia's Canadian Light Infantry, a regiment recruited in Canada, but whose units had seen service in almost every corps of the British forces. On this same spot, in the later years of the war, when the place had been

253

transformed into a permanent camp with concrete huts and mess rooms, many thousands of United States troops spent a period of training before proceeding to the Western Front.

On the left of the main road is the long stretch of down which was the site of the Morn Hill Camp, where many thousands of Londoners spent their period of training for service in the war. Some of their practice trenches may still be discerned on the southern scarp. Across the valley, a mile to the south (*L*), and behind the conical hill of St. Catherine, lies Hazeley Down, well known to many other Londoners, Canadians, and Newfoundlanders, who spent their time of training there. For, during the Great War, Winchester, which was the gathering point of the bowmen who were to win on the fields of Crécy, Poitiers, and Agincourt, again became the place of preparation of hundreds of thousands of troops destined for service in France and Flanders.

The war has passed, but the downs overlooking the city still bear the marks of that terrible time. Most of the war huts are gone. The few which remain are now peaceful cottages. Though many huts have been cleared the concrete floors remain in many places, defying the weeds and creeping couch grass. Broken asbestos, rusty iron, fragments of concrete, lie in heaps waiting for patient Nature to reduce to dust and cover with verdure these ugly relics of an ugly time.

The road drops downhill, and the city comes into view. The long valley of the Itchen, with its lush meadows, is beautiful at all times, but is best of all in spring, and in early morning for preference. The city lies as in a green cup, and in the centre, "like some great prehistoric monster," sits the cathedral.

The City

On the other side of the valley, on the slope west of the city, is an object which arrests the eye. It is the ventilating shaft of the county prison, that sinister erection immortalized by Thomas Hardy in the concluding chapter of *Tess of the D'Urbervilles*.

A yet more striking view of the city may be obtained from the brow of St. Giles's Hill. This can be reached by car, turning down Stratton Road (*L*) immediately the downs are left behind; then first to the right, which will bring one out to the open sward where, in medieval times, the great Fair of St. Giles was held every September. From this vantage point the city lies at one's feet, the narrow High Street running up to the West Gate; the Guildhall immediately in front, dwarfed, however, by the immense mass of the cathedral just behind; immediately to the left the ruins of Wolvesey Castle, with the bishop's palace close by, and the grey buildings of the college just beyond in the same line; and a mile farther away in the same direction the fine old Church of St. Cross, with its hospital, founded by Bishop Henry de Blois. To the right may be seen the Church of St. John, built in the thirteenth century, contrasting sharply with the new Roman Catholic Church visible half a mile distant in the same line.

Proceeding a short distance (*R*) the main road is again reached; then, dropping downhill very steeply for a quarter of a mile, the city is entered over the old stone bridge, successor to that which tradition says was built by St. Swithun. A convenient motor-car park is found in the Broadway, under the shadow of Thornycroft's statue of Alfred the Great.

The Guildhall (*L*) is modern, dating from 1878. The old cannon on the right came into the possession of the city after the Crimean War. It has been the

255

occasion of two riots by the citizens (in 1883 and in 1908) when attempts were made by the Corporation to remove it to other sites. St. John's Rooms (*R*), an uninteresting and barn-like eighteenth-century erection, was for a time the Guildhall. The little chapel adjoining is medieval, and still serves as the worshipping place of the inmates of the Hospital of St. John immediately behind.

There is quick access to the cathedral by way of Abbey Passage (entrance at the left-hand corner of the Guildhall) and the Water Close. This walk affords good opportunity for observing the external characteristics of the edifice on the east and south, and on the way, the quaint back streets of the city. But, if time permits, it is preferable to walk back a few yards to the City Bridge, where the old City Mill may be inspected; then, entering the Weirs walk, to follow the river round to Wolvesey, and the college. A great part of the high flint wall seen on the right of the walk is medieval. It formed the outer defence of Wolvesey Castle, and was constructed by Bishop Henry de Blois in the Stephen-Matilda faction; it probably followed the line of the earlier wall which defended the castle of King Alfred. It is even possible that in some parts the wall is the original Saxon, restored and strengthened by de Blois, for in places can be seen red bricks, which, judged by their size and texture, are Roman. The Saxons were ignorant of brick-making, but they frequently used Roman bricks as rubble in the construction of their walls.

In the course of this walk by the river the swiftness of the stream will be noticed. The evidence of the Ordnance Survey is that the fall between Winchester and Southampton is nine feet per mile. Looking across the river (*L*) some quaint old houses may be

CATHEDRAL AND COLLEGE FROM THE CASTLE OF WINCHESTER

(Photo by F. A. Grant, Winchester)

seen. A brief deviation over the wooden bridge by the mill to the left will enable the visitor to inspect a curious suburb of old Winchester, known as the Wharf. A seventeenth-century dwelling, a few yards

"THE DOG AND DUCK," A SEVENTEENTH-CENTURY DWELLING,
FORMERLY A TAVERN

from the mill, and skirted on every side by a thoroughfare, was until recent years a hostelry, known as the "Dog and Duck."

Returning to the Weirs walk, the entrance to Wolvesey is reached (*R*). A postern gate in the wall gives access to a path which leads to the ruins, passing, on the left, the official residence of the Bishops of Winchester, designed by Wren, and built by Bishop

S

Trelawney, one of the famous Seven Bishops who defied James II. The more beautiful part of the palace, built a little earlier by Bishop Morley, Trelawney's predecessor, was pulled down in 1781 by Bishop Brownlow North, because he was too mean to spend the money on its upkeep. After the division of the diocese of Winchester, when the Bishop of Winchester ceased to live at Farnham Castle, Wolvesey palace was in 1928 repaired and reconditioned as an episcopal residence.

Returning to the road, and proceeding westward along College Street, the college is reached (*L*). Over the entrance will be noticed a statue of the Virgin and Child, a fourteenth-century piece of art which had the rare good fortune to escape the fury of the iconoclasts at the Reformation, and again, in the Civil War of the seventeenth century, the vandalism of the Puritan troopers. The gateway and the old brewhouse are part of William of Wykeham's original foundation. The red-brick addition to the left of the gate, the warden's house, was erected in the seventeenth century.

The buildings may be visited on application at the porter's lodge, entrance within the main gate (*R*). Passing within the gate and viewing it from the south side, some idea of the troublous times when the college was built may be gained. It was being built when the echoes of the great upheaval of 1381, known as the Peasants' Revolt, had scarcely died away, and only fifty years after Southampton had been burnt by the French.

Passing through a second gateway the visitor arrives in Chamber Court, a quadrangle around which are the rooms of the scholars, the Second Master's apartments (N.W.) Dining Hall (S.W.), and Chapel

(S.). It is at the entrance to Chamber Court that distinguished visitors are received by the whole college, assembled in hollow square, the head prefect reciting an address of welcome in Latin. This ceremonious welcome is termed an "Ad Portas."

In these old chambers live the seventy scholars who are upon the original foundation; hence "Foundationers." Those scholars not upon the foundation, who live in "houses," south of St. Swithun Street, are termed "Commoners." None below the rank of prefect is allowed to cross Chamber Court with covered head, no matter what the weather.

The severity of the architecture of these old buildings is nevertheless pleasing to the eye. Wykeham, in his building, made free use of the local material, flint, using ashlar where strength was needed. He apparently considered flint not dignified enough for the chapel, so used quarry stone alone for its construction.

Chapel is original as far as the shell is concerned. The seating and wainscoting are entirely modern, although in perfect keeping with the structure itself (built probably under the direction of William Winford, Wykeham's architect in the transformation of the nave of Winchester Cathedral). The tower is not Wykeham's. Originally circular in form, it was rebuilt in square style in the fifteenth century, and then, becoming insecure, it was pulled down and rebuilt in 1863.

Dining Hall, reached by a stone staircase in the south-west corner of Chamber Court, contains much of interest: the massive trestle tables on which many generations of young Wykehamists have dined and supped; the square wooden trenchers from which they used to eat their food, using ramparts of potato

259

for the conservation of the gravy, and, the first course disposed of, turning the trencher to use the other side for pudding; the old chest into which fragments of food were placed for the poor; the painting of the Founder, the oldest in existence, dating from the end of the sixteenth century; some fine tapestries, said to have been brought to College about 1570; and not least, some superb examples of modern stained glass designed by Professor R. M. Y. Gleadowe, the present art master.

In the kitchen, at the foot of the stone staircase leading to Hall, may be seen a curious emblematical painting, the work of a scholar of the seventeenth century.

Through the archway (S.) between Chapel and Hall, Old Cloister is reached, with Fromond's Chantry standing in the centre of the garth. The chantry was built about fifty years later than the original fabric, of which Old Cloister formed part. In former times burials took place here of deceased Fellows, and the gravestone is shown of one scholar who "went to heaven instead of to Oxford," while still in his teens. On a pillar of the arcading at the north-west corner may be seen incised the name of Thomas Ken, afterwards Prebendary of Winchester, and later Bishop of Bath and Wells. On the walls are many brasses and tablets commemorating Wykehamists of several centuries. Flint forms the principal material of the walls, and the roof slabs are of stone.

Immediately to the west of Old Cloister is School, a red-brick building erected towards the end of the seventeenth century. There is no certainty that Wren had any hand in the actual designing of the place, but it is evident his influence is there, in the style. On the wall may be seen a curious symbolical admonition to students, urging industry or departure,

BREWHOUSE, WINCHESTER COLLEGE

and threatening corporal punishment as an alternative. In this room, immediately before the break-up for the summer vacation, the whole School with Warden, Fellows, Headmaster, and Staff, assemble for the annual prize-day—in Wykehamical parlance, "Medal-speaking." In the evening of this day the old college song, *Dulce Domum*, is sung in Meads, the enclosed field to the south of School. Immediately before the break-up for the Christmas vacation another more curious ceremony is observed by the students, and called by them "Illumina." In the old stone wall surrounding Meads are many small niches, cut by the penknives of bygone Wykehamists. These are termed "temples," and on a given night these niches are filled with lighted candles, the effect in the darkness being impressive.

The red-brick buildings to the west, Moberly Library and the rest, are modern, as also are those farther to the south, with the exception of the sanatorium, called by Wykehamists "Sick House," which belongs to the seventeenth century. By far the most interesting building among these modern erections is New Cloister, built as part of the College Memorial to those Wykehamists who fell in the Great War. Visitors must seek entrance via Kingsgate Street.

Returning to College Street, and proceeding west, the Headmaster's house is passed, a modern building, but interesting for its façade of squared flint masonry, a fine example of local craftsmanship. Almost next door will be seen the house where Jane Austen, the novelist, lived her last days. The beautiful Italian gardens opposite show the present trend of Wykehamical aspiration, initiated by the former Headmaster, Dr. Rendall.

The City

At the end of College Street, turning left into Kingsgate Street, the entrance to the College War Cloister is reached (L) after about two hundred yards. It is questionable whether at any public or private institution in England there has been set up so perfectly conceived and constructed a memorial. It was designed and placed in such fashion that twice or thrice daily in term time "commoners" should pass through it and, in their passing, be reminded of the five hundred and more who went from the college and died on land, sea, or in air, during the Great War.

The details of this War Cloister say nothing to dull minds, but to those gifted with a spark of imagination they sing a pæan of delight and thanksgiving. It is a quadrangle full of symbolism, a volume in stone, a temple in which are laid up the banners of the British Empire, a bridge linking past with present and future, a crown in which have been set gems from the four corners of the Empire.

Here is an insistent proclamation of the oneness of the Empire; here is a trumpet call of courteous service of humanity which is the keynote of Wyke-hamical teaching and tradition; here is the quiet, awful record of human anguish and bereavement, of swift, irremedial translation of young lives of highest promise, and here is also the silent record of zealous service rendered by the living to the dead. For, not only those who worked with cultured brain to perfect design and ornament, but those who came after to put stone to stone, and flint to flint, worked, as unto God, to make of this place a monument of perfect workmanship for the sake of those whose names their work enshrines.

The stately prose inscription around the four walls

embodies the spirit of the place. The workmanship which set the words in flint within incisions of white stone, and the artistry which grouped the phrases in such position that significant words might appear at the end of each vista, need indicating, lest they be overlooked.[1]

On the walls are tablets bearing the names of those who fell; on the corbels of the arcading and on the roof beams are the badges of the many units of the British and Colonial forces; and in each of the four corners are symbols indicating the three great Commonwealths of the Empire, and India. In the floor at each corner are set stones brought from British Columbia, Table Mountain, New South Wales, and Delhi, while at Meads entrance are set in the floor stones from the ruins of Ypres. Above this entrance, on the east side, is set a modern representation of the Madonna and Child. It is instructive to contrast this with the fourteenth-century work over the old gate in College Street.

Retracing one's steps along Kingsgate Street in order to visit the cathedral, Kings Gate must be

[1] The inscription, the composition of Dr. M. J. Rendall, former Headmaster, runs as follows: "Thanks be to God for the service of these five hundred Wykehamists who were found faithful unto death amid the manifold chances of the Great War. In the day of battle they forgat not God, Who created them to do His will, nor their country the stronghold of freedom, nor their school the mother of godliness and discipline. Strong in this three-fold faith they went forth from home and kindred to the battlefields of the world, and, treading the path of duty and sacrifice, laid down their lives for mankind. Thou, therefore, for whom they died, seek not thine own, but serve as they served, and in peace or in war bear thyself ever as Christ's soldier, gentle in all things, valiant in action, steadfast in adversity."

passed. It stands at the junction of Kingsgate and
College Streets, and is a thirteenth-century erection,
built after an earlier gate had been burnt during the
de Montfort fighting in the reign of Henry III. Over
the gate is the little Church of St. Swithun, which is

PILGRIMS' GUEST HOUSE IN THE CLOSE

one of the very few instances in England of a church
built over a thoroughfare. It was the place of
worship, before the Reformation, for the lay workers
of the Monastery of St. Swithun who lived outside
the monastery. Until the Great War services were
held there regularly, it being the church of the
parish of St. Swithun.

Passing through Kings Gate the lofty wall of the
Cathedral Close faces one, and to the right is the main
gate of the Close, through which a pleasing view is
obtained of the façade of Cheyney Court, a Tudor

building in which, until 1820, successive bishops of Winchester held their courts for the administration of affairs in the Soke; that is, all that part of Winchester which lay outside the walls, and, therefore, beyond the jurisdiction of the mayor and his fellows.

Entering the Close the visitor will notice the irregularly-built timber and brick wall abutting on Cheyney Court at its east end. This is the western wall of the monastery stables, and is a very early example of the use of brick by English builders. Following the road the visitor comes first to a house of one of the residentiary canons of the cathedral, a building uninteresting in itself, but having on its left or northern side the remains of the old Guest Hall of the monastery. Permission is necessary before it can be inspected.

Turning to the left the way leads to the Deanery, formerly the Prior's Hall, with its beautiful Early English Cloister of pointed arches. Viewed from a little distance it is perhaps the most beautiful building in the Close. The red-brick wing on the right is the Long Gallery, erected for the accommodation of Charles II in his last years, when he was contemplating the building of a royal palace in Winchester. In the floor of the entrance porch may be seen a fragment of Roman pavement, found when excavating on the south side of the nave of the cathedral; also some medieval tiles.

The modern building opposite the Deanery is the Judges' Lodgings, where the Judges of Assize stay when on circuit three times a year. The narrow cul-de-sac to the west is Dome Alley. The last house on the right is that in which Izaak Walton lived out his closing years, with his son-in-law, Dr. Hawkins, and where he died in 1683.

The greensward to the west of the Deanery is the remains of the cloister garth of the monastery. It was originally surrounded by a cloister, the only remaining fragment of which may be seen on the right, five Norman arches linking the south transept wall of the cathedral with the Deanery buildings. On the south wall of the cathedral may be seen grooves in which were set the wooden trusses carrying the Cloister roof. The flying buttresses of stone, supporting the south wall of the cathedral, are modern, being part of the preservation scheme carried out in 1905–12.

Before entering the cathedral the visitor may observe the external characteristics of the edifice. From the garth much Norman work is visible, the outer walls, the tower, and the south transept. Later work appears in the window heads of the nave, and in some of those of the transept, but the tower remains practically as it was constructed by Bishop William Giffard in the twelfth century, after the first tower fell in 1107. The tower is an excellent example of Decorated Norman architecture.

Turning to the right the visitor may pass through the slype, over which is the cathedral library. The southern wall of the south transept is bolstered up by this medieval addition, and with reason, for the wall at its highest point is more than four feet out of the perpendicular. Hence, when the work of preservation was in progress (1905–12) massive buttresses were built to counter this deflection. Moving round to the east end of the building several interesting architectural details will be observed. The first that will strike the eye will be the faulty alignment of the southern wall of the retro-choir, the work of Bishop de Lucy (thirteenth century). It is obvious that the wall is much out of the perpendicular, especially at its easternmost end. Moreover, if the last four courses of stone in the parapet are carefully examined it will be seen that the masons increased the thickness of each course as they worked from west to east, in order that they might make their last course level by the plumbline. This is clear evidence that de Lucy's building had sunk down upon its foundation of beech logs even while it was being constructed, and that it was considerably out of the level before the parapet was completed. The Lady Chapel at the extreme east end was built about the end of the fifteenth century, and the transformation of the Norman windows of the presbytery to the style of Wykeham was carried out early in the sixteenth. The eastern part of the cathedral was threatened with collapse early in the twentieth century, owing to the drying of the foundations, and the consequent shrinking of the timber raft upon which much of the building had been reared. The preservation works carried out under the late Dean Furneaux included the removal of the timber foundations, and the substitution of concrete and masonry.

Retracing one's steps to the garth it is preferable to pass the south door, and go through Laud's Passage at the south-west corner of the cathedral to the north side of the building. Following the paved walk until one arrives at a point opposite the north wall of the presbytery, the best view of this elevation of the cathedral is obtained. The immense length of the building will be noted (it is the longest cathedral in Europe, save St. Peter's at Rome). The original length of the Norman building can be seen, except for the apse at the east end, which was removed by de Lucy when he extended the retro-choir. De

Lucy's work is not so lofty as that of Walkelyn's, but the grace of the Early English style is very manifest. The north transept stands almost untouched in its Norman massiveness, but there is in the north wall a Catherine Wheel or rose window, of later date. The north wall of the nave is especially interesting, architecturally, because it presents a comparison between the styles of Bishop Edyngton and Bishop William of Wykeham. Edyngton pulled down the Norman west front, with its flanking towers, and he began to reconstruct the cathedral from the west end in the English Perpendicular style. The first two windows, counting from the west, are his; the remainder are Wykeham's. By contrast with the later graceful work of Wykeham, Edyngton's style appears squat and clumsy; yet by comparison with the rude Norman of three centuries earlier it marked an immense stride forward.

While contemplating the cathedral from this point it will perchance be of interest to the visitor to be reminded that upon this very spot stood the rival of the old church, New Minster, erected by Edward the Elder at the wish of his father, Alfred the Great. In 1110 it was removed to Hyde, half a mile to the north, thereafter being known as Hyde Abbey.

Some of the windows of the north transept are interesting (as also are those of the south transept) as showing the crude transformation which was wrought in endeavours to replace Norman with Early English work. Often the ribs and mullions of the newer style are inserted within the original window opening, so that the window is now a mixture of both styles.

Before retracing one's steps to the west front it will be of interest to walk a few yards down a narrow

269

walk to the north to inspect the ancient tower of St. Michael's Church, with its doorway in the Decorated Norman style, and an old sundial on the wall above. The church itself is modern and uninteresting.

Proceeding now westwards past the lime avenue and the King's Royal Rifle Corps Memorial (*R*) and the Hampshire War Memorial (*L*), a vantage point is reached from which the west front of the cathedral may be viewed. This front is of interest as a specimen of the English Perpendicular style of architecture, but its severity of outline, and almost entire absence of anything in the shape of adornment, makes it resemble nothing so much as a gridiron reared on end. The empty niches on either side of the central doorway at one time contained statues of saints, but these were destroyed at the Reformation. The statue of St. Swithun at the apex is modern.

Entering the cathedral by the west door a glorious vista confronts the visitor. There are probably few finer specimens of human architecture to be found in the whole world. Many there are with more ornate finish, with exquisite intricacies of workmanship, but there is none so perfect of its kind as this superb Gothic nave, the longest in Europe. Here may be seen the full beauty of English Perpendicular, a style which displays the supreme character of line in architecture, unbroken by unnecessary ornament. It is a marvellous canopy of stone, conveying in the length of its vista and the loftiness of its graceful arch, something of the mystery and impressiveness of the forest glade. The massiveness of the huge pillars, an inheritance from the Norman builders, is in perfect keeping with the soaring roof which is ornamented just sufficiently to satisfy, and not enough to surfeit. The carved bosses along the line of the apex of the arch, and the smaller cusps at the points where the ribs meet each other, are all the carved details in this wonderful creation. The same beauty of style is seen in the arcading which separates the north and south aisles from the nave, and in the aisles themselves. Standing at the west door and looking eastward one may see the two styles of architecture, Perpendicular in the nave and Norman in the great arches of the tower. These latter, like the north and south transepts, were left untouched by Wykeham and his successors. Standing at the west end of the south aisle one may see three styles of architecture, for at the extreme east are visible the Early English arches of de Lucy.

Having noted the graceful lines of the window heads as put in by Wykeham, it is interesting to observe from the inside the simplicity of the design, and see how, from practically the same curves as characterize the Early English arch, the Perpendicular style is achieved. On either side a vertical mullion is inserted, to strike the arch midway in its curve, the space thus created being filled in with stone panelling.

The internal appearance of the edifice before it received its Perpendicular transformation may be judged in some measure by a contemplation of the north and south transepts. The arcading between nave and aisles was practically the same as now appears in these transepts, with a timber roof carried upon huge oaken rafters. The massive cushion capitals, and square abaci, of the pillars carrying the arches, and the wide mortar joints of the masonry of the transepts, indicate the earliest type of Norman workmanship.

Another interesting architectural feature will be

271

seen in the retro-choir. That is the curious coffin-like effect which was made by the later transformers of the edifice at the point where Walkelyn left an apse. Behind the great stone screen the arcading narrows perceptibly to meet a wall of less width than the screen.

In the presbytery, or choir, there are several striking features. The principal item to notice is the enormous size of the great piers which carry the tower. They are oblong in shape, and larger than those in any similar church in England. The builders evidently were determined that the tower should not fall a second time. Not only were the piers designed on a vast scale, but much greater care was taken with the work of laying the stones, the mortar joints being much finer than in the nave piers and in the transepts. Moreover, within and without, the window openings were very finely decorated. For some centuries after completion the whole of the interior of the tower was visible from ground level, but in the seventeenth century the tower was roofed in with timber groining, as the remainder of the presbytery had been roofed in earlier in the style of the nave. This wooden groining was painted to look like stone. The best that can be said for it is that it improved the acoustics of the choir. The stone arcading enclosing the presbytery on the north and south was practically the last considerable addition to the building; it was put in during the episcopate of Bishop Fox, and is dated 1524. Builders had been busy on the fane for over four hundred years, each building to the taste prevailing in his own period. There are upwards of one hundred and seventy masons' marks in various parts of the edifice.

The great screen, or reredos, is a thing of striking

beauty, although its archæological interest is limited to the screen itself, which dates from the fifteenth century. The figures which fill the niches were put in towards the end of the nineteenth century. The face of Queen Victoria, as well as that of a Mayor of Winchester, appears in the screen.

There was a Renaissance screen, the work of Inigo Jones, in the choir for many years, it having been put there in Stuart times, but a return of the sense of the fitness of things caused the removal of this anachronism.

The elaborate service books upon the altar were the gift of Charles II to the church, and the carved altar rails are the work of Grinling Gibbons, of the same period.

The somewhat cumbrous throne of the bishop, on the south side of the choir, was built during the episcopate of Trelawney, one of the Seven Bishops who dared to oppose the will of James II. It was of him that west-country folk sang:

> And shall Trelawney die?
> And shall Trelawney die?
> Then thirty thousand Cornishmen
> Will know the reason why.

The superb oaken stalls date from early in the fourteenth century. The carving is exquisite, and as fine as any that can be seen in the country of medieval workmanship. The carving on the choir "miserere" seats is curious, and in some instances shows the exuberant humour of the monkish craftsmen. These seats were designed to give a measure of rest to the monks taking part in the services, but are so poised that at the slightest appearance of somnolence the sitter would be thrown forward, a clever device to prevent sleeping on duty. The very

T

finely carved pulpit is of somewhat later date, having been put in by Prior Silkstede in 1520. His name is commemorated in the skeins of silk in the panels, and a black horse. The wooden screen at the west end of the choir is modern. It is a memorial to Bishop Samuel Wilberforce (known to the profane as "Soapy Sam") and to Dean Garnier.

The tomb in the centre of the choir is popularly referred to as Rufus's tomb, but considerable doubt is entertained whether the remains of the Red King lie there. He is said to have been buried immediately under the tower, and the tomb is certainly in that position; but there are traditions that his bones were removed elsewhere, and ultimately found a resting-place in one of the mortuary chests. The tomb was opened in 1868, and a skeleton of a man probably 5 ft. 8 in. or 5 ft. 9 in. in height was found within. This did not settle the problem, for while some were satisfied that the skeleton was that of Rufus, others thought it was more probably that of a great cleric.

The mortuary chests, or coffers, which stand on the Renaissance side-screens of the choir, are reputed to contain the bones of Saxon kings, queens, and bishops. Some destruction was done to those on the north screen by the Parliamentarian troops during the Civil War, and two new chests were constructed, and such bones as could be gathered together after the troops had used them as missiles to smash the stained-glass windows of the church were put in the new receptacles.

The organ is largely the work of Willis, and was exhibited by that great organ builder in the Great Exhibition of 1851. Samuel Sebastian Wesley was the organist of the cathedral at the time, and the instrument was purchased by the dean and chapter

WINCHESTER COLLEGE CHAPEL AND SCHOOL FROM MEADS

upon his recommendation. It has been considerably added to in recent years. Its action is tubular pneumatic, and the energy to provide both action and speaking-wind is supplied by a gas engine stowed away in a recess off the north transept. The engine is required to lift a weight of over three tons in order to operate the action.

Returning to the nave, it is worth while to note the effect when standing upon the dais. The eye will inevitably be drawn to the great west window, which is 53 ft. in height, and 34 ft. wide. It is interesting not only for its size, but also for the quaint patchwork of stained glass with which it is filled. This is said to have been the work of zealous churchmen after the destruction wrought at the Reformation; they gathered together all the stained glass which could be found after the spoliators had done their work, and then, with infinite pains, assembled the fragments into the strange picture which now arouses the interest, and often the admiration, of visitors. Here and there about the cathedral may be discerned fragments of medieval stained glass in the window heads, but the so-called reformers did their destruction pretty thoroughly in the larger openings.

The nave contains many monuments, several of outstanding interest. At the west end are a large number of military memorials, chiefly of officers belonging to the King's Royal Rifle Corps, the Rifle Brigade, and the Hampshire Regiment, the depots of which are at the barracks on the site of the old castle, and what was later to have been the palace of Charles II. Elaborate caskets contain the books in which are recorded the names of the officers and men of those several regiments who fell in the Great War.

The two statues just within the west door are by

Hubert de Sueur, a seventeenth-century sculptor, and they represent James I and Charles I. The bodies were cast in the same mould.

The font of black Tournai marble on the north side of the nave is of twelfth-century date. It was the gift of Bishop Henry de Blois. In this font were baptized Henry III, and Arthur, firstborn son of Henry VII, the prince who died too soon to be king. The quaint carvings depict scenes in the story of St. Nicholas, patron saint of sailors and children. One of the stories shown is of the restoration to life by the saint of three children who had been murdered by a wicked innkeeper, and whose bodies had been salted down for food.

Opposite the font on the south side is the chantry of William of Wykeham. He is said to have chosen this spot for the erection of his chantry and tomb because it was here that he worshipped as a boy. Like the buildings and other things at Winchester College this chantry and its effigies escaped destruction during the Reformation, and in the Civil War, by the zealous defence of Wykehamists. The effigy on the tomb, and the little figures at the feet, are contemporary. These three figures are said to represent the three chief assistants of Wykeham in his architectural works, William Winford, Simon Membury, and John Wayte.

On the south side, near the dais, is the chantry of Wykeham's immediate predecessor, Bishop Edyngton. On the sculptured adornment of the vestments of the effigy may be seen a representation of the ancient swastika, or fylfot cross. On a pier on the south side of the nave, opposite this chantry, may be seen the seventeenth-century brass commemorating the bravery of Colonel Boles at Alton in the Civil War.

Passing to the retro-choir, by way of the south transept, the visitor will notice the iron gates at the top of the steps. These exhibit what is believed to be the oldest example of wrought-ironwork to be found in England. These gates were used to shut off the monks' part of the church from the army of pilgrims constantly visiting the shrine of St. Swithun during medieval times. In passing the south transept an ancient muniment chest and two quaint old settles may be inspected.

At the east end of the retro-choir will be found the Lady Chapel (centre), Bishop Langton's Chapel (S.), and the Chapel of the Guardian Angels (N.). Langton died of the plague on the eve of his translation to Canterbury in 1501.

The most beautiful chantry as far as intricate workmanship is concerned is that of Waynflete (N.), the founder of Magdalen College, Oxford, the authorities of which keep the chantry in repair. Waynflete was Headmaster of Winchester, and was appointed by Henry VI to be the first Headmaster of Eton, the idea being that he should implant into the new college the spirit of Winchester College. Opposite (S.) is the chantry of the great bishop and cardinal, Beaufort. The effigy of his victim, Joan of Arc, the work of a French artist, stands at the side of the Lady Chapel looking over at her one-time judge. Near Beaufort's chantry is the tomb of an unknown crusader. The remaining two chantries are those of Fox (S.) and Gardiner (N.). Each has a "cadaver" in stone in a cavity at the side.

In the north transept may be seen the renovated Chapel of the Holy Sepulchre, also a modern and very beautiful tomb, the work of Bertram Mackennal. It is the tomb of General Buller, of South African fame.

About the church may be seen many monuments, or memorial windows and tablets, some having wide interest. Such is the memorial to Izaak Walton whose work, *The Compleat Angler*, is a classic. His memorial window and tomb may be seen in the little chapel on the south-east of the south transept. Another memorial of more than passing interest is the window commemorating the work of Jane Austen, the novelist. This is near the black font, on the north side of the nave. Her tomb slab may be seen in the floor of the north aisle close by the window. Another memorial of slight literary interest is that in the south aisle of the nave, close to the south door, erected to the memory of Joseph Warton, Headmaster of Winchester College, and a close friend of Dr. Johnson.

For those who are interested in statistics it may be here set down that the total length of the cathedral is 556½ ft. The length of the nave is 250 ft. The total breadth of the building at the transepts is 217 ft. The tower is 138 ft. high, and the height of the nave to the external ridge of the roof is 109 ft. Internally the height of the nave to the ridge rib is 77 ft.

SECTION II

WHEN arriving in Winchester by Southern Railway, or by car over the London-Southampton main road, a different itinerary should be followed. If walking from the railway station, the visitor may either leave the Station Approach via City Road and Jewry Street to reach the High Street at the George Hotel, or, as is preferable, he may take the Station Path, following the railway for a little distance southwards, then turning down Upper High Street to reach the West Gate, with the Plague Monument close by. This would be to approach the West Gate as a traveller from the west would have done in medieval times.

The West Gate, which is scheduled as a national monument, dates back to the thirteenth century in its oldest part, but the west side was constructed in the fourteenth century. The grooves in which the portcullis slid still remain, and on the western side, the battlements, through which heated substances could be poured upon attackers, are in good preservation. The passageway on the south side is modern. The gate itself was used for long periods as a prison, and in its lower parts were confined poor debtors who used to importune passers-by for alms, holding out collecting-boxes on poles. The upper floor of the gate is now used as a museum in which are kept many interesting relics, including the standard weights and measures, the ancient moot horn, with which in medieval times town's meetings were summoned, felons' wrist and ankle shackles, and a "suit" of irons in which a condemned felon was to have been hanged after execution. Tradition says he was measured for his "suit" by a local blacksmith immediately after his condemnation, but a fortunate reprieve arrived, and the irons were not required. From the roof a fine view of the High Street and St. Giles's Hill can be obtained.

From the West Gate the visitor should proceed up Castle Hill, past the new County Council buildings to reach the Castle Hall, one of the most historic buildings of the country; for here on a number of occasions the English Parliament assembled. It is the only part remaining of the great castle of Norman and Plantagenet kings, and it has for centuries been the centre where the king's justice is dispensed for the County of Southampton, or Hampshire. Many notable trials have taken place here, such as that of Sir Walter Raleigh for alleged conspiracy in 1603, and that of Dame Alice Lisle before Judge Jeffreys in 1685. On the west wall hangs the reputed Round Table of King Arthur, a piece of Early English carpentry which it would be hard to match anywhere. It is of oak, 18 ft. in diameter, adze-finished. Mortice holes at the back seem to prove that the table once had legs, but for many centuries it has hung in this Great Hall, an object of interest to the curious. A writer of the second half of the fourteenth century speaks of the table as a hoary relic in his time. It originally hung on the eastern wall, being moved when the modern assize courts were constructed in 1872, and the eastern wall pierced for their entrance.

To the left of the Round Table may be seen an ancient speaking-tube. Popularly termed the King's Lug, it is supposed to have been constructed to enable the king to listen to the progress of business in the Great Hall while concealed in a chamber behind.

The dais at the foot of the east wall has disappeared save for a few fragments. In front now stands Sir Alfred Gilbert's statue of Queen Victoria, in bronze.

Originally of Norman construction, evidence of which is to be seen in a piece of masonry at the north-east corner inside, the Great Hall has undergone reconstruction at least twice. A great amount of work was done upon it in the thirteenth century, during the reign of Henry III, and it was then transformed in its appearance from Norman to Early English style, the window and door openings being constructed with pointed in place of round arches. The beautiful fluted pillars are of Purbeck marble, and were put in during this reconstruction, and glass window frames were introduced. They were not fixed, but hung upon huge iron staples, some of which are still in their original position. A little over a hundred years later further reconstruction had to be undertaken because the thrust of the heavy roof was pushing the roof pillars out of the perpendicular. Consequently, in the reign of Richard II, the outer walls were raised in height, and the roof altered, but the roof pillars could not be returned to the upright. This is obvious even to the most casual eye. On the north side of the hall there are the remains of a sally port, and on the south may be seen the floor and part of the walls of what may have been a dungeon.

Around the Castle Square are the buildings of the Hampshire County Council. A quarter of a mile up the Romsey Road (*L*) are the County Prison and the Royal Hampshire County Hospital.

The High Street (*R*) may now be traversed. It contains much that will be of interest to the visitor, although most of the buildings have been modernized.

not always in keeping with the old-time architecture of the place. The George Hotel (*L*), the oldest hostelry in the city, still preserves much of its eighteenth-century atmosphere, that being the period of the present building, but there has been a hostelry on the spot for upwards of five hundred years. A little farther down the street is the hostel of God Begot, a Tudor building (modern front) erected upon the site of the tiny manor of God Begot, which was given to the Church by the widow of King Cnut.

On the opposite side of the street is the quaint bow-fronted office of the *Hampshire Chronicle*, one of the oldest journals in the country. The office front is cotemporaneous with the founding of the newspaper in 1772. Just below is the old Guildhall, with the town clock hanging over the street. The curfew is tolled from the tower above at 8 o'clock each evening. The statue on the front is of Queen Anne. It is of lead, and is one of many which were cast and distributed among provincial towns about 1713. The clock and the statue were given to the city by the Members of Parliament of the time, and were to commemorate the Peace of Utrecht.

The City Cross, sometimes called the Butter Cross because in former days it was the centre of the butter market, is a relic of which the citizens are proud. It was built in the fifteenth century in the Perpendicular style, but it has been impaired architecturally by some modern restorations. The city nearly lost it in 1770, for the Corporation sold it to the owner of Cranbury Park, four miles distant, but popular outcry made them reverse their decision.

Immediately behind the City Cross is a fine old Tudor building, probably older than God Begot House. It screens the fifteenth-century Church of

283

St. Lawrence, the entrance of which is on the east side of the archway leading to the square and the cathedral. At this church, which is entirely surrounded by buildings, every new bishop of the diocese "rings himself into" his episcopate, thereafter going in procession with his clergy down the beautiful lime avenue to the west front of the cathedral for his enthronement. Opposite the entrance to St. Lawrence will be noticed a Norman pillar and capital. This is considered to be a relic from the palace of William the Conqueror which stood upon the spot.

Passing for a moment into the square the visitor will find it worth while, if time permit, to visit the City Museum, in which are stored a number of interesting local relics. The museum itself is a modern building standing on or very close to the site where took place the public executions until the close of the seventeenth century. Here it was that Dame Alice Lisle was beheaded after sentence by Judge Jeffreys in 1685. The lime avenue, stretching from the entrance to the museum to the west front of the cathedral, was planted early in the eighteenth century. On either side in earlier days was the principal church-yard of Winchester. Several curious tombstones still stand, notably one to a certain grenadier, quartered at Winchester, who died of a fever through drinking small beer.

The overhanging shops below the City Cross go by the name of the Pentice, or Penthouse. In Tudor times it was carried as far as Market Street. Several of the buildings are of Tudor date, but the fronts have been reconstructed.

In the lower part of the High Street are the Guild-hall (S.), St. John's Rooms, St. John's Hospital, and Chapel (N.), the Abbey House (S.) (the official residence of the Mayor of Winchester), and Abbey Grounds, the site of Nunnaminster, the nunnery founded by the queen of Alfred the Great, and Hamo Thornycroft's superb statue of that great king. By the side of the Town Bridge is the City Mill (N.), now a national monument and a hostel for strolling pedestrians. Passing over the bridge into what was in medieval times the Soke, the visitor arrives at the Oldest House, at one time the rectory of the parish of St. Peter Chesil. The rectory house is believed to date from the middle of the fifteenth century. Close by is the ancient and curiously planned church. The earliest part of the church is the lower part of the tower, which is Norman. It is a church nearly as broad as it is long, and there is no separate chancel. The font is Norman.

One other church in the Soke is worth inspecting. This is St. John's, in St. John's Street. This also is on a singular plan. The architecture ranges from the twelfth to the fifteenth century. An Early English window, and an Easter sepulchre, are interesting.

Returning to the High Street the visitor should now visit the Hospital of St. Cross and its church, about a mile distant. A pleasant means of journeying to St. Cross, if time is not pressing, is to walk through the Cathedral Close and Kings Gate, through College Street, into College Walk (*R*), and then to traverse the footpath which follows the stream flowing from the Headmaster's garden, and past the College Mill. A quarter of a mile farther south this footpath crosses Garnier Road (otherwise Bull Drove), and then continues for a few hundred yards until the pedestrian comes in view of the village of St. Cross, and the walls of the Hospital enclosure. It is said that it was from one point in this approach that the artist, Dendy

Sadler, painted his renowned picture "Thursday," which depicts monks fishing in a pleasant stream, with the walls and towers of monastic buildings in the background.

St. Cross village itself is worth spending a little time upon, for here, especially on a pleasant day in spring or summer, there is an old-world atmosphere not easy to come by elsewhere. Several old timbered cottages, with massive external chimneys, are interesting.

The entrance to the Hospital of St. Cross is through a splendid stone gateway erected by Cardinal Beaufort, the hospital's second founder. The original founder was Bishop Henry de Blois in the early part of the twelfth century. Beaufort's foundation, which had for its object the benefiting of men of noble birth, who had fallen on bad times, dates from 1446. The two orders comprise twenty-seven brethren. Those of the de Blois foundation wear black gowns with a silver Jerusalem cross on the breast; those of the Beaufort foundation wear plum-coloured gowns with a badge depicting a cardinal's hat and tassels. There are also a number of out-pensioners.

The Hospital buildings are full of interest. There is the great hall, and the ambulatory, the houses of the brethren, and the porter's lodge, where daily (as long as the supply lasts) bread and beer are given to all who call for it. It is termed the Wayfarer's Dole.

The church is interesting from every point, both from within and without. In architectural style it is of the Transitional period. The east end is Norman, the choir and transepts late Decorated Norman, and the west end is Early English. The west window is a fine specimen of the Decorated style. The west doorway is a good example of the same.

In the floor of the church are a number of medieval tiles. The church also possesses a brass of the fourteenth century, executed to commemorate John Campeden, who was master during the episcopate of William of Wykeham. There is also a well-preserved piscina in the north aisle of the chancel or choir.

Formerly the Master's apartments were in the old buildings, but now there is a modern house for the use of the Master on the north side. The Master's old garden, to the east, is a delightful retreat, but is not generally open to visitors.

If the visitor should desire to visit the site of Hyde Abbey on the north of the city he will proceed from the High Street, along Jewry Street and Hyde Street, as far as Hyde Church (*R*). Fifty yards down the road, past the church, originally the place of worship for the domestics of the abbey, will be seen the entrance gate of the abbey, a plain erection of the fifteenth century. Passing through the gate the visitor may see two small ancient arches spanning the stream which was the lockburn of the place, and which supplied the domestic offices with water. The gate, and these two arches, are all that remain intact of the great Abbey of Hyde, in whose church were buried King Alfred the Great and his son, Edward the Elder.

MADE AT THE
TEMPLE PRESS
LETCHWORTH

GREAT BRITAIN